# Contents

CW01500467

# Waiting for the Revolution to End

# Waiting for the Revolution to End

*Syrian displacement, time and subjectivity*

Charlotte al-Khalili

First published in 2023 by
UCL Press
University College London
Gower Street
London WC1E 6BT

Available to download free: www.uclpress.co.uk

Text © Charlotte al-Khalili, 2023
Images © Copyright holders named in captions, 2023

The author has asserted her rights under the Copyright, Designs and Patents Act
1988 to be identified as the author of this work.

A CIP catalogue record for this book is available from The British Library.

ISBN: 978-1-80008-505-3 (Hbk)
ISBN: 978-1-80008-504-6 (Pbk)
ISBN: 978-1-80008-503-9 (ePDF)
ISBN: 978-1-80008-506-0 (ePub)
DOI: https://doi.org/10.14324/111.9781800085039

*To the detainees and the martyrs*

*To Rita and Mohammad*

# List of figures

# Preface

When I started to hear about the Syrian uprising through friends and relatives, I was in Rio de Janeiro finishing a master's dissertation in philosophy on anthropologist Eduardo Viveiros de Castro's Deleuzian-inspired theory of anthropology as a 'practice of permanent decolonisation of thought' (2009). What I then heard about the Arab Revolutions of 2011 and, more specifically, about Syria's, led me to believe that what was happening there could potentially lead to the emergence of a different form of political imagination, practice, institution, and regional order. At the time, my friends and interlocutors imagined that the Syrian revolution would lead to a total reorganisation of the Levant region; they saw it as the first time Syrian people would be able to access self-determination and they dreamed that this would lead to a redrawing of the regional borders inherited from the colonial past.

The Arab revolutions in general, and the Syrian uprising in particular, have generated dreams and hopes in many (see Wedeen 2013: 873). As I began my PhD in September 2013 I had high hopes in the Syrian revolution's transformational power and alternative politics. Having in mind the ways in which anthropology can teach us to think otherwise, I then imagined that the study of the Syrian revolution would be a project focused on doing politics differently. Inspired by Viveiros de Castro's work (2003; 2004; 2009) and teaching in Rio de Janeiro (2011), I believed that radically different political thought and practice were coming to Syria. When I started this project I quite naively tried to locate this political practice, thought, and imaginary through an ethnography of displaced local councils and of grassroots revolutionary organisations.

In March 2014 when I first visited Gaziantep in Turkey, to which many Syrians had fled, my interlocutors were still hopeful about the revolution and sincerely believed that it would succeed in the near future. These hopes were sometimes inflated by Free Syrian Army (FSA) victories on the ground or the belief that a foreign intervention that would lead to the downfall of the Assad regime was imminent. But the situation gradually took a turn for the worse with Russia's intervention, the internationalisation of the conflict, and the mass displacement that caused the so-called 'refugee crisis' in Europe. Through these events, my Syrian interlocutors were deprived of their revolution and dispossessed of their (own) political future in Syria. Rather than attaining self-determination, they saw their country being 'occupied' and 'ruled' by foreign forces.

The situation inside Syria, and the hopes my friends and interlocutors had in the revolution, had a dramatic impact on their spatio-temporal horizons and on pragmatic decisions about their futures. The evolving situation in Syria had led some of my friends and interlocutors to go back when revolutionary victory seemed closer, but when all hope for its success failed, they fled to Turkey en masse. The oscillation between hope and despair has also marked the writing of this book: how should an unfolding revolution that has fuelled so much hope and sacrifice be described?

When I returned to Gaziantep in March 2017 to write up my findings, I found a city totally changed: most of my interlocutors had fled to Europe; some who were still living in Syria at the time of my fieldwork were now in Gaziantep; new people had also arrived after the enforced displacement of entire populations from besieged areas. Those of my friends and interlocutors who were still in Gaziantep were defeated, disillusioned, and depressed by the ongoing situation; most of the liberated areas had now been retaken by the regime, making any hope of a revolutionary future inside Syria almost impossible.

Writing this text as the events were still unfolding and I was still living among my interlocutors has required me to accept the revolution's defeat. This has not been an easy task, but it was a necessary one. Analysing the consequences of the 2011 revolution on my interlocutors' and friends' lifeworlds has only been possible once I recognised that my own and my interlocutors' hopes had been disappointed. Throughout my fieldwork and the writing up of the thesis that led to this book, I witnessed the sacrifices of my friends and interlocutors and their investment in the revolutionary project. Moreover, it was difficult to accept that the revolutionary process, if it had not actually stopped, had reached a temporary dead end; this acceptance has, however, been key to the writing process and to anthropological analysis.

On a more personal note, one of the things that prompted me to study the Syrian revolution and its connections to displacement is my family history. On my mother's side, family members fled the Russian Empire and the USSR as the revolution and then civil war unfolded from 1917 onwards. As they sought refuge some relatives first fled from Odessa to Istanbul, Turkey where they spent a few years before continuing further south to Athens and later crossing western Europe before arriving in France. Some have died fighting for the 'white' or the 'red' armies in the revolutionary and civil wars. It is this biographical resonance and personal interest in the relations between revolutionary war and displacement that have also led me to try to make sense of this rich nexus in the Syrian case. This parallel became even more poignant as Syrians fled from Turkey to Europe, following similar migratory routes as my ancestors. It became very vivid when I was asked by interlocutors that had become close friends to carry their precious belongings from Turkey to Germany, which they hoped to reach by sea.

# Acknowledgements

I would like to thank from the bottom of my heart all the Syrians in (Gazi) Antep who have contributed to this research and made it possible. Their trust and generosity in sharing their stories, and the help and encouragement they offered by introducing me to their friends and relatives, allowed this text to see the light, and I hope that it is worthy of their trust. Despite being displaced and dispossessed they have continuously hosted me and made me feel at home; this generous hospitality and their way of including me in their fictive kinship network helped me carry on with fieldwork through good times and bad. I cannot thank them enough for this. I am particularly grateful to Nura and Omar for introducing me to many relatives and friends; Mariam and Zaher for always being ready to share a coffee; Lubna, Rand, Mayada and Nisrin for always offering a warm home; Thanaa and Ahmad for trusting me with their stories and taking the time to explain the situation 'inside' in detail; and the ones I have called Umm Yazan, Umm Khaled, Umm Ahmad, Umm Nidal and Umm Zayd, for being true friends and real mothers. Writing in Gaziantep with a small baby would have not been possible without the help of Asma and Sima; without Lina's and Umm Yamen's delicious food; or the generous hospitality of Nour, Bilal, Lina and Nashat.

There are also many people in London to whom I owe a great debt of gratitude: I must thank Masa, Ranya and Eyad for their introductions to their friends and relatives in Turkey; my supervisor, Martin Holbraad, for his patient reading of all my drafts during five years, for his encouragement, and for believing in my work even when I did not believe that I would be able to finish it with a newborn to take care of; Elizabeth Fox and Aeron O'Connor for their friendship, support and for reading and giving thought-provoking feedback on chapters at different stages; my fellow CARP and PhD colleagues (Narges, David, Sofia, Alice, Igor, Kaya, Myriam and Nico), who have all enriched my thinking through discussion of early drafts. The fieldwork for this book was financed through a PhD studentship from the ERC project Comparative Anthropologies of Revolutionary Politics (2013-CoG-617970). Its writing was made possible by a postdoctoral fellowship at MRU financed through Professor Elena Fiddian-Qasmiyeh's Philip Leverhulme Prize (PLP-2015-250), a LaBex Hastec postdoctoral fellowship (2021–2) and a Leverhulme early career fellowship (2022–5).

I have received very rich feedback when I presented my work during research seminars in Cambridge University, EHESS, Goldsmiths University,

IFPO Amman, Koç University, ÖDTU, the University of Copenhagen and SOAS. Insightful comments on various stages of the work were also made by Farha Ghannam, Elena Fiddian-Qasmiyeh, and Charles Stewart. Maria Kastrinou and Charis Boutieri have also made generous readings at various stages of the writing. Andreas Bandak and Alice Wilson have been true mentors and have continuously encouraged me throughout the writing process. I am also grateful to Emma Aubin-Boltanksi and Nisrine Al-Zahre, who have welcomed me into their research project, the Living Lexicon of the Syrian Revolution and War, through which my thinking matured and evolved greatly. I would also like to thank Pinar Şenoğuz and Birgitte Holst Stampe for discussing fieldwork challenges and research results in Gaziantep, and Janine Su for always being ready for a study date in Istanbul and for reading many parts of this book.

I also thank Farouk Mardam-Bey and Yassin al-Haj Saleh for their generous engagement with my work since our first encounter in a round-table on the Syrian revolution in Toulouse University. For final but crucial suggestions, I thank Sherry Al-Hayek who made inspiring comments. For the pictures I wish to thank Manal Shakhashirou, Fadi Dabbas, Muhammad Shehadeh, Ali Haj Suleiman and Zouhir al-Shimale for providing pictures and facilitating communication with photographers. And for suggestions on transliteration, I am grateful to Jean-Christophe Peyssard.

It has been a pleasure to work with UCL Press, in particular with my editor, Pat Gordon-Smith, to whom I am very thankful for her patience in delivering the manuscript as I was delayed in finalising it due to the earthquake in southern Turkey and northern Syria that strongly touched the cities that had been my home for many years, and the places that are still home to many of my family members, friends and interlocutors. Many of them are now living with the devastating consequences of the earthquake.

I also want to thank my family from the bottom of my heart: my parents for always supporting me without questions; my sister Olga for reminding me to take care of myself, for always introducing new critical theories and for being a lifelong comrade; my grandparents for being such an inspiration with their life choices and history; and Ediz for coming with me to Gaziantep the first time, and for his thought-provoking comments. Above all I thank Mohammad who has been a real teammate and a tremendous support throughout the entire process, and Rita for being such a beautiful motivation and distraction.

An earlier version of Chapter 1 has previously appeared in *Condition Humaine/conditions politiques*; of Chapter 3 in *American Ethnologist*; and of Chapter 6 in *Social Anthropology*.

# Note on transliteration

I have transliterated Arabic words based on the simplified system recommended by the *International Journal of Middle Eastern Studies*. I do not use diacritics or long vowel markers. The *'ayn* is marked, following convention, by ', the *hamza* by ', and the *ta marbuta* is transliterated either as 'a' or 'eh'. I have also tried to stay as close as possible to my interlocutors' Levantine dialect in transliterating terms, except for proper nouns and words for which an alternative transcription is dominant in English. In this case I use the most commonly known form or the closest to the Syrian dialect. For instance, *shaheed* rather than *shahid* and Deraa rather than Dar'a. All the transliterations have been done from dialectal Arabic, with variation in the vocalisation following the regional dialect of my interlocutors. I have anonymised all my interlocutors for safety and privacy reasons.

# Glossary

| | |
|---|---|
| abu | father |
| 'adaleh | justice |
| al sha'b | the people |
| 'aysh | life |
| barra | outside |
| dayif (*pl.* diyuf) | guest(s) |
| fasad | corruption |
| haram | forbidden |
| harb ahliyya | civil war |
| hayat | life |
| hurriyya | freedom |
| juwwa | inside |
| karama | dignity |
| khuf | fear |
| laje' | refugee |
| muhajir | follower of the Prophet from Mecca to Medina, and by extension, migrant |
| nasheteen | activists |
| nizam | regime |
| qada wa qadar | destiny |
| rif dimashq | Damascus countryside |
| shabab | youth |
| shabbiha | pro-regime thugs |
| shaheed (*pl.* shuhada') | martyr(s) |
| sheghel b-l thawra | revolutionary work |
| ta'fiyyeh | sectarianism |
| thawra | revolution |
| thuwwar | revolutionaries |
| umm | mother |
| zulm | oppression/ injustice |

# Acronyms and organisations

Daesh   ISIS (Islamic State in Iraq and Syria). 'Daesh' represents the word formed by the equivalent acronym in Arabic.

FSA   Free Syrian Army.

IDP   Internally displaced people.

PYD   Partiya Yekîtiya Demokrat. Kurdish political party, in English, Democratic Union Party.

YPG   Yekîneyên Parastina Gel. Kurdish armed force, in English, People's Protection Units, associated with the PYD.

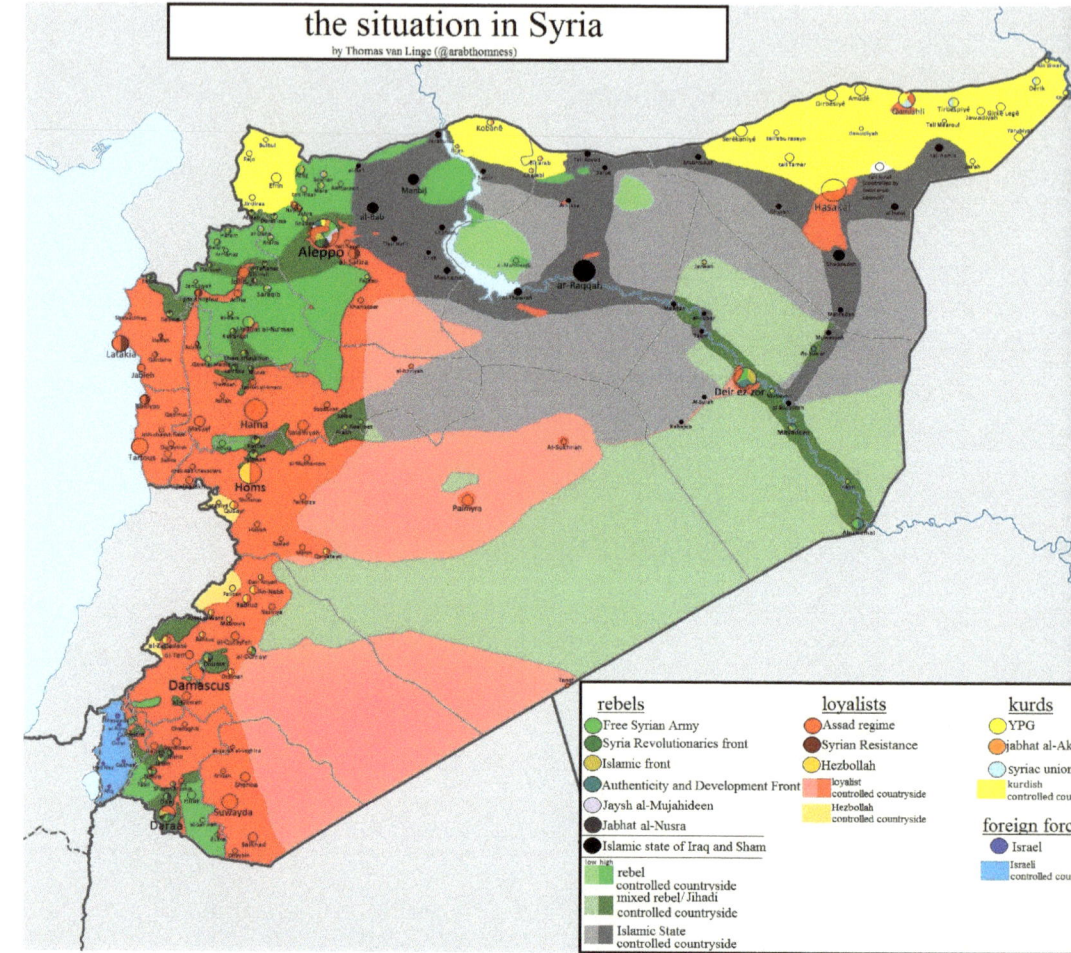

**Figure 0.1:** Map showing areas of control in Syria as of January 2014. © Antiracista, available at https://commons.wikimedia.org/wiki/ File:Map_of_the_Syrian_Civil_War,_January_2014.jpg

# Introduction: living in the midst of defeat

*In a revolution as in a novel …*
*the most difficult part to invent is the end*[1]

'Look! All the paths are closed!' Hanan tells me, pointing at the pattern made by the grounds of the coffee we have just drunk from small white cups decorated with a blue eye. She continues to lament while turning her cup in her right hand: 'Everything is closing down, everything is dark. There is no hope! There is nothing good coming. There isn't even a small path!' It is early morning in the autumn of 2015; the two children are still asleep on the floor of the living room, undisturbed by our morning coffee reading. Hanan has been obsessed with coffee reading for the past couple of weeks as she is looking for signs and answers to the conundrum of her future. Will she stay in Turkey? Will she go back to her parents' village in Syria? Or will she cross into Europe?

We turn to look at Dina's cup. Hanan asks me what I see in it. I see a lot of people running towards a place that is white and open. Bearing in mind her recent preoccupations and the news,[2] I suggest that the space is an open road for refugees to Europe, but Hanan does not agree. She sees a lot of people standing together, which to her represents the protest we are attending later that day. 'The white opening is the positive outcome of today's protest', she says, pointing to the part of the cup that is clear of coffee grounds. This references the weekly protest in which we participate, replicas of those that used to occur in the early days of the revolution in Syria. Hanan also sees two people hugging one another behind a dark shape. She reads the same shape at the bottom of the cup after pressing her thumb on it, saying that they are friends reunited after a long time apart.

Hanan, a former civil servant in her fifties, and I are living at Dina's, a former teacher in her forties. Hanan is a Kurdish woman who comes from a small village near the Turkish border but used to live in a city in the north of Syria. Dina, although originally from eastern Syria, used to work in a city in the centre of the country. Hanan shares Dina's room and I sublet the second room of the apartment in Gaziantep, a city near the Turkish–Syrian border. The two boys sleeping on the floor of the living room, aged 10 and 12, are Dina's nephews, recently arrived from their war-torn city in eastern Syria, where the situation is deteriorating. Their mother sent them to stay with her sister while they wait for visas to join their father in Europe.

For a week I have been woken by Hanan's early Skype calls with relatives and friends, either in Europe or in Syria, and daily we drink and read – literally 'open' (*iftah*) – coffee together. Since the summer of 2015, the number of Syrians fleeing to Europe has increased greatly, and every day she reports that a relative, friend, or acquaintance is on her way to, or has arrived in, Europe; this paralleled the opening of the 'Balkan road'. For Hanan, however, leaving the border town where we live means abandoning her country and, most importantly, giving up hope that the Assad regime will eventually fall and the revolution succeed. 'As long as I can stay here I will, but as soon as the border opens I will be on my way home', she once told me, referring to her in-between situation. In order to be able to stay in Turkey, however, she must find a job, since she will not be able to survive for long on the modest savings she brought out of Syria when she fled.

We follow Hanan to the kitchen where she elaborates on her reading by flipping the cup in the saucer above the sink. She observes the designs again, but she cannot identify any relevant pattern so we decide to leave it there for the day. In this morning's cup, rather than offering direction or wide openings as it does sometimes, the coffee has just shown that the future is dark and without much hope. 'Let's see what we have tomorrow,' she concludes as we go back to the living room. By the time we finish our morning ritual it is already late but the boys are still asleep and will probably not wake before the early afternoon as they usually go to bed in the early morning hours.

Smuggled through the border, which had been closed for several months, they arrived with three of Dina's siblings and now spend most of their days indoors, watching the news, archive videos of the revolution, or television series on Arabic channels. They were not admitted to school, as they do not have a *kimlik*, a document all Syrians in Turkey must have but which is no longer distributed in the city in which we live. Their lives have thus become little more than enforced and indeterminate waiting, as they do not know how long it will take for their visas to be delivered. Their everyday is shared between memories of the past and Skype or WhatsApp calls with their parents in Syria and Europe respectively. When I am home, I often find them watching videos of the revolution's first protests, one of their (and their aunt's) favourite pastimes – along with participating in the weekly protests – or trying to find an adequate connection so they can speak with their mother and younger siblings in Syria.

This book is an ethnographic study of life in the aftermath of a thwarted revolution and in the midst of war and displacement. It explores the 2011 revolution in Syria, its roots, actors, legacies and impacts on Syrians' lifeworlds. It simultaneously gives an emic description and analysis of the revolution's evolution into an armed rebellion from 2012 onwards and a conflict that quickly became internationalised after 2013. It also depicts the main unexpected consequence of the revolution's repression: mass displacement inside and outside the country since 2012, and thus analyses the rich nexus between revolution and displacement.

## Ethnographic timespace

When I left Gaziantep in autumn 2019, the Syrian revolution was largely overshadowed by descriptions and analyses of what was called a 'civil war', a 'never-ending conflict' and a 'humanitarian crisis'.[3] In this book I invite the reader to go back to a different timespace. This is an ethnography of a clearly bounded period of the Syrian revolution and its associated displacement: a moment that has now disappeared, a moment characterised by hope and a sense of community among Syrian revolutionaries and the displaced. The fieldwork for this research is inscribed in a context of ongoing war inside Syria and displacement of its people to neighbouring countries. It cut across different phases of the revolutionary process: from a peaceful revolution (2011) to a proxy war and mass displacement (2015), and from local victories of the FSA and the establishment of liberated areas (2012) to the regime's taking over most liberated areas (2016). This moving landscape forms both the ethnographic and analytical background of the book.

For most of my interlocutors, the war was however part of the revolutionary process, and displacement was perceived as an unforeseen consequence of the revolution's repression. Hence, in speaking of *al-thawra* (revolution) I stick to my interlocutors' use of this term to describe the unfolding events. This book does not therefore attempt to speak about all Syrians but rather focuses on Syrian revolutionaries who fled to the city of Gaziantep in southern Turkey when the peaceful protests that broke out in March 2011 were violently repressed by the Assad regime, and who were later forced to flee the country as the revolution became armed and its actors were targeted not only by the regime and later by Daesh (also known in the West as ISIS), other Islamist factions, and the Kurdish Democratic Union Party, or PYD (along with its armed wing, the People's Defense Units, or YPG).

This book's main argument is that despite the revolution's overall defeat – that is, the Assad regime was not overthrown at the scale of the state – revolution survives its defeat in the present in exile. Throughout its ethnographic exploration, the Syrian revolution appears as a process that has a powerful and lasting impact on all aspects of Syrians' lifeworld: it is an ongoing and unfinished process that has deep roots in the local and regional histories and that is conceptualised as espousing a cyclical rather than a linear temporality. In this sense, al-thawra does not fit classic definitions of revolution that are inherited from the European Enlightenment philosophy and historiography (see Ghamari-Tabrizi 2015; Trouillot 1995)[4].

Revolutions have indeed been classically defined, according to a model of before-and-after, as a historical rupture that leads to a new political order and temporal cycle because of a change in political regime – the ancient regime is replaced by a new one (see Arendt 1965; Koselleck 1985). Such a definition therefore glosses over the transformative potential of apparently defeated and failed revolutions. Because of such definitions, failed or defeated revolutions end up in history's dustbin. The ethnographic enquiry of the Syrian revolution thus calls to an expanding of our conceptual framework and methodological tools[5] to fully grasp what revolution, and in particular a defeated one, is and can be.[6]

Arguing that revolutionary transformations outlast revolution's defeat, this book maps out the ruptures (intended changes) and disruptions (unexpected shifts) that the revolution engendered beyond what is usually defined as the political field: within the self, in the intimate sphere of the home, in Syrians' everyday lives, social relations, and sense of time, and in their experience of Islamic cosmology, thereby shifting the analytical focus to the revolution's long-lasting and in-depth consequences.[7] Revolution becomes a multi-layered and multi-dimensional entity: it affects Syrian lifeworlds in all domains and scales. These very transformations are themselves being interpreted in ways that evolve as Syrians' theorisations, experiences, and imaginations of al-thawra (the revolution) are themselves being transformed. This book has thus two overall aims: the location of the traces of the early stage of the 2011 revolution through my interlocutors' narratives, memories, activities and artefacts; and the mapping of the transformations that revolutionary moment, space and experience create in exile.

## Bashar's Syria: a reign of terror, atrocity and abjection

Syria has been under the rule of the Assad family since 1970, when Hafez al-Assad led a successful putsch within the Baath ruling party. It was initially a pan-Arabic socialist party that was founded in 1947 with the goal of overthrowing European-backed governments in the Middle East. The 'Baathist revolution' (1963) led to important reforms such as the democratisation of education, the development of modern media, the wave of nationalisations (banks, industrial companies, natural resources and so on), and agrarian reforms (such as the limitation of land property) that privileged the impoverished peasantry and working class over big landowners and the merchant bourgeoisie. The rural and urban proletariat soon became disappointed, however, as Baathist politics largely benefited the new state bourgeoisie composed of civil servants (Picard 1980).

After his coup, Hafez's 'corrective movement', Syria was built as a Baathist populist state dominated by Alawi officers (members of the Alawite minority, a sect that is usually considered to be an offshoot of Shi'ism) in a country predominantly Sunni: the regime was a 'presidential monarchy' supported by Alawi clients who were in charge of key military and intelligence machinery (Picard 1980). The political system, based on the control of one man, created an authoritarian regime that ruled the country with a strong secret service. Moreover, with the state of emergency, in place since Hafez's accession to power, an authoritarian rule based on the three branches of the security services, the army and the Baath party (Ziadeh 2014), the Assads managed to build a regime structured to prevent military coups (Munif 2020: 14). The state of emergency allowed the Assad regime to act outside the legal framework and to incarcerate thousands of opponents and dissidents throughout its reign.

Bashar al-Assad came to power on his father's death in the summer of 2000, raising hopes that he would implement economic and political reforms that would bring more freedom. He instigated liberalising reforms of the country's economy, destabilising its traditional social base of the working and lower-middle classes (farmers, industrial workers and civil servants) as the state abandoned its protective role, disinvested in public services, and stopped its support for development. This simultaneously led to the emergence of a growing upper-middle class made up of businessmen and entrepreneurs who supported the regime; on the political level, the regime's reforms led to an 'authoritarian upgrading' (Hinnebusch and Imady 2018b). The violence and the arbitrariness of the Assad carceral system, already visible since the 1980s, continued to spread through the 1990s and 2000s (Ziadeh 2014; see also Al-Khalili 2021).

The memory of the 1982 Hama massacre was omnipresent in most of my interlocutors' recalling of the uprising, and so were the memories of arbitrary arrest, detention and killing since then (see Chapter 1). Virtually all of my interlocutors had either been arbitrarily arrested and subjected to state violence, or had relatives who were. Aleppo and Hama were the two main scenes of the revolt that started with targeted assassinations of Alawi soldiers, officers, and university professors, among others. In 1979, a member of the Muslim Brotherhood killed 32 Alawi students of the Aleppo artillery school; in 1981 there was an assassination attempt against Hafez al-Assad (Saouli 2018). The army was sent to Aleppo and Hama in order to stop the insurgency.

This resulted in the death of over 20,000 people as the army besieged the city of Hama and almost erased it from the map, using heavy weaponry against the population (Al-Sarraj 2011; Chatty 2018; Coquio et al. 2022). Thereafter, a crackdown on Syria's opposition – mainly the Muslim Brotherhood and other dissident political parties: the Nasserist, non-aligned Baath and later the Communist Party Political Bureau (*al-maktab al-syassi*), among others – led to hundreds of arrests and to the massacre of hundreds of unarmed political prisoners, detained in the infamous Tadmor prison, by special forces sent in to kill them.[8]

## Revolution in/and displacement

It is in this history of mass political violence and repression of any political dissent that the 2011 revolution and its aftermaths have to be seized. There are many ways in which the Syrian revolution's beginning is recounted. In this introduction, I present one of its most widespread versions while I discuss the variations in this story – its historicisation and contextualisation – by my interlocutors in Chapter 1.

The Syrian revolution is said to have started when protests erupted in the southern city of Deraa on 18 March 2011[9] after children were arrested and tortured by security forces in the city for having written on their school's walls: 'The people want the fall of the regime', and, 'It's your turn next doctor', echoing Tunisian and Egyptian slogans (see for instance

Chatty 2018; Ruiz de Elvira Carrascal 2014). The protests were immediately met with high levels of violence as the regime deployed security forces and soldiers in Deraa and other Syrian cities where protests were taking place.[10] They were soon to be joined by snipers and tanks, locking down cities and districts that were rebelling and shelling them from the first months of the uprising leading to the killing of at least eight thousand civilians in the first year.

The protests quickly grew in size, reaching four hundred thousand protestors in Hama in July 2011, and started to move from peripheral to central cities. The militarisation of the uprising marked a turn in July 2011 when the Free Syrian Army (FSA) was created by regime army defectors joined by armed protestors. From November 2012, the armed conflict was no longer limited to rebels vs the regime as the rebels and YPG were fighting over the border city of Ras al-Ayn. In the winter of 2013, the rebels were successful in Damascus's suburbs and seized Raqqa in March. In April 2013 Daesh (ISIS) was created in Syria as the al-Nusra Front split between it and the organisation now pledging allegiance to al-Qaeda. From January 2014 the rebels and Daesh started an open war with each other, and the latter took Raqqa. The armed conflict turned into a proxy war with the US making its first airstrike against Daesh in September 2014. Foreign states also armed the opposition: the US trained and armed Syrian rebel groups from January 2015 onwards, while Jaysh al-Fatah was backed by Turkey, Qatar, and Saudi Arabia. In December 2015 France and the UK formed a coalition with the US and started bombing Daesh in Syria. The Russian army began its intervention in Syria in September 2015, allegedly shelling Daesh but in fact targeting 'moderate' rebel forces in opposition-held areas.

As a result of the sieges, shelling, and enforced disappearances of protestors and inhabitants of revolutionary strongholds by the Assad regime, Syrians started to flee their homes as early as April 2011. At first, internal displacement was organised around kin logic and solidarities – those who helped the displaced were criminalised, arrested, and killed by the regime – but as the uprising turned into war, displacement became increasingly external. A turning point was the shelling of Aleppo in February 2012. Between 2011 and 2012, 250,000 Syrians were internally displaced, and only 50,000 crossed international borders (Chatty 2018: 228). The intensifying of the armed conflict between the Syrian regime and non-state armed actors led to the massive and sudden flight of about two million Syrians between 2012 and 2015. With fighting starting in the region of Idlib (along the Turkish border), the Turkish government built a refugee camp in 2011 that soon hosted 10,000 people. About 20,000 people were said to have crossed the border in 2011 and 2012 (Chatty 2018: 226), yet the populations were going back and forth between the two countries as the fighting stopped and resumed. This ease of movement was due to the open-door policy of the Turkish government.

The ongoing conflict led to mass displacement inside and outside the country from 2012. At the beginning of 2015 the UN estimated that 8 million Syrians had been displaced internally and abroad. With Russia starting to support the regime's forces and shelling opposition's neighbourhoods and towns, flight to neighbouring countries intensified. Those who could pay smugglers started to cross from Turkey to Europe in 2015 in massive numbers, giving birth to a phenomenon soon called the 'refugee crisis'. After a few weeks, the European borders started to close under the EU strategy of containing Syrian refugees in Syria's neighbouring countries. 'By 2017 more than half of Syria's population of 23 million had been displaced: 7 million internally and 4.9 externally by March 2017, at which time the number of Syrians who reached European shores was under a million' (Chatty 2018: 243). By 2017, in Gaziantep, a city located in the Syrian–Turkish borderland where I did most of my fieldwork, 17 per cent of the city's population of 350,000 was Syrian (Carpi and Şenoğuz 2019: 126).

## Ethnography of a defeated revolution's afterlives

The opening description of one of the regular coffee readings in the home I shared with a Syrian family gives a glimpse of the extent to which the revolutionary process and its repression inflected Syrian life. Families were scattered, and displaced Syrians lived a precarious present and an uncertain future, hoping that the revolution would reach a positive ending or looking for a personal ending through migration. This book focuses on people, like Hanan, who have been involved in various ways in the Syrian uprising, and on families, like Dina's, that have been scattered by revolution, war, and displacement. Like these two women and their relatives, the Syrians I encountered in Turkey were waiting for the revolution to succeed, the war to end, the chance to go home, or the opportunity to migrate elsewhere – often contemplating several of these horizons at once. Most of the people with whom I lived defined themselves as *nasheteen* (activists) or *thuwwar* (revolutionaries), a term deriving from *thawra* (revolution) with the root *th-w-r* (to rise up and rebel) (Achcar 2013: 14; Said 1979: 314–15).[11]

The *thuwwar* are those who participated in the revolution and shared a specific set of demands (freedom, justice, and dignity) rather than referencing a circumscribed identity and a clear political programme. The *thuwwar* were involved in a wide range of activities: cooking for protestors and rebels, preparing banners and slogans, collecting clothes and medicines for IDP (internally displaced people) and injured protesters, and supporting the revolution and rebellion materially. Others had participated in protests and/or been detained for years; many of their relatives had been martyred or incarcerated. Some had sung in protests, treated injured protesters, or joined the armed rebellion. Moreover, they had dissimilar political orientations and projects, came from various social, religious, and ethnic backgrounds, and belonged to different generations. In this book, the *thuwwar* are understood as taking an ethico-political position (see al-Haj Saleh 2016b) and sharing a common ethico-political and often religious language that encompasses a wide variety of people not traditionally seen as revolutionaries: people who stand on the margins of what is usually defined as revolutionary action, yet who are at the heart of its transformations and without whom revolutions could not happen (see Abu-Lughod 2012; Winegar 2012).

In displacement, some *thuwwar* continued their revolutionary activities by working in organisations providing aid and relief or in political bodies and structures, by volunteering in schools and orphanages, supporting revolutionaries still in Syria, or going to weekly protests. Others had ceased their activities as they lost hope in the revolution, feeling that it had already failed or been defeated, or because they were too busy trying to survive in exile. Yet, even when they were not directly involved, all the families with whom I lived were deeply affected by the revolution and its repression. No family was left without a martyr, someone under siege, a detainee, or someone who had fled to another country as a result of the revolution and its repression. Everybody's life was marked by multi-layered loss, by scattering and forced displacement. Ruptures and disruptions, which I respectively define as intended and unintended transformations, were felt in every aspect of their lives.

The young people and the families, despite being linked by kinship ties and/or their involvement in the revolution, had different characteristics. The families were scattered: they had members still in Syria (often detained or besieged), others in neighbouring countries or Europe, and some had disappeared or been martyred. The households all had female heads, were often marked by the absence of male relatives, and belonged to the working and lower-middle classes. Before displacement, my interlocutors came from families of small shopkeepers and farmers, low-ranking administrators, taxi drivers, small land- and business-owners, *shyukh* (plural of sheikh) and teachers. Displacement and involvement in the revolution affected all of them strongly, however, and for the majority of my interlocutors, who could not secure proper employment or depend on relatives' remittances, living conditions were rather poor. Many had spent large amounts of money trying to free relatives detained by the regime; others had paid for their children's crossings into Turkey and to Europe; many had lost their properties and businesses in Syria and could not secure employment in Turkey.

On the other hand, youths – the *shabab* – came from the working classes to a wealthier part of the middle classes. Those who managed to find employment in local and international organisations were usually university graduates and/or prominent and well-connected revolutionary actors. Those employed in Gaziantep lived rather comfortably in comparison to the locals and the Syrian population, as their salaries could range from US$200 up to US$2,000.[12] Working with both revolutionary *shabab* and families allowed me to enrich my experience as I was offered different points of view on the same topics and I could discuss and compare what I saw in one context in a different one and with people from different generations and backgrounds.

The majority of displaced Syrians in Gaziantep are from northern Syria, and mainly from the city of Aleppo and its region because of the cities' proximity, common history, and economic relations. However, I had interlocutors who came from south, central, and eastern Syria. My main interlocutors were overwhelmingly Sunni Arabs, although a few were Ismaeli, Druze, Shia, a fewer still were Alawi, Orthodox, or Catholic, and others were Kurds or Armenians. However, unlike the *shabab*, the families I worked with were exclusively Arab Sunni, defined themselves as pious (*multazem*) and were defined by fellow Syrians as socially and religiously conservative, which led many youth to describe them as *islamiyyin* or *akhuan* (Muslim brothers) in opposition to their self-definition as '*almaniyyin* (secular).[13]

What brought my interlocutors together however was their involvement in the revolution and their displacement to Gaziantep. My book thus presents an account of the perspective and experience of the nexus between revolution and displacement of revolutionary families and *shabab*, who were predominantly Sunni Arabs from the working and lower-middle classes.[14]


## Revolution's landscape and soundscape

The Syrian revolution's presence was pervasive in Gaziantep, marking everything and shaping the city's landscape and soundscape. Its traces could be perceived in marriage ceremonies, 'eid celebrations, departures to Europe, arrivals from Syria, liberation of detainees, coffee readings, women's meetings, and protests. It was widely present visually in the city: the revolutionary flag was increasingly seen at the opening of official institutions of Syrian governance in exile – the temporary government, local councils, civil society organisations – and signage was often in its colours of red, green, black, and white, conspicuous when walking in the streets of the city and visiting offices. The flag was also frequently exhibited on everyday items such as bracelets, phone covers, T-shirts, scarfs, and other accessories. The visual presence of the revolution was likewise manifest in pictures of martyrs, protests, and videos of sit-ins and attacks on rebel areas. Houses were often decorated with revolutionary flags, and some displayed pictures of detainees, revolutionary slogans, and other imageries, which were also present online – as profile pictures on WhatsApp and Facebook, for instance.

The revolution also formed a soundscape as it was made audible during the weekly protests that reached their peak during Aleppo's stiffening siege (autumn 2016), as the main square of the city hosted a giant *dabkeh* (traditional Syrian dance) in the colours of the flag. In such protests, as well as during commemorations, wedding ceremonies, and funerals, revolutionary songs and slogans were widely used. Furthermore, it was rare to visit a house in which the TV was not showing the events unfolding in Syria. The visual and audible presence of the Syrian revolution in the city was in fact linked to the increasing 'Syrianisation' (Al-Haj Saleh 2016a; 2017a) of the city: Arabic signs appeared on shops and offices; Arabic speakers were increasingly present in shops and administrations; Syrian women with their distinct hijabs were recognisable in the streets; Arabic music was often heard in passing cars, in flats, or in wedding halls; Syrian restaurants, schools, and medical practices flooded the city. Syrian products were also imported and could be seen in Turkish shops and supermarkets: Syrian *za'tar* (dried thyme), *mlukhiyya* (a local spinach-like vegetable), olive oil, coffee, and so on.

Due to its spatial, historical, and political proximity Gaziantep rapidly became a refuge of choice for many Syrians. The city is located 60 kilometres from the Syrian border and a hundred from Syria's second city, Aleppo. Moreover, it was part of the Ottoman region of Aleppo for five centuries until the tracing of modern Turkey's borders (1923) split this territory and separated communities that used to live together. In 2011 and 2012, most Syrians fleeing to Turkey only stayed temporarily while their towns or villages were being shelled, returning home when the shelling stopped, but with the intensification of the repression many were forced to flee and settle more permanently in Syria's neighbouring countries. Turkey maintained its open-door policy although it frequently closed its border to Syrians until May 2015. Throughout my fieldwork, the Syrian presence dramatically grew and was increasingly visible in Gaziantep. When I first visited the city in 2014, it was rather discreet, but it was omnipresent in 2016.

Gaziantep has also been an attractive city for Syrians for at the time of my fieldwork there had been fewer tensions with the local population than in the neighbouring cities of Antakya and Şanliurfa. Moreover, the Syrian territories along the Turkish border near Gaziantep were liberated early on (July 2012), spurring a series of attacks by the regime and giving rise to the need for aid and relief that local and international NGOs established in Gaziantep could bring to these areas. Gaziantep was also a 'friendlier' city as its mayor (representing Turkey's ruling AKP) was welcoming to her 'Syrian brothers and sisters', aligning herself with Erdoğan's discourse of hospitality and friendship with Syrians and support for Assad's opposition. By 2016 Gaziantep officially hosted 300,000 Syrians and it had become the headquarters of the opposition's political bodies and of many local and international NGOs; it has also hosted the Syrian provisional government and its administrative apparatus from mid-2013, and became the home of hundreds of Syrian businesses and firms. In January 2015 there were 1,622,839 Syrians in Turkey. In 2016, 2,749,000 Syrians were settled in Turkey with only 10 per cent living in camps and more than 50 per cent comprising youth under 20 (Betts et al. 2017). And in 2019 the total was about 3.6 million.

Syrians' presence was also visible with the growing number of Syrian shops, restaurants and businesses; Arabic script started to appear everywhere and local business owners employed Syrians in order to facilitate relations with Syrian customers. With the influx of Syrians, the city's shape also changed as new buildings were constructed, especially in the university area and in wastelands. The city centre was renovated and embellished and foreign brands were increasingly available, thus marking the flourishing of the local economy due to the raised numbers of Syrians and INGOs dealing with the 'Syrian file'. Yet the presence of the displaced was also visible in the impoverished Syrians (often children and youth) begging in the streets, selling small items such as tissues, water bottles and roses, and/or collecting items that could be recycled from the garbage.

Some districts, blocks, and buildings of the city became predominantly Syrian. The families with whom I worked lived in the poorer parts of Gaziantep, in the old city and its peripheries where the rents were more affordable. The young people displaced without their parents often lived around the university and closer to the city centre in newly built, tiny studio flats. Syrians were also increasingly visible and audible in the streets because of the women's characteristic dress and the widespread use of Arabic. Syrians were sometimes obliged to stay indoor during elections, national celebrations, and when crowds gathered in the streets – during football tournaments or demonstrations – fearing violent incidents, since their presence was not positively received by some of the city's inhabitants. Otherwise they tended to be seen in the streets and parks in the evening, later than the Turkish population, especially during Ramadan, as they liked to break their fast outdoors and wander in the city.

## Towards an anthropology of defeat

This book proposes an anthropology of defeat that is both an exploration of the unexpected consequences of the 2011 revolution and a mapping of the material and immaterial traces left by this event in exile. It investigates a series of unfulfilled actions, events, aspirations, and projects, and analyses their unwanted, unexpected, and uncertain outcomes. Through revolutionary ruptures and disruptions, the Syrian world – that is, Syrians' selves, everyday life, sociality, relations, and religiosity – appears radically transformed. The anthropological exploration of the consequences of failed projects, actions, and aspirations remains underdeveloped.[15] It has, however, been the topic of Samuli Schielke's ethnographic enquiry (2015) into life in Egypt before and after the 2011 revolution and David Scott's monograph (2014) on the failed Grenada revolution of 1979–83. Schielke's 'theory of the unpredictable' does for instance propose an account of life in the midst of unintended consequences resulting from the pursuit of unreachable horizons (2015).[16] Scott's concept of 'tragic consequences' – that is, uncontrollable outcomes – in relation to political and revolutionary actions is another way to seize my ethnographic object. In Scott's work, tragedy becomes a conceptual tool to understand the temporality of political action: the ineradicable contingency of human action in general, and of revolutionary actions in particular, make them vulnerable to failure and often lead to tragic outcomes.[17]

I draw on both these works to analyse the unpredictable outcomes and unintended consequences of defeated and failing political events on displaced lifeworld. In this book I examine the (tragic) consequences of a revolution that did not reach its primary goals, yet I expand this examination from time and temporality to Syrians' entire lifeworlds: I explore how new worlds can emerge as intended and unintended consequences of unattained political projects and uncompleted events. Moreover, I do not only focus on the consequences of failed aspirations but widen this focus by exploring the ways in which such actions and projects are being reframed: Syrians' ideal horizons themselves shifted over the time of my fieldwork. Furthermore, I invite the reader to look beyond the notions of failure and success, proposing to think of the Syrian revolution as defeated.

To describe the Syrian revolution as 'defeated', following Walter Armbrust's suggestion (2017), helps to transcend the dichotomy of failure/success.[18] Whereas the notion of failure points to an internal cause of the lack of success, that of defeat implies a cause from outside, whereby the central responsibility is external. There is therefore something guilt-inducing in the concept of failure: it would be linked to the revolutionaries' actions themselves, something some interlocutors claimed in their darkest moments (see Chapter 1). By contrast, the idea of defeat implies that one has been vanquished while still having made every effort and sacrifice one could. The notion of defeat is of interest for it allows one to think about the revolution beyond failure/success and vanquished/victors and to interrogate the question of the 'end' of the revolution and its potential open-endedness (see Haugbolle and Bandak 2017). How does a revolution end? Does a revolution ever end? How and where is this end visible?

This book thus offers a reflection on the ways in which anthropology can study a defeated revolution in displacement – a revolution whose very existence is contested, for it did not reach its primary objective of toppling the existing regime. But I also propose that an anthropology of defeat has to simultaneously be an anthropology of traces (Napolitano 2015): an anthropology of defeat becomes a tracing of life in the aftermaths of mass political violence, a tracing of the erasure of revolutionary utopia since there has been a partial deletion of the Syrian 2011 revolution.

The Syrian regime's tentative erasure of the uprising and revolution on a local and regional level  has been amplified by its allies on the international level. This process is not unmindful of the way in which the Assad regime dealt with the 1982 revolt and the Hama massacres, when more than 20,000 people were killed and the city destroyed.[19] This presents theoretical questions about the tools that anthropologists use to retrace 'unwitnessed' events (those that happened elsewhere and in the past), of which the very occurrence are denied, and whose traces are being deleted. The non-violent revolutionary moment described in this book has thus become a non-event, in Michel-Rolph Trouillot's sense (1995), for it has been widely invisibilised by the regime's narrative and actions as well as by the definition of the events as a civil war and a humanitarian disaster (Al-Khalili 2022; 2023).[20]

In this context, what remains of the 2011 revolution and its defeat, and where might it be located? In other words, how can it be ethnographically seized? I draw on anthropological studies of the aftermaths of mass political violence to answer these questions (e.g. HadžiMuhamedović 2018; Kwon 2008; Napolitano 2015; Navaro 2020; Taneja 2017). Here, anthropology's 'ocular-centricity' (Bubandt et al. 2019) that is particularly salient in its primary tool of enquiry, participant-observation, appears as a critical challenge to the study of revolution, and especially a defeated one that can be overcome through an anthropology of traces, absence and the invisible.[21] The study of a defeated revolution's aftermaths thus has to bring together the visible and the invisible, the present and the absent, and redefine these categories by questioning the relationship between invisibility and hypervisibility (see Mittermaier 2019a).

This has led me to focus on the material and immaterial traces of the defeated revolution that belong to the intimate and public domains, and inscribe themselves on individual and collective scales: linguistic and mnemonic traces such as narratives of the regime's repression and stories of incarceration; and material traces left on individuals' genealogies and on people's bodies that is the loss of a close one, or of a part of oneself. Moreover, the invisible, the missing, the absent appears not only as the unknown future and the destroyed past, but also as the invisible and the unknown in cosmological and historical terms.

## Al-thawra: an ethnographic theory of revolution

Taking revolution as an ethnographic object – that is, examining it through Syrians' experiences, narrations and understandings of the events – this book sheds a new light on its causes, developments and evolving definitions. This contributes to extending the concept of revolution, showing what a revolution can be when it is understood from the perspective of its very actors. Heard through Syrian voices, or its mnemonic and linguistic traces, *al-thawra* (the revolution) appears as an ongoing process that inscribes itself in a national and regional history of uprisings, rebellions and revolts, rather than merely a failed uprising. It is presented as having deep roots in Syria's past, creating a radical rupture in Syrians' present, and having long-lasting consequences in their lives. Moreover, *al-thawra* appears as a transformative entity that is itself subject to change: from a peaceful uprising to an armed rebellion against the regime's and, later, the jihadists' and islamists' oppression (*zulm*), leading Syrian revolutionaries from hope to doubt and despair in their political project.

Here, looking at revolution ethnographically means putting the concept of revolution itself 'under ethnographic scrutiny', in other words, deconstructing revolution using my interlocutors' conceptualisations and experiences as analytical tools (Elliot 2021: 15). Such endeavour allows for a redefinition of what revolution *is* and *can be* by ethnographically showing how Syrian events have been experienced, conceptualised, and imagined by my interlocutors as *thawra*. This shows that a revolution engenders a series of transformations that transcend the paradigm of success and failure and can be found outside the (narrowly defined) political realm.

In taking revolution as an ethnographic object, this book's central argument is that the Syrian revolution is understood as open-ended: despite having been defeated in the political domain at the scale of the state, the Syrian revolution still has a transformative power that can be identified at the level of the constitution of subjects, social relations, modes of dwelling, temporality, future horizons, and imaginative modes. Moreover, the Syrian revolution witnessed a displacement: rather than a political rupture at the scale of the state, it produced a series of transformations that dramatically reshaped Syrians' lifeworlds. Here, *al-thawra* appears as a transformational entity that can reorganise an entire world even when a revolution has been defeated.[22]

My argument is therefore that a revolution defeated in the political domain can nonetheless produce ruptures and disruptions in the social realm, as well as on micro (intimate) and macro (cosmological) scales. It thus suggests stepping away from the dichotomous definition of revolution as either a successful or a failed rupture and shifting the research focus to its marginal and often unexplored dimensions in order to grasp more fully what a revolution is. Rather than looking at the epicentre of revolutionary action – protests, occupations, and political organisations – it proposes to explore what is often seen as peripheral and apolitical: everyday life, kinship relations, religious imagination, and spatio-temporal practices.

By grounding my research within families, my ethnography was able to grasp the in-depth and long-term effects of the 2011 revolution on Syrians' lifeworlds. This echoes Jessica Winegar's (2012) suggestion of focusing on what usually appears as non-revolutionary spaces and actors – women in the intimacy of the home – and Lila Abu-Lughod's (2012) suggestion to look at the margins, rather than uniquely at the epicentre of the uprising, in her case, non-urban peripheries outside Cairo.[23]

## The politics and pragmatics of fieldwork

This book is based on eighteen months of fieldwork and an additional two years of ethnographic engagement with Syrians displaced in the city of Gaziantep. After a one-month visit in the summer of 2014 I lived in Gaziantep for a period of 16 months from January 2015 to April 2016 and a further one-month visit in the autumn of 2016. I then moved back to Gaziantep in March 2017 and stayed there until September 2019, which allowed me to be in constant contact with my Syrian interlocutors and friends and have feedback and input throughout the writing of my doctoral dissertation, and later working on my book project. This book is therefore the fruit of multiple layers of conversations and encounters: first from 2014 to 2016 when I was still doing my doctoral fieldwork and then from 2017 to 2019 as I wrote my doctoral thesis and started turning it into a book. The latter discussions were about the first ones and about the ways I recount and analyse them. I chose to live and work in Gaziantep after first visiting southern Turkey in March 2014, although I had initially planned to settle in Antakya, located 20 kilometres from the Syrian border about 140 kilometres south-west of Gaziantep. But Gaziantep had become the 'capital of revolutionaries in exile', whereas Antakya had a greater role in cross-border relief and aid. Grassroots organisations, local councils, and provisional government all had their offices in Gaziantep. Furthermore, despite being further from the border it hosted a larger Syrian population, as obtaining documents was easier there than in Antakya at that time.[24]

I was introduced to my field site by Lina, a Syrian friend I met in Istanbul (where I lived for a few months in 2013 and 2014). This played a decisive role in my access to the field since the context in which I worked was rather sensitive and my interlocutors were suspicious of strangers and foreigners. During my fieldwork, particularly until the summer of 2015, my interlocutors were still entering Syria regularly, and the parents of many *shabab* still lived in regime-controlled areas and the children of many families were detained or besieged; speaking with a stranger, particularly a foreigner, was thus not always perceived as a safe thing to do. Lina, as well as Syrians I met in London, put me in contact with relatives and friends living in Antakya and Gaziantep. These people were my first contacts, interlocutors, and friends in the field. They generously hosted me in their homes from my very first stay. This warm welcome and the trust it expressed were also linked to the fact that during my first visit to the field I was with my partner, who came from one of the iconic revolutionary bastions.

Being connected with someone who was related to the people with whom I lived granted me a sense of strange familiarity and led most of my interlocutors to treat me as, and call me, their daughter-in-law (*kenetna*). Despite being a foreigner, a white European non-Muslim woman, I did have deep connections with the Syrian revolutionary project on a political level and I could personally relate to the Syrian experience through my own familial history of life in revolution and exile, albeit in the Soviet context. But being a French citizen also led to bitter jokes, Syria having been a French mandate from 1923 to 1946. Young people sometimes laughingly said that they would have been resisting and fighting my relatives a few generations earlier, referring to the liberation war against France.

Over the months, my network of interlocutors grew from the few names I was first given by my London- and Istanbul-based Syrian friends, who had been particularly crucial in the early months when I sought accommodation and organisations that would accept me as a volunteer. When I first moved to Gaziantep, I lived in a studio flat in a building mainly occupied by Syrian *shabab*, on the same floor as a Syrian couple who worked in the organisation in which I volunteered for around half a year. Through this volunteering work, I developed a network of interlocutors and contacts in organisations and local councils and I also started to meet the families of the young people in the building as I was invited for lunches and sleepovers in their homes.

In the first months I would often spend my mornings visiting the house of a 50-year-old housewife who had offered to help me further develop my Arabic, which I felt the need to constantly improve in order to grasp the subtleties of the oral language in more detail, to understand different accents and dialects and to be able to engage with as wide a range of written and visual works as I could.[25] This was a great opportunity to read online articles and posts, a place where Syrians expressed views on the revolution and the current situation and where many shared personal experiences, feelings, and ideas; it also allowed me to read the testimonies and personal stories of the revolution and the war, as well as extracts of published 'prison literature',[26] accounts of the 1982 uprising and later novels and plays about the uprising, revolution and war (e.g. Al-Attar 2013; 2014; 2017; Al-Haj Saleh 2015; Al-Dik 2016; Karabet 2010; K. Khalifa 2006; 2013; 2016; M. Khalifa 2007; Yassin Hassan 2009).

Moreover, informally learning Arabic with local women was a great way to be introduced to topics that were crucial to them, offering the opportunity for them to teach me and speak about topics that most mattered to them, often religion and personal experience in the revolution. These 'classes' turned out to be more of an excuse for my teacher to speak of her family's and her own experiences in the uprising, the revolution and her children's life under siege, and in detention. The daily visits became longer over time as her children started to join our conversations and I became part of the everyday routine: I helped her eldest daughter prepare breakfast and tea in the morning and, after I had sat with my 'teacher' or accompanied her on her errands, I spent the rest of the day cooking with her daughters. I would sometimes spend a night or two at their place, and up to a week when her eldest daughter's engagement party was approaching so that I could help with its organisation. My 'teacher' was living in Turkey without her husband and with two daughters and a son at the time I arrived, and later for several months she hosted a daughter who had fled a besieged area with her husband and two other children. Through this rather typical family, I met many other families whom I visited regularly throughout the duration of my fieldwork.

In addition, as a woman living alone during the first months of my fieldwork, I was often invited to share dinner, and spend a night or the weekend at my interlocutors' places, which led me to build strong ties, become integrated into the daily routine and often become a friend or a virtual daughter-in-law of the family and the young people with whom I lived. On a typical day of fieldwork, I would visit friends' and interlocutors' homes to drink coffee, then help prepare breakfast (usually eaten around 11 or 12). In the afternoon, I would volunteer with grassroots organisations, run errands with the housewives I befriended, and queue at administrative offices where my friends were applying for documents, or at NGO offices tasked with providing support to Syrians. I would then cook and eat dinner with one of the families I befriended, spend the evening at youths' houses, or visit widows of martyrs who lived in *dar al aytam* (orphanages) with their children.

I later shared a flat for a few months with a young couple, and so came to spend a lot of time at my flatmate's family home on the outskirts of the city. We used to spend the weekends there as her husband was mostly absent, travelling to Syria where he might be stuck for weeks when the border closed without warning. I left this flat after the couple went back to Syria, and I settled for the last year of my fieldwork with Hanan and Dina and her two nephews; I became part of this unusual 'family', extending the idiom of kinship to our home. As neither of the women had a formal 9-to-5 job, we had a lot of visitors; and our home hosted the weekly meeting of a local revolutionary group. Moreover, family members who had just fled Syria or were en route to Europe often stayed for a few days or weeks. During this time I continued to spend periods ranging from a single night to a whole week or more at interlocutors' houses, accompanying them on their visits to relatives or friends in distant neighbourhoods and nearby towns. Moreover, I was often invited to marriage and engagement ceremonies and expected to be present at religious celebrations such as 'eid. Ramadan was a particularly rich period of my fieldwork as I spent a large amount of time in houses cooking with women, breaking fast with their families at *iftar* (the meal after sunset), and often staying until *suhur* (the pre-dawn meal), chatting with the family on their balcony.

'So, what are you gonna do with all these stories?' asked Naya, the young woman with whom I was to share a flat for a few months, as we sat eating fast-food in one of Gaziantep's popular malls as her husband just came back from Syria and was craving this food, which was not available there. 'I'm going to write a book about the Syrian revolution', I answered half-convinced and expecting my response to attract more scepticism. But Naya seemed quite convinced that writing a book was a good enough reason to be in Gaziantep, sharing displaced Syrian revolutionaries' lives and listening to their stories. I often asked myself, given the high stakes of the situation for my friends, what would be the outcome of my project: What was the aim or utility of it? How could it ever help my interlocutors?

Despite the precarious conditions and, for some, desperate situations in which my interlocutors lived, I was never asked for any form of material compensation in exchange for their time and help. On the contrary, I was always treated as a guest in the households I visited and served delicious food even in the most humble of them (see Kastrinou and Knoerk n.d.). I returned this hospitality by bringing presents – usually sweets and small gifts for children – as is expected in such reciprocal relations. I did, as many anthropologists do, make gifts, help with visa applications and the writing of asylum stories, give language classes and did some translation and editing work for Syrian grassroots organisations and local councils. I also helped organise campaigns and co-organised some myself, I co-created grassroots initiatives along with Syrian activists and refugees, and fundraised to help Syrian and Palestinian youths to support their activities. Yet, academic writing is far removed from decision-making, and despite having tried to write some more public newspaper articles on the one hand, and more policy-oriented briefs on the other, I do not believe I could escape the paradoxical position in which many fellow anthropologists find themselves: our academic work has very little impact on the real world (see Mittermaier 2019: 14–15). I do hope, however, that such an ethnographic description and analysis of the Syrian revolution and its aftermaths can contribute to writing a heterohistory of these events by giving voice to its often invisibilised actors, Syrian working- and lower-middle class housewives, which show a different genealogy and trace a counter-history of these events.

## Ethnography in times of political turmoil

Working in a context of revolution, war, and displacement created specific challenges to ethnographic work. First, my fieldsite was constantly in movement. On the one hand, Gaziantep's location at the border with Syria's liberated areas and the government open-door policy[27] meant that there were frequent new arrivals. Revolutionaries freed from jail would usually be smuggled through Syria and cross into Turkey as they were often still wanted by the regime and could not easily cross into Lebanon or Jordan. Moreover, the shelling of regions near the Turkish border, their liberation by the rebels, or occupation by the regime led to a continuous arrival of Syrians. On the other hand, because of the deteriorating situation in Turkey, many attempted to reach Europe by sea, especially during the summer of 2015 when the Balkan route opened, a movement that never stopped though it greatly decreased in the following years. This meant that some of my interlocutors left and new ones constantly arrived. I managed to maintain coherence in my fieldwork as departures rarely involved an entire family and arrivals were usually family members of my circle of friends and contacts. For instance, my flatmate's moving back to Syria led me to find a new living arrangement but did not disturb the course of my research. Similarly, when my first teacher's family suddenly left Turkey I had to deepen my relations with families I already knew but with whom I was less close. These movements became an integral part of my research methodology and analysis. Quite unlike multi-sited ethnography (Hage 2005), I lived these movements of people by staying put, watching them happen and pass through the place where I was settled, creating an interesting inversion that one could call a Syrianisation of the research tools. It became a structuring part of my analysis as the concepts of inside (*juwwa*) and outside (*barra*) became methodological and analytical tools in my book.

In addition to this spatial dimension there was a temporal one, or rather the structuring spatial division between inside and outside was also temporal. I studied an event that started in 2011 and that was still ongoing at the time of my fieldwork yet had taken different shapes and was understood differently over time and was constantly changing and being transformed by current circumstances. Most of the events that affected my fieldsite happened elsewhere and had different temporalities: the revolution, the war, and migration. Some were ongoing while others already belonged in the past, although the temporalities of these events were always subject to debate. Throughout this book I thus map out the transformations occurring in people's lives as a consequence of events that were happening elsewhere, and which, for some, had already ended. I simultaneously study the transformations to which these events bore witness: they were ongoing changes in the situation on the ground but also through Syrians' (re)interpretations of it.

While the spatio-temporal divide (inside *juwwa*/outside *barra*) structured my field, there are geographical, historical, and political reasons behind Gaziantep's specific status. The city constituted a liminal space where ephemeral communitas was formed. This liminal positional as well as a common past and present (the revolution) explained why, despite the variety of my interlocutors in terms of religious, ethnic, social, and regional backgrounds, they nonetheless formed a coherent group of interlocutors. Indeed, Gaziantep formed an in-between, a bridge between inside and outside: a place where revolutionary youth and families stopped for a while before going back inside or continuing their journey towards an outside elsewhere. Some, however, settled for a longer period, and it is they who are at the heart of this study.

But Gaziantep was also a hostile place for my interlocutors and a taxing fieldsite for the researcher. Despite Syrian hospitality and generosity, even in precarious situations, the atmosphere in Gaziantep remained rather antagonistic. Syrians were living in a limbo as they struggled to obtain residence permits, to access education and healthcare, to find jobs. Moreover, discrimination and acts of xenophobia were daily occurrences. Hostility also came from the fear that spread with the series of attacks in Turkey,[28] the murder of Syrian activists,[29] and the tense political context in the country. The election periods (such as in summer and autumn 2015) were particularly strained; the situation in the city was modified as the borders were closed and Syrians could no longer travel freely inside Turkey. Fear within the Syrian community and tensions with the Turkish locals increased in this period. Each of these events further destabilised the Syrian community and increased the precariousness and uncertainty of its present and future in the country.

Being a woman in a partially gender-segregated society could have been a major obstacle to my fieldwork, except that most of the households I visited were exclusively composed of women. Moreover, as a foreigner, I was not expected to follow the rules of gendered segregation. For instance, during a friend's engagement party, the young female guests stayed with the fiancée in her room while the men ate with the future groom, whereas I could navigate the house freely with the mother. Similarly, when my teacher's daughter arrived from Syria with her husband and sons I could access both the kitchen where the women were eating and the living room where the mother sat with the men. The main limitation I had to observe was not to sit alone with a man except in a public place. This would have sent ambiguous messages both to the man himself and to the rest of my interlocutors, my female friends explained.

This book is divided into six chapters that trace the (un)intended consequences of the revolution and its unexpected outcomes on Syrian lives and the subsequent reshaping of their world, describing Syrians' evolving conceptions, theorisations, experiences, and imaginations of *al-thawra* (the revolution). The book maps out these transformations on both cosmological and intimate scales – the reshaping of spatio-temporal coordinates and horizons, and the constitution of new selves – and also through the shift from the political to the social domain, resulting in the modification of relations, everyday life, gender norms, and types of alliances among my interlocutors. It thus attempts to understand *al-thawra* as a cosmogonic (that is, world-shaping) entity. The division into chapters is not only thematic, but also follows the spatio-temporal logic of the events studied and the constant redefinition of *juwwa* (inside) and *barra* (outside). It begins with an account of the uprising inside Syria, follows my interlocutors in their displacement to Gaziantep and their movement between Turkey and Syria, examines the reconstitution of their lives outside Syria, and reflects on the consequences of the events on Syrians' lives, while the conclusion focuses on Syrians' flight from Turkey to Europe. In following the chronology of the events inside Syria and Syrians' geography of displacement, the book thus places the intimate relation between revolution and displacement at its centre, both as an ethnographic object and an analytical device. Through the simultaneous depiction of revolution and displacement, the book sheds light on their influences on one another.

# Notes

1 These words were written on a wall in Saraqeb in 2017. The graffiti was photographed and archived on the 'Walls of Saraqeb' Facebook group and on Creative Memory of the Syrian Revolution's website, https://creativememory.org/fr/archives/164258/dans-la-revolution-comme-dans-les-contes__trashed/.

2 This was in the context of the 'Balkan road', which opened in summer 2015 and later closed with the flow of refugees, and the hope that it would re-open again or that another way from Greece and the Balkans would open towards central and northern Europe.

3 In his book, Yasser Munif (2020) gives a lengthy description of the political and academic discourses that erase the Syrian revolution.

4 Revolutions are thus often understood and defined as macro-events, as breaks with history and in history, and as points where time restarts, marking a new beginning or a new phase (see Arendt 1965; Koselleck 1985). In this sense, the concept of revolution is still very much marked by Enlightenment philosophy and Western historiography (Ghamari-Tabrizi 2016; Trouillot 1995).

5 Revolutionary events represent both a methodological and an analytical challenge for anthropology as a discipline that has traditionally focused on continuity rather than rupture, using analytical language and conceptual frameworks that privilege continuity and stability over fracture and change (Robbins 2007; see also Humphrey 2008; Worsley 1961). More precisely, the conception of time underlining the discipline presents an obstacle to the study of revolution because it is considered a rupture in time, while anthropology traditionally assumes that its objects of study are not subjects of change (Robbins 2007; see also Scott 2014: 5). Hence, while there are a few ethnographies of unfolding revolutions – for it is rather a matter of chance to find oneself in the field during a revolution (for instance Hegland 2014; Manning 2007; Starn 1991) – there are plenty of ethnographic monographs of post-revolutionary societies, states and subjects (such as Davis 1986; Holbraad 2004; 2014; Humphrey 1983; Ssorin-Chaikov 2006; Yurchak 2015; Khosravi 2017; Varzi 2006; Lan 1985; Potter and Potter 1990; West 2005).

6 The literature on the so-called Arab Spring directly challenges anthropological methodology by underlining that research into such ongoing social and political changes pushes anthropologists to 'rework the tools of their discipline' (Elyachar and Winegar 2012: para. 3). For instance, the notion of 'ethnographic distance' and the balance between 'immersion in the field' and 'distance necessary for writing', since none of these methodological precepts apply in the case of anthropologists addressing the revolution from within its action, because of the 'intensity of affect' that emerged from the events and the blurring that takes place between thinking and acting (Sabea 2012: para. 11). Moreover, they question the kind of theory that can emerge from the study of unfolding (and therefore shifting) events whose outcome is inconclusive, asking whether the events under study can be called a revolution with a capital *R* or whether they should rather be labelled a revolt with a small *r* (Elyachar 2012a; Sabea 2012). Finally, politically, qualifying the events of revolution as they still unfold can only be partisan – and even *has* to be – for one does not know whether the events will qualify as a revolution (i.e., will succeed) in the future (see Schielke 2012b).

7 Studies of revolutions in exile have shown the importance of shifting attention to displaced revolutionaries' everyday life, pragmatic choices, marriage patterns, social life and economic conditions (such as Allan 2014; Peteet 1991; Wilson 2016).

8 See Chapter 1 on the prison literature of biographical and fictional testimonies of the 1982 uprising and of detention by the regime in the '80s and '90s in Syria (for instance al-Haj Saleh 2015; Karabet 2010; M. Khalifa 2007; Yassin Hassan 2009).

9 There has been controversy about this date, as others claim it started three days earlier with small protests in downtown Damascus (see Chapter 1).

10 Rami Farah's movie *Our Memory Belongs to Us* (2021) recounts this story in the city of Deraa based on videos filmed by citizen journalists and three of the actors describing these events.

11 This word first appeared in its substantive form and its current 'positive' meaning in the Arab press of the 1850s (Ayalon 1987: 145).

12 Whereas the Syrian population is on average living on US$100 to US$200 per month and the Turkish on US$6,000 per year (Mahmud 2016).

13 These self-definitions were however very dynamic: constantly evolving, moving and often overlapping. Most of my interlocutors started using these terms to define themselves in contrast

to the al-Nusra Front in 2012. Whether they initially supported or opposed it, many *islamiyyin* stopped supporting al-Nusra as soon as they understood its political aims. Despite defining themselves as *islamiyyin* in opposition to the *'almaniyyin*, most of my interlocutors would be defined as secular in Western terms, for they similarly asked for a secular state. *Islamiyyin* in the Syrian context rather signifies one's social and religious conservatism when used by *'almaniyyin*, and is used self-referentially to differentiate oneself from the *'almaniyyin*, who were often caricatured as atheists (see Asad 2003, 2018 and Schielke 2019 on the notion of secular).

14　See Dahi (2011) on the revolutionaries' social composition.

15　Failure has however been the topic of a number of studies (for example Carroll et al. 2017; Llera-Blanes and Oustinova-Stjepanovic 2015; Oustinova-Stjepanovic 2011; 2017).

16　By defining the pursuit of grand schemes – ideal horizons such as romantic love, religious piety, revolutionary action, and capitalist consumerism – as unrealisable, Schielke crucially draws our attention to the 'ambivalence, contradictions, and experiences of failure' rather than the 'successful ordering of social experience' (2015: 19). He thus presents failure and its unintended consequences as inherent to human actions and intentions.

17　The specific temporality of revolution makes revolutionary action more vulnerable to tragic endings, for it rejects the past and projects itself towards an unknown future, aiming to establish a new order that is being resisted by existing powers.

18　See also Amar 2021; Al-Aswad 2020; Seifan 2020.

19　See M. Khalifa (2007); Al-Sarraj (2011).

20　The level of violence that has unfolded on the Syrian population since the start of the 2011 revolution has been called 'genocidal' by Syrian intellectual Yassin al-Haj Saleh (2021); while the levels of destruction have led other scholars to speak of 'urbicide' (Munif 2020; Vignal 2021). Survivors' testimonies, pictures leaked from the military intelligence and the work of forensic architects show that torture and executions have been conducted on an industrial scale by the Assad regime, with, for instance, a crematorium in Sednaya prison (Weizmal 2019). Chemical weapons were used against civilians living in revolutionary strongholds and entire towns were besieged and systematically bombed, with barrel bombs and other heavy weapons (Al-Haj Saleh 2021; Coquio et al. 2022; Munif 2020).

21　This also strongly resonates with what Amira Mittermaier has called 'an anthropology of *'al-ghayb'* that is an anthropology of the hidden, the unseen, the invisible, but also the absent, in that it encompasses both what is in the here and now and the thereafter, what is in the historical and cosmological realms (2019).

22　See Cherstich et al. (2020) and Holbraad (2013) on the notion of revolution as cosmogony.

23　Emphasising that the majority of Egyptians were not in the streets during the revolution, they respectively argue that, by conducting research on revolution outside its emblematic places and with its hidden actors, one can grasp revolution in all its complexities. Furthermore, one can assess whether and how revolutionary aims and slogans materialise in people's everyday life.

24　Syrians' situation was more precarious in Antakya as the municipality did not issue *kimlik* (identity document for Syrians in Turkey). Moreover there were sometimes tensions with the local Arabic-speaking community that is largely Alawi and are rather sympathetic to the Assad regime.

25　See Schielke (2019) on the constant learning of spoken Arabic, especially the religious idioms, in the field.

26　There is a literary genre called 'prison literature' in Syria that focuses on biographical and fictional testimonies of the 1982 uprising and of detention by the regime in the '80s and '90s.

27　This was the case until the summer of 2015, although the border was sometimes closed before this date (Longuenesse and Ruiz de Elvira 2016).

28　There were a total of 37 attacks in Turkey between 2014 and 2016, and around ten of them happened in Gaziantep (https://140journos.com/terror-attacks-in-turkey-between-2011-and-2017-4b5981c974ca).

29　Prominent activist and film-maker Naji Jerf was murdered in December 2015, among other activists (https://www.telegraph.co.uk/news/2016/06/26/isil-murders-five-media-activists-for-exposing-syria-atrocities/).

Part 1
# Revolution inside

**Figure 1.1:** Walking towards the revolution. © Daraya Local Council

# 1

# The Syrian revolution: a struggle for dignity

'The Syrian people will not be humiliated' (*al sh'ab al suri ma byindhal*); 'dignity, dignity, dignity' (*karama, karama, karama*); 'either live in freedom or die in dignity' (*ya na'ish b-hurriyya, ya nmut b-karama*) the protestors sang in demonstrations across Syrian cities and towns, stressing the demand for dignity that largely fuelled the 2011 revolution. The idea of a dignified life reflected in these slogans resonates strongly with my interlocutors' narratives about the revolution when they spoke about its causes, its nature and its outcome.

> *Zulm* was everywhere [before the revolution]. When the revolution started, all my sons participated in it. They were all out to ask for their rights. They were just against the *zulm* … This is why we got into the revolution, so we can live properly.

Umm Ahmad,[1] a mother of three martyred sons and two others forcefully disappeared from a working-class neighbourhood of Aleppo, told me this in one of our conversations as she explained her sons' motivation for participating in the uprising. The protestors' demands pointed to the absence of dignity that marked their life under the Assad regime, a life my interlocutors described as characterised by *zulm* (oppression/injustice), *khuf* (fear) and *fasad* (corruption). The definition of dignity given by the Syrians I lived with was often elaborated in relation (and opposition) to different forms of *zulm* (injustice/oppression): oppressive regime practices in the political and religious fields that constituted their everyday lives before the uprising; socioeconomic injustices; as well as the unjust and violent repression and humiliating treatment of unarmed protestors during the uprising.

The unjust and oppressed life my Syrian interlocutors described under the Assads is vividly rendered in what Yassin al-Haj Saleh (2021) calls the 'palmirisation' of Syria, in reference to the infamous prison of Tadmor (Palmyra) where members of the Muslim Brotherhood were massacred after the 1982 rebellion (M. Khalifa 2007; Saouli 2018). The palmirisation of Syria is actually not a phenomenon that started with the 2011 uprising, although it then spread on a larger scale with the mass repression of the revolution. The weaponry and levels of violence deployed on the part of the regime, prior (iconically in Hama and Tadmor) and during the uprising, have led Yasser Munif (2020) to define the regime's politics in terms of 'necropolitics' (Mbembe 2019), describing the taxonomies of death by the Assad regime from its accession to power in the 1960s till the late 2010s.

It is in this context of constant terror and daily humiliation (see Mardam-Bey 2022; Ismail 2018) that the Syrian concept of *karama* (dignity) developed as a revolutionary call to put an end to the oppressive rule of the Assad regime. It is in response and in opposition to the 'abject' and the 'atrocious' that Syrians rose, asking for *karama*. Dignity, in its 'Syrian' definition, has thus to be understood, in Nisrine al-Zahre's terms, as the 'opposite of the Assadist abject' (2021: 45) or what Yassin al-Haj Saleh calls the atrocious (2020; 2021), something my interlocutors name *zulm* (oppression/injustice) and which is characterised by a lack of *hurriyya* (freedom) and *'adaleh* (justice): a life governed by *khuf* (fear) and *fasad* (corruption). Moreover, by stating that death is better than humiliation, the protesters show that dignity is the capacity to face death while simultaneously attempting to live and to access a political life (Al-Zahre 2021: 46; see also Chapters 2 and 6 on this point).

This chapter describes, through at-length quotations of my interlocutors' stories, how the 2011 revolution started in Syria: What were its historical, political and ideological roots? Who were its actors and their motivations? What was the initial project and how was it transformed over time? Through my interlocutors' life stories and genealogies as well as through their own historicisation of the revolution within local and regional history, one sees how the revolutionary project inscribes itself in the *longue durée* and resonates with regional events happening in the early 2010s. Moreover, such contextualisation of the revolution and its actors show how notions of justice, freedom and dignity, the central revolutionary claims, are grounded in my interlocutors' historical and everyday experiences. Overall, through the descriptions, analyses and theories offered by my interlocutors, a history of the revolution 'from below' – what could be named a counter-history or 'heterohistory' (Chakrabarty 2000) – appears: a history that goes against the official historiography of the Assad regime, for which the 'revolution' was their 1963 coup celebrated each year as the 8 March Revolution, and in which narrative the 2011 revolution is a 'foreign conspiracy' (*mu'amarah kharjiyyeh*) or a 'terrorist plot' (*tamarud al-i'rhabiyyin*). In the counter-history presented here, the revolution is rather defeated or paused, thus offering a first definition of *al-thawra*.

## Revolution: dignity or death

You want to know why we started the revolution? It is because of the *zulm* ... We all used to live in *zulm* and *khuf* [fear]. We didn't live before the revolution. Maybe we ate and drank but this was not a life!

I first met Umm Ahmad when accompanying Umm Nidal as she ran a few errands and took Umm Ahmad some cash collected by the friends of her martyred sons; Umm Nidal's own son numbered among them. Umm Ahmad is a pious woman in her mid-forties, she comes from a socially and religiously conservative family and used to live in one of Aleppo's most impoverished suburbs. She was married when she was fourteen and did not finish middle-school. She is a housewife and her husband used to work in a local garage as a mechanic. 'Umm Ahmad is a living symbol of the revolution; she is the one that will help you understand it the best,' Umm Nidal told me on the way to visit her. Umm Ahmad is sometimes referred to as Umm Saber (mother of patience) for three of her sons have been martyred in the revolution, while two had been detained for over four years at the time; no one has heard from them since their arrest. 'Everybody thinks they are also martyrs', Umm Nidal confided to me.

After our first encounter in 2015, I visited Umm Ahmad weekly, listening to her stories of revolution, loss, displacement, and hope. I used to sit with her, her daughter, and her daughter-in-law on the floor of one of the two small rooms of her flat and listen to her stories for hours drinking coffee, tea and sometimes eating a light meal. Umm Ahmad took pride in the fact that, despite not having any formal education herself, she had managed to push all her children to study hard and enrol in institutes or universities. She also insisted on sound moral and religious education for her children and told me how her sons used to volunteer in the local mosque and give lessons to the neighbourhood children while her daughter studied sharia. They were also hardworking, with the sons working alongside their father to help with the household's expenses.

During wintertime, we sat on folded blankets that replaced the usual mattresses or sofas around the only heating device in the house, a *subya* (wood-burning hearth) that they lit during the night and when I was visiting. During my first visit, hearing that I was researching the Syrian revolution, Umm Ahmad proffered as its cause something that she termed *zulm* (oppression/injustice), presenting the revolution as the logical outcome of the absence of life – an existence in *zulm* and *khuf* (fear) – prior to it.

In the quote above, Umm Ahmad links the revolution with the absence of real life under the regime – a life that is defined not by the absence of basic needs ('we ate and drank') but by the absence of humane values, since it is a life of oppression, without dignity and justice. Umm Ahmad implicitly contrasts two kinds of life: a humane life (*hayat*) without oppression (*zulm*) – the life *b'ad al-thawra* (after the revolution); and the kind of life common to all living beings ('*aysh*) – the life *qabl al-thawra* (before the revolution), under the regime.

The distinction between *hayat* and '*aysh* that starts to appear in Umm Ahmad's words was clarified in a conversation with Rami, a young man from a rural town in central Syria who witnessed the Egyptian revolution in Cairo. Rami's family were originally farmers but his father benefited from the early Baathist reforms and secured employment in the state administration after graduating from a local institute. The family lived on his civil servant salary, which Rami's father augmented by working on his own father's land.[2] Rami's family was socially and religiously conservative and close to the Muslim Brotherhood, which led the rebellion in Hama in 1982, in which some of Rami's uncles had participated. For Rami's as for Umm Ahmad's family and most Syrians, education was a priority and the only means of social mobility.[3]

Rami was sent to study engineering in Egypt, where he had relatives, as his baccalaureate results did not allow him to enrol in this faculty in Syria, but he came back when the uprising started. In his attempt to define the Syrian revolution, Rami contrasted the concepts of *hayat* and '*aysh*. *Hayat* and '*aysh* both mean 'life' in Arabic, but the young man explained that the Syrian revolution, unlike the Egyptian, was not a matter of '*aysh* but a matter of *hayat*. 'The Egyptians asked for bread ['*aysh*],[4] but we demanded justice ['*adaleh*], dignity [*karama*], and freedom [*hurriyya*]!' the young man proudly said. People in Syria already had '*aysh*, Rami argued: they were living well in the sense that their everyday needs were fulfilled, but they did not have and wanted *hayat*, a human life, a dignified one, in contrast to the mere life of the body. Yet, this clear opposition is complicated by my interlocutors' recounting of their everyday life prior to the revolution (see below). In Rami's definition, however, *hayat* and *'aysh* appear as Arabic equivalents of the Greek *bios* and *zoe* as defined in Agamben's work (1998). Here *'aysh/zoe* seems to be the equivalent of a bare life while *hayat/bios* is a political (and dignified) life.

This resonates with protestors' slogans. In March 2011, they chanted: '*Ya Bouthaina, wa ya Sha'ban, al-sha'b al-suri mu ju'an*' ('Oh, Bouthaina, and oh, Sha'ban, the Syrian people are not hungry'); this was also inflected as, '*Ya Bouthaina, wa ya Sha'ban*, the Hawrani [inhabitants of the Deraa region] are not hungry, we want freedom!' (Wedeen 2013: 847).[5]

The grievances against the regime were also religious; many wanted religious (as well as political and personal) freedom. In a country with a predominantly Sunni population, all Sunni religious institutions were nevertheless under the strict control of the Assad regime (see Pierret 2013; Pinto 2007a; 2007b). Many of my interlocutors shared their fears and frustrations about the impossibility of practising their faith freely.

> I took my wife's gold because maybe they [the regime's army] would come and enter our home. I took the gold and I bought a gun. This was at the beginning of the revolution. I was not ready to let them enter our house and kill us … I had my children, my wife, my mother … Did I want to sit there and see what happens next? I wanted to defend my family and I was ready to die for it! … The kids in Deraa who wrote on the wall, they [the regime forces] came and took their nails off. This is *zulm*! They were just children! … So was I supposed to sit and see what happens?

Abu Zein, a pious man in his early thirties close to the Salafi movement, worked in a religious bookshop in his native city after he came back from studying sharia in the Gulf. I met him at the home of Umm Yussef, his mother, a woman from Homs in central Syria whom I often visited. In the above extract of one of our conversations that took place in the spring of 2015, after Abu Zein arrived from his besieged neighbourhood where he was fighting on the side of the rebels, oppression also appears as central to his decision to join the protest and to become a fighter. Here oppression is also linked to honour – which he presents as the protection of women and children against oppression – and to the central claim of the Syrian uprising: dignity (*karama*). But Abu Zein's linking oppression with honour and dignity was far from an exception.

As in Egypt and Tunisia, the spark that started the Syrian uprising was arbitrary police violence towards children and people struggling to make a living.[6] A protest erupted in Damascus on 18 February 2011 after a policeman violently beat a street vendor in the old city, and the uprising is said to have begun after children in Deraa were arrested and brutally tortured by the regime forces. This brought Deraa's community together, as tribal leaders, family members, and local notables went to the security office to ask for the children's release. They were met with a violent answer by the head of security who allegedly told the men that he advised the fathers of the detained children to make other children with their wives and that if they could not, the security officers would do it for them. This was experienced as a strong affront to the men's honour,[7] unleashing the first protest in the city in which men and women from other families joined.

## Rising against fear and corruption

Simultaneously to the opposition to oppression that materialised in the call for dignity, Syrian revolutionaries positioned themselves against corruption (*fasad*) and fear (*khuf*), two other defining realities of Syrians' daily pre-2011 life (*qabl al-thawra*), calling for freedom and social justice.

> I had the feeling that I was born again (*waladet min jdid*)! I could speak. I was happy that I was finally free! I could say whatever I wanted ... Until then we couldn't even speak in our own houses! We couldn't speak with anyone!

These words of Abu Leila,[8] a man in his late sixties from *rif dimashq* (Damascus countryside), expressed the feeling of freedom that emerged with the possibility of speech without fear brought by the revolution. As we sat around the wood-burner waiting for Umm Leila to finish preparing 'lunch'[9] with her daughters, Abu Leila told me how he too had participated in the revolution, sharing with me the feelings that overwhelmed him. He was proud that not only did his daughters protest against the regime but that he did too. In the protests he felt like a new person: for the first time in his life he was free, he did not have to fear that he would be overheard and that a report would be written against him, he could express his opinion and speak about everything to everyone. He did not have to abide by the logic of 'as if' anymore (see Wedeen 1999).

One of Abu Leila's main motivations to participate in the protest was his deep knowledge of corruption. The father of five daughters, he used to work in the army before opening a small shop in his native town and starting a career as a local sheikh. In a later conversation, he recalled how he used to participate in the regime's corruption logic, as his low-ranking officer's salary did not allow him to feed his growing family. He told me that, during his decade-long service in the army, he took part in cross-border smuggling activities, explaining that it was something everyone did in his unit: they all used to smuggle goods that they sold on the black market or kept for themselves. The higher one's position in the hierarchy, the more one took.

Abu Leila must have done something that displeased higher-ranking officers, however, as he was arrested and jailed for nearly two years for his activities. This reveals how many Syrians participated in a regime with which they coped by applying the modality of 'as if' (Wedeen 1998; 1999; Al-Kallas and Aubin-Boltanski 2022): neither Assad's propagandists nor the Syrian people believed in the regime's propaganda, yet it functioned as a coercive and disciplining device. But such a system also led to what sowed the seeds of the uprising, as it generated moral trouble and anger.[10]

In addition, the deteriorating economic situation from the 1990s onwards pushed many functionaries to participate in the regime's corruption and/or to adopt the strategy of moonlighting (taking on another job or two in addition to their main occupation), which had previously been exclusive to the working class.[11] In the early 2000s the situation worsened with the opening up of the market and the state's divestment of responsibilities, which led to a series of privatisations. State employees saw their income level dramatically diminish and a career in the state administration, previously a means of social mobility perceived as eventually leading to a middle-class lifestyle, began to be synonymous with poverty. In the 1990s and 2000s not only lower-ranking functionaries but also engineers and doctors[12] started to diversify their source of income, indexing the worsening of the economic situation for traditional lower-middle and middle classes. Abu Leila recalled how local sheikhs started to ask for *zakat* (alms), reserved for the poor, for state functionaries.

While it brought together people from various social backgrounds, impoverished labourers, disgruntled students, civil servants, and civil rights activists, the biggest contingent of the uprising consisted of people who, like my interlocutors, belonged to the working and lower-middle classes.[13] Before the revolution, the men had been bus or taxi drivers, shopkeepers, policemen, farmers, state engineers, traders in local bazaars, low-ranking military officers, local sheikhs, small shop owners, or had cultivated small pieces of land. They had all had two or three jobs in order to make ends meet. Most of the women had been housewives and those who worked had been schoolteachers or civil servants; the young were students and graduates of high schools, military academies or universities, apprentices in farms or workshops, civil servants, or working for a parent in a local business, although some were unemployed. Most of my interlocutors came from suburban and small towns, fewer from the countryside and big cities. Their families were mainly socially and religiously conservative: most were raised with strict Sunni morals that are close to the Salafi reading of the Quran, although the majority followed Sufi practices (see Pinto 2007a; 2007b). Some of the *shabab* with whom I worked belonged to the wealthier middle classes. Their parents, who still lived in Syria, were bigger landowners, traders or wealthy doctors. Yet, despite the opening of the market, the corrupt system led to frustration as merchants and traders had to share their business profits with the Assad clan;[14] they could also be arrested, or forbidden to work, as the regime could stop providing them with authorisation to operate.

*Kunna n'aysh b-khuf* (we were living in fear), my interlocutors often said, qualifying the overwhelming and omnipresent feeling that their life under an unjust and corrupted regime had. A mother was scared that her son would be arrested because he prayed regularly at the mosque; another worried each time her son returned late at night from a friend's place in case he was arrested on his way home by the plain clothes officers believed to be present everywhere. People were scared to speak even in their own houses, Abu Leila explained. 'The walls have ears' was commonly repeated to me by Syrians to characterise life before the revolution. *Khuf* (fear) and *fasad* (corruption) as causes of mobilisation in the revolution were also highlighted by Umm Khaled.

> I feared for my children, and hoped that we would succeed [in overthrowing the regime]. I just wanted the regime to step down and hold new elections; I wanted the corruption to end; I wanted us to have laws. I wanted people to live in *karama* [dignity]! Why did my husband need to work three jobs for us to live? Why should I always be scared that my son would be arrested if he says this or that, or if he prayed at the mosque? … Before the revolution, you were always scared for your future and the future of your children …

Umm Khaled used to live with her husband and four children in a provincial, predominantly Sunni, town. As was the case for most of my interlocutors, despite being an engineer employed by the state, her husband had to take on extra jobs for his family to make ends meet. He was thus working his father's land with his wife, who was selling their small surplus, in addition to his civil-servant job. Abu Khaled blamed the regime's corrupt practices for his situation: his superiors in the hierarchy used cheaper and weaker materials than those required but still charged for better, more expensive goods, so they could pocket the price difference. This inevitably resulted in the country having defective infrastructure, he lamented to Umm Khaled. Describing how the corruption worked, he explained to his wife that the higher you got in the hierarchy the more money you stole, underlining that only Alawis could get to the top of the system regardless of qualifications; then came the members of other minorities, but Sunni were always at the bottom of the scale, according to him.

In fact, under the Assad regime, corruption was omnipresent in Syrians' everyday life. My interlocutors recalled paying bribes to get just about anything: an ID, a passport, a licence to open a shop, a permit to build a house, or for a son to be able to visit his family while doing his military service. Corruption existed at all levels and in all domains, as many stories attested: before 'eid celebrations, for example, policemen stopped pedestrians and drivers and fined them on any pretext so they could finish their rolls of tickets. Moreover, corruption was supported and driven by sectarianism (*ta'fiyyeh*), manifested in the monopolising of resources by a small (often Alawi) elite,[15] particularly in state services and administration, and most critically in the army and in universities. Yet, more than merely a reference to Shi'i heterodoxy, the term 'Alawi' connoted for my interlocutors the notions of privilege, links to the regime, and profit from these links (see Salamandra 2013).

*Khuf* and *fasad* were thus constitutive parts of the *zulm* that the Assad regime had erected into a ruling tool: Syrians were governed by oppression and fear, and lived in a country ruled by widespread corruption and arbitrariness. These realities were omnipresent in my interlocutors' narratives of Syria before the revolution. *Khuf, fasad* and the encompassing notion of *zulm* constituted that which *karama* opposed and sought to replace through revolutionary action.

## History from below

On the second of February [2011], we [a small group of about twenty *shabab* who used to meet and discuss politics] started to discuss what we should do on the fifth. We tried to organise a protest but it didn't work as there were too many security agents on the square where it was meant to happen. We waited until the fifteenth of March [national day of protest] and organised a small protest near the Umayyad Mosque [in central Damascus]. We gathered about forty people near the old market. Many of us were arrested, but after this first experience we knew it was possible to organise protests even in the heart of Damascus. We started to be more organised and more efficient. We organised a protest after the Friday prayer near the Umayyad Mosque on the eighteenth of March [2011] as it is always crowded and the old city is a labyrinth where we could escape easily. We tried to follow the instructions of Egyptian revolutionaries in facing the security forces: walk alone, avoid crowds, don't run. But most of the protesters were too scared and started to run away as the security forces arrived. It happened to be one of the most spontaneous protests as people who were praying inside the mosque joined us. But there were too many security agents surrounding us to escape; my brothers and I were arrested.

Zakaria, a university student from *rif dimashq* (the Damascus suburbs) who took part in the peaceful protests at the beginning of the uprising before joining the armed rebellion in his small town, explained how he helped organise protests in his town and in the capital. His account of the first protests in Damascus shows that they were both organised and spontaneous, thus playing on preparation and surprise. Zakaria explained how the first protests were organised on secret Facebook groups, and through friends and acquaintances, so no one knew if the call would be heard; there was also an element of surprise in that the organisers never knew if people would join, how the crowd would react,[16] and whether they would be able to gather in highly surveilled squares. Zakaria recalled that the first protests in central Damascus did not even have time to form as the security forces intervened directly and arrested the protesters. That the Syrian revolution was inspired by the Tunisian and, even more so, the Egyptian revolution is undeniable, as Zakaria mentions. However, the Syrian revolution was not simply an answer to other revolutionary events; it had its own logic and chronology which this chapter traces in the local and regional history.

'The question, as for all Syrians, was how were we going to start the revolution?', Zakaria said.

We gave ourselves a deadline: if the revolution survived in Egypt, we could do the same. When the revolution was over in Egypt, the atmosphere was ready in Syria. One of my friends thought of immolating himself to start the revolution [referring to the way in which the revolution in Tunisia started with Mohammad Bouazizi's immolation].

Although these words seem to stem from the exceptional position of a political activist, Zakaria was a rather ordinary student. He was from a conservative family; his father owned a small shop in their suburban town and he did not belong to any political party or have any political experience before the revolution. Yet, with the uprisings starting in Tunisia and Egypt, he began to meet with like-minded friends to think of ways to organise. Zakaria's words show that the anticipation was linked to the spreading of uprisings around the region, and to internal dynamics within Syria's history. In fact, the 2011 uprising extended both backwards (historically) and outwards (geographically) in a series of revolts ('abortive revolutions') and revolutions ('a radical upheaval including, at the very least, a change in the political regime' according to Achcar 2013: 14–16).

'It will take a long time [to tell you my story]; it all started in 1948!' So said Yassar, a graduate student who had taken part in the uprising in *rif dimashq* and his native Deraa, in answer to my request, when we first met, that he tell me about his experience in and thoughts about the revolution. The uprising was thus both a spontaneous event influenced by the Tunisian, Egyptian, and Libyan revolutions and something that was part of a long national and regional history. The year 1948 referenced Palestinian resistance to the establishment of the Israeli state; 1923 and 1936 were sometimes offered as dates when the circle of revolts and rebellions began, as they marked struggles against the French colonial power. The 2011 uprising was also linked by my interlocutors to the rebellions against Hafez al-Assad. In the late 1970s and early 1980s the Muslim Brotherhood organised themselves against the regime, underground resistance that culminated between 1978 and 1982 when the regime faced an armed revolt led by the Brotherhood. As a result the Brotherhood and all oppositional parties that did not integrate with the ruling National Progressive Front[17] were forced underground and severely repressed.

The regime's violent repression of any political dissent and activity, characterised by the campaign of arbitrary arrests and detention in appalling conditions, are elements that marked many of my interlocutors' biographies and family histories, constituting a shared collective memory that played an important role in their participation in the uprising. Some of my interlocutors had, as youths, rebelled against the regime in the 1980s; some had spent several years in jail as a result of their political opposition, while most of my interlocutors who were old enough in 1982 had memories of the repression. One, a woman in her sixties, had been jailed for over a decade with her children due to her kinship ties with a leader of the rebellion. Another was detained for four years for her peaceful activism in the Communist Party Political Bureau as a student. Umm Ahmad, whom I presented above, although still a child at the time, vividly remembered the bodies of the young men killed in the streets by the army in Aleppo and 'left there to teach a lesson to the local population' as she told me.

Moreover, many of my interlocutors had been affected in one way or another by repression of that revolt: a brother, fiancé, or uncle had disappeared and never been heard of again, someone else had been killed or detained for decades. The memory of the uprising was also vivid in young people's minds, as it had been transmitted within the private sphere of the family, sometimes as revolutionary genealogies, and more generally through the widespread fear of discussing – and consequent silence about – political matters of any sort, even within the home. The memory of the uprising's repression was also kept alive, although only for a minority of my interlocutors, through the literary accounts of direct witnesses, victims of the repression, and former political detainees that some had read;[18] these were published in Beirut and smuggled into Syria, or were sometimes found on the internet. The regime's violence was thus perceived by my interlocutors as a reason why it should be toppled: it was yet another proof of its oppression (*zulm*), cruelty, and illegitimacy.

Re-placing the 2011 revolution within a local history of political dissent, Yassin, a former political detainee in his forties who had spent eight years in prison for being a member of a party belonging to the wide spectrum of political Islam, recalled the following story about a riot (*asta'sa'*)[19] at the infamous Sednaya prison in March 2008:

> After the US invasion of Iraq many jihadists[20] were jailed in Sednaya [prison] where I was detained. The number of detainees grew dramatically. The situation became tenser as torture became systematic. The prison is structured like the Mercedes sign [Yassin draws it on a small piece of paper with a smile on his lips]: there are three wings leading to the central building and each of them has three floors and a basement … On one day in March 2008, the head of the prison, accompanied by military police, came to a cell on the second floor [the jihadists' floor] and started to bring the men out one by one and torture them in the corridor.[21] There were about 20 to 30 men to a cell. We could hear them screaming: fear and tension increased in the whole wing [on all three floors]. We knew our turn would come, as they opened one cell after the other and tortured all the men. We had to revolt! As one man, without any instruction given or previous plan set, we started to bang the doors and the walls of the cells, some starting to scratch the walls between the cells with some small tools[22] we were hiding. When they reached the

third cell, the men ran out and attacked the guards, who retreated outside the wing. Then they used the opened door to break the other cells' doors and walls. Within an hour all the [inner] walls of our prison wing were down! We even took the main door off [the one that leads to the central building] and occupied the three floors of our wing.[23] This proved to us that not everything we saw as stable is stable forever; everything can fall! After this, we started to feel that this could also happen in Syria [with the regime], because no one knew this could happen [in the prison] but it did.

Yassin had been arrested just as he had graduated from medical school and come back to his small town. Several of his relatives had been involved in the Muslim Brotherhood 1982 revolt and others had joined the Islamic jihad in Iraq in the early 2000s. I met Yassin through Yassar, his cousin, as I became interested in revolutionary genealogies and stories of political dissent before 2011. This interest led me to meet with former political detainees imprisoned in the 1980s and 1990s: most had been Communist Party Political Bureau or Muslim Brotherhood members, the historical opponents of the regime alongside the dissident Baath and Nasserist parties. I also met former detainees who had been involved in other Islamic and Islamist parties and were detained in the 1990s and 2000s.

When Yassin was arrested in the 2000s, after a decade of underground political work, he was subsequently detained at Sednaya along with most of the political prisoners labelled Islamists.[24] In his story of a riot inside the prison in March 2008,[25] Yassin suggests an analogy between the penitentiary system and the Assad regime: both were believed to be indestructible as they seemed to control people with an iron fist. However, the fact that the prison's walls could fall so easily invited the detainees to think that Syria's regime could also be overthrown if the Syrian people were to rise against it. This description of actual events appears as an allegory of the revolution itself and simultaneously reveals that, for those involved in politics for years, the Syrian revolution was inevitable. The revolution was thus presented as unavoidable and necessary for political prisoners and grassroots activists, as well as for people like Umm Ahmad, Umm Khaled or Umm Nidal who did not have any previous experience of political activism.

Tracing the roots of the uprising within Syria's political history and mapping out the ideological landscape prior to the uprising through my interlocutors' lives, genealogies, and narratives offers a history from below of the Syrian revolution that goes beyond the sometimes reductive analyses of events.[26] This shows that the revolution and its demands did not emerge in an ideological vacuum,[27] but rather that is was embedded in a specific socio-political context and determined by my interlocutors' social class, and was rooted in political and religious thinking, practices, and traditions. Such perspective avoids the pitfalls of the post-ideological reading of the so-called Arab Spring that tends to suggest it emerged in a political vacuum.[28] Indeed, it interrogates the relationship between the 'exhaustion of ideological traditions underpinning the ruling regime' (Haugbolle 2016: 6); the frustration of young people as their opportunities to attain available and competing 'grand schemes' diminished (Schielke 2015); and global revolutionary upheaval.

## Revolution and counter-revolutionary forces: a continuous struggle against *zulm*

With the militarisation of the uprising, opposition to the regime became increasingly fragmented and new forms of *zulm* appeared with the emergence of new revolutionary and counter-revolutionary actors on the ground, thus leading my interlocutors to redefine their position towards *al-thawra* and to redefine *al-thawra* itself. 'There are two revolutions now: against the regime (*al-nizam*) and against Daesh',[29] said Reema, a graduate student from Aleppo's countryside in her thirties, as we discussed her involvement in the revolution's non-violent movement. This statement was quite common among my interlocutors although, to them, the major fight was still against the regime. Daesh was perceived as an avatar of the regime that hid the latter's crimes by staging and filming the executions it carried out, while the regime's crimes were said to be far more horrendous, affecting a greater number of people, but hidden from people's eyes in the underground levels of the security facilities.[30] My interlocutors argued that Daesh had effectively been created by the regime and that the regime and Daesh were the two faces of the same problem: they recalled how jihadists had been released from the regime's jails in 2012 and saw it as a way to use the Russian strategy in Chechnya. Playing on the global fear of jihadi insurgency, the regime could then frame the uprising as an Islamist rebellion so they could repress it without having to worry about 'red lines'. Moreover, they were both defined as comparable sources of *zulm*.

With the growing presence of Islamist armed groups, the armed face of the revolution became increasingly marked by sectarian language. These groups started to appear in the first half of 2012 and they framed their fight against the regime following a sectarian logic. The revolutionaries' anti-sectarian discourse was replaced by these groups as a 'jihadists or believers vs. infidels or heretics' formulation, hence aiming to get the support of the Syrian Sunni majority (Bartolomei 2018: 299). Such discourse, as well as the regime's own sectarian discourse and logic, have spread since the beginning of the uprising and eventually led to the dramatic increase of violence among opposition groups that targeted those from rival sects without distinguishing between pro- and anti-regime supporters. Illustrating this polarisation of discourses, Abu Leila once told me:

> I knew from the beginning [of the revolution] that there would be a lot of problems. After we saw the revolution in Egypt and Tunisia my wife told me it would take three months for us. I told her if it takes three years we would be lucky! I know how the army is. The regime used to say, 'It's either us or we burn the country.' So they burned the country! The regime's answer to the peaceful protests was really tough for it turned to an armed revolution and so [in the regime's thinking] justified their use of unlimited violence. The regime also wanted the revolution to become an Islamist one so it let all the Islamists out of the prison. They were all in prison! It wanted to show: either me or them. We don't want either!! The regime is the biggest supporter of the Islamists …

To my interlocutors Daesh and *al-nizam* formed a Janus-like figure. Zakaria illustratively spoke of the revolution's struggle against the regime as a struggle against cancer, saying: 'If you take it out you can save the rest of the body. But you need to attack and kill the tumour.' He further elaborated that Daesh was only a symptom of this tumour (that is, the regime) and that if one killed the tumour this symptom would disappear. On another occasion he told me: 'The regime played the card of the Islamic martyrs: they freed Islamist leaders from jail and started their military actions against the protesters.' The idea that Daesh was an avatar of the regime was very widespread among my interlocutors. Umm Ahmad once said:

> See, we are not terrorists [referring to the regime's designation of the protestors]! My boys were normal kids, not extremists, smart and hard-working kids, but they were all killed by the regime. The problem is Bashar al-Assad. We need to take him down! If we take him down we will all fight against Daesh because we don't support Daesh. We don't want them! There was no Daesh in Syria before [the revolution and the war] and there wouldn't be if it wasn't for Assad …

If Daesh was not seen as the primary enemy, it was, however, discussed in the context of attacks in the region and in Europe. Moreover, in the house where I lived during the last part of my fieldwork, it was a common topic of discussion, as Dina, one of my housemates, was from Raqqa, the so-called capital of Daesh in Syria.[31] The main topic of discussion was the Muslimness of the organisation. Dina did not tire of repeating that Daesh could not be considered Muslim: it looked Islamic for those who did not know Islam, as it borrowed some elements of the Islamic law. Yet Dina argued that it turned exceptions into a general rule:

> They claim that in Sharia, someone who steals bread will have his hand cut off. But they don't say that there are many conditions to amputating a thief's hands. This doesn't apply in time of war or famine, if the thief has children who need to eat, if he is hungry … And one needs four direct witnesses for the court to order such an amputation. See, it's nearly impossible to reach the point that a thief's hand is cut off!

Moreover, Daeshi were said to be largely foreigners, which fed many conspiracy theories and led some of my interlocutors to argue that Daesh is not a Syrian but a European organisation composed of intelligence officers.[32] My friends and interlocutors not only differentiated themselves from Daesh, but also opposed themselves to the PYD and YPG.

Their revolutionary project was distinct from that of the PYD/YPG (usually referred to as 'Kurdish'), which they did not perceive as a revolutionary group but rather as another oppressive party. Moreover, in opposition to the independentist programme of the PYD, the Syrian revolution was said to be for all Syrians, as illustrated by the slogan 'Wahid, wahid, wahid, al-shab al-suri wahid!' (One, one, one, the Syrian people are one!). Many Kurds did join and participate in the Syrian revolution, such as Hanan who shared the flat with Dina and me. Living, like most of my Kurdish interlocutors, in non-Kurdish areas before the uprising, she had participated in the uprising from the very beginning. As the Syrian revolutionaries started to lose territories and the PYD/YPG to gain some, she thought of going back inside and living in her parents' village. Hanan sometimes embraced the PYD's project and entered into heated arguments with fellow (non-Kurdish) Syrian revolutionaries that were sometimes quite uncritically anti-Kurdish, rather than specifying their anti-PYD position.[33] However, she could not go back to PYD-controlled areas as she reluctantly conceded that she feared being arrested for having participated in the revolution. Indeed, she acknowledged that the regime was still operating in PYD-controlled areas, arresting those who participated in the revolution and therefore making these areas unsafe for people like Hanan.

Most of my interlocutors were bitter about the PYD, as they felt it had betrayed them by allying itself with the regime, and as they found its project equally authoritarian. They were particularly angered by the alliances the PYD had made with the regime in Aleppo. By letting the regime fight on a single front they had weakened the FSA (Free Syrian Army) and their allies terribly. 'How could they believe that the regime, which had never treated them well, would respect their agreement of non-aggression?' some asked. Although they could not blame the Kurds for wanting their independence, given the history of repression of Kurds in Syria and the region,[34] some of my interlocutors argued that sooner or later the regime would turn against them and their independence projects would fail as they had in the past. Their opposition to the PYD/YPG was later reinforced by the Kurdification of Arab regions that had been won with the support of the US Air Force.[35]

My interlocutors, who were mostly part of what has been labelled the 'non-violent movement',[36] thus opposed themselves to the regime, Daesh and more widely to any armed groups taking control over parts of the territory, for they were all defined as forms of *zulm*: '*Zulm, zulm*! Both of them [Daesh and the regime] just bring *zulm*,' Dina's sister, for instance, told me as she arrived from Raqqa. The injustice and oppression (*zulm*) they brought was made particularly clear by their sectarian discourse and practices, and my interlocutors presented themselves as deeply anti-sectarian. Despite the current conflict being widely framed in terms of sectarian and civil war (see for instance Baczko et al. 2017), the original 2011 revolutionary movement was profoundly anti-sectarian in its claims, and the protestors as well as the protest locations were cross-sectarian. The movement thus called for an inclusive civic state and gathered cross-class, cross-ethnic, and cross-sectarian adherents. Such positioning was not only made clear in slogans[37] but was also present in public statements, the founding documents of grassroots networks, local coordination committees and opposition political bodies outside and inside Syria.[38]

Yet, unlike the situation in the first and peaceful phase of the revolution, the sense of communitas deteriorated inside Syria as the revolution turned into an armed conflict. In the armed phase of the conflict (from 2013 onwards) sectarian language was increasingly used in Syria. The indiscriminate violence against peaceful protesters, and its sectarian character as entire neighbourhoods and cities were attacked by *shabbiha*[39] (pro-regime Alawi militias) and the regime's army, provide however a convincing explanation for the growing sectarian character of the armed revolution. The militarisation of the uprising and the polarisation of the discourses and parties along sectarian lines spread doubt and disillusion among my friends and interlocutors.

## Of doubts and disillusions

My interlocutors' understandings and definitions of the revolution changed over the years of my fieldwork. If defining *awal al-thawra* (the first [phase of the] revolution) was quite unproblematic, the militarisation of the revolution and its turning into a conflict were objects of debate among my interlocutors. The discussions became more complex with the evolution of the situation in Syria and its turning into a proxy war and an international conflict. With the marginalisation of the non-violent movement, and armed conflict taking centre stage, the revolution's aim was no longer to overthrow the regime and establish a new one but turned to the control of local territories; assessment of the revolution's success was framed in terms of the gain and loss of territory. Moreover, the meaning of the revolution had to be reinvented with the changing situation on the ground and the flight of the actors of the non-violent movement.

The Syrians I lived with usually framed the ongoing war (before its growing internationalisation with the Russian and US interventions in the summer of 2015) as a revolutionary one, inscribing this war into the revolutionary process, often comparing it to the French revolution, which had similarly, they argued, been marked by a series of setbacks and wars. They thus refused to call the current situation a civil war, arguing that the events were revolutionary in nature, for they were inscribed within revolutionary dynamics (cf. Agamben 2015). My interlocutors were actually growing more and more certain that a revolution was a process belonging to the *longue durée*, and were prepared not to see the results of the uprising they had started (see Chapters 4 and 5).

As I discuss in this book, the Syrian revolution was sometimes understood as a paused project, an ongoing process or a process that could still succeed in the near or distant future (see Chapter 4), while for others the revolution had already failed or been defeated. I encountered this phenomenon in a discussion between members of a small civil-society organisation where I volunteered during the first months of my fieldwork. In the context of a battle over narratives – the regime described the protestors as Salafi terrorists, the revolutionaries presented the uprising as non-violent and anti-sectarian, and the Islamist groups used a sectarian rhetoric similar but opposite to the regime's – the terms being used to speak of the 2011 revolution were under discussion among my friends and interlocutors. As I sat in the meeting room with them I listened to their review of the adequacy of the terms used to describe the situation in Syria since 2011. The aim of the meeting was to select which could be used in a project aiming to present the current situation in Syria. To this end the different terms used by diverse media and actors were listed on a white board and a vote was taken as to which were acceptable.

On the board the team leader wrote in different columns: *thawra* (revolution), *intifada* (uprising), *harb* (war), *harb ahliyya* (civil war), *azmeh* (crisis), *syra'a* (conflict), *niza' taye'fyi* (sectarian conflict), and *jihad*. While everybody agreed on revolution as the best term to use, everyone rejected civil war outright, seeing it as some sort of regime propaganda to discredit their revolution. Next, they discussed the term *harb* (war): although most were unhappy about using it, they had to agree that descriptively the situation was increasingly one of war. This term was also being used more frequently by revolutionaries in everyday conversations: first with reluctance – people corrected themselves when they used the word and replacing it with *thawra* – and later with regret, acknowledging that the situation had shifted from the revolution they had started to a war they had not wanted and over which they had no control. However, *harb ahliyya* (civil war) was never used by the people with whom I lived; nor were religious terms such as *jihad* (holy war) and *fitna* (civil strife);[40] these too were strongly rejected by the group.

In fact, for most of the people I lived among, and for most of my fieldwork, the only term used to describe the situation in Syria was *thawra*, despite the ambivalent and ambiguous situation on the ground. Abu Leila's eldest daughter, a widow in her early thirties who was a school-teacher in Syria, gave me her views as we drank coffee in Gaziantep's main park.

> I want people to know our story, I want them to know that the warlike situation started with a revolution. My husband didn't die in a civil war; this is not a civil war. He died because we had a goal, we had demands. We wanted freedom, justice, you know … these things!

The insistence in calling what was happening inside Syria since 2011 a revolution was shared by most of my interlocutors and was presented as an ethical and political stance that was also ideological and sometimes sentimental. On the one hand, people could not give up on their revolution because they had lost too much in it and for it; on the other, the revolution was still alive, not only in people's minds and hearts, but inside Syria in the liberated areas. This was echoed by Amjad, a high-school student from Aleppo whom I met during my first visit to southern Turkey in March 2014:

> The revolution is an orphan ... it started well, in a good way; now the situation is much more complex but it is not a civil war. It's a war, yes, but led by revolutionaries, even though the goals are not clear [any longer]. The FSA [Free Syrian Army] started as defence groups against the regime forces that attacked the protests. When the regime forces had sticks they had sticks too; when they started to carry weapons they did the same. Stick against stick, weapon against weapon. It was still a revolution because the armed branches did not attack civilians. It is a revolution as long as we act according to revolutionary values against the regime's values and practices.

I was introduced to Amjad, who was in Turkey only for a couple of days, by the friends who were hosting me during my first trip to Turkey. They insisted that I record his story as he was soon to return to Syria. At this period in my research I used to collect the life stories of revolutionary youth through semi-structured and unstructured interviews that I recorded manually during or after they took place. As we discussed his involvement in the revolution and his view on the recent developments in Syria, Amjad made the above statements. His reasoning was that the situation could only be defined as a revolutionary war, since it started as a revolution and embraced revolutionary values. Yet one has to note that, with the growing internationalisation of the conflict, mainly at the end of my fieldwork (spring 2016) and my following visits (autumn and winter 2016), Syrians' understanding of the situation changed. Umm Yazan (whom I write about in Chapter 4) once told me, echoing other interlocutors' views, 'It is the third world war happening in one country'. With the situation slipping out of Syrians' hands, and with the revolutionaries seeing their actions as less and less effective, doubts started to emerge about the revolution and its legacy.

But others who had first supported or participated directly in the revolution became disenchanted and turn against the revolution. 'They [the revolutionaries] destroyed the country; we used to have a life (*kunna n'aysh*),' Umm Riyad, the mother of a friend who was deeply involved in the revolution, once told me. Umm Riyad was the first person I met who openly criticised the revolution and the revolutionaries. I was surprised at first by her comment since her children were dedicated revolutionaries and she had herself participated in the first protests in her native city. A retired teacher who had worked in the Gulf for twenty years and had moved back to her city for her children to go to university, Umm Riyad had finally accomplished her dream of buying a flat and settling back in her homeland. Yet everything evaporated when the home she had bought with her hard-won savings was destroyed in the regime's shelling. She had spent her life away from home in order to build a better future for her children and to attain what she perceived as a good life, but it had been taken away from her.

The feeling that a lifetime of effort and investment had been put into building a home was not uncommon for Umm Riyad's generation. Buying, building, or having a home was a central element in what a good life meant for many of my interlocutors, since having one's own home, or building a top floor on one's father's home, meant being able to get married, a point I develop further in Chapter 5. In a society where getting married played a central part in defining a good life, many of my interlocutors had chosen to leave the country and make money abroad to facilitate this. Young qualified graduates, for example, had made plans to work abroad for a decade before coming back and establishing a home in Syria, as economic pressure was especially high for youth.[41] These life trajectories were cut short with the beginning of the revolution as hopes of establishing a 'good life' at home receded.

During one of our weekly meetings Umm Ahmad addressed the critique she and many revolutionaries faced, a critique that seemed to answer Umm Riyad's words:

> When people say that people like my sons are responsible for the war I can't stand it ... The regime is responsible for the war; these young men were peaceful and they were fighting for justice and for our rights ... they didn't start the war ... People sometimes tell me, 'Why didn't you keep them home?' They blame me for having let them join the protests. But my sons were right, they were fighting for justice ... they were not doing anything wrong ... It is the son of the dog [*ibn al-kalb*, i.e. Bashar al-Assad] who is wrong. He is the one who killed them; they didn't kill anybody ... Our neighbourhood was bombed by the regime ... these young men were helping other people.

She refused to be accused of having destroyed the country. To her the regime was responsible for its destruction: it bombed revolutionaries' neighbourhoods and peaceful protests. These critiques – which in her case came from her own siblings, who remained in regime-controlled areas and cut all ties with her, fearing the regime's violence would fall on them – as well as perceptions and imaginaries of the revolution, evolved throughout my fieldwork. In the autumn of 2015, in the face of the massive level of destruction in their country, some revolutionaries started to criticise themselves in the same terms, saying, 'We destroyed the country'. Reema summarised the spirit of Syrian revolutionaries rather bleakly: 'In a way it's best to be dead; we wouldn't see our defeat if we were dead! I'm telling you, today we are defeated! We lost. I think we lost.' This pessimism was tinted with an intense sense of guilt that appeared in the rest of her monologue:

> Each time I heard of a building or a house being shelled I would go and I would apologise to the family. I would say, 'I'm sorry, I'm sorry', because I thought that it was our [the revolutionaries'] fault. We are the ones who went out to protest, but they are the ones who got killed. We are the ones that should have died, and they could have continued to live. Now we live with this guilt every day. We feel that we are the ones who started it [the revolution], but we are the ones who left. We are the ones who left and who live. It's like people have died for nothing! Before it was like they died for a higher cause, but not anymore. They died for nothing. That's why we feel guilty. We didn't finish what we started. We couldn't make their dream – our dream – live.

In addition to the pessimism and the guilt that started to undermine the opposition, the revolutionaries became increasingly divided. For some of my interlocutors, a revolution could only be peaceful. They thus defined the militarisation of the revolution as the cause of defeat. They believed that if the revolution had stayed non-violent, the revolutionaries would have retained the moral high ground and the regime would have eventually failed. They thought that the use of violence on their part had allowed the regime to increase its use of violence and to legitimate it. Some also believed that if the uprising had not become armed, it would have had a chance to gain the support of the international community. Ussama, a young man who had been arrested several times by the regime for delivering medicines and medical supplies to besieged areas, told me that after he was freed from jail he no longer recognised the revolution. An armed revolution was nonsense to him. 'There is no revolution anymore!' he concluded, disenchanted. On the other hand, some thought that arming the revolutionaries was the only possible way to defeat the regime. In the words of Tareq, a young man I introduce in detail in the next chapter, who had lived in the besieged city of Ghouta for three years, and who described himself as a pacifist:

How can these people speak so badly of the people who are liberating areas? It is not a revolution any more, it is an armed conflict. Being peaceful and writing messages or believing in peaceful protests is not enough anymore. Now people have to fight a revolutionary war. It is not correct to call it a civil war as the regime tries to do, as that will allow it to kill civilians. The problem is that the people who are now speaking about the liberation in bad terms are putting themselves on the side of the regime. We need to create – as in the battlefront – a unification of the different tendencies in civil society. Today we are totally fragmented between seculars ('almaniyyin) and Islamic (islamiyyin).

The above narratives demonstrate the great shifts in understandings of the revolution among my interlocutors as they evolved throughout my fieldwork: from an unfolding event that could still be successful to a long process that was temporarily defeated, the revolution increasingly appeared as paused or suspended in the present, with my interlocutors hoping that it would start again in the future (see Chapter 4). The rest of this book follows this evolution and shows how the evolving understandings and experiences of al-thawra, as well as the changing nature of events inside and situation outside Syria, had direct and indirect consequences on my interlocutors' spatio-temporal horizons, social and familial relations, and life trajectories.

## Al-thawra: an ethnographic redefinition of revolution outside the Enlightenment frame

Is it possible for a people to envision and desire futures uncharted by already existing schemata of historical change and patterns of social changes? Is it possible to think of dignity, humility, justice, and liberty outside the Enlightenment cognitive maps and principles? (Ghamari-Tabrizi 2016: 1)

Behrooz Ghamari-Tabrizi poses these questions in the preface to his book on the Iranian revolution as he reflects on the Arab revolutions of the 2010s. A similar point is raised by Guillaume Mazeau's diagnosis of the incapability of most commentators to think about the Arab revolutions outside a Western time frame that places these revolutions in a unique and universal time, one oriented towards progress and liberal democracy (Mazeau 2013: 2).

Taking revolution as an ethnographic object – examining it through Syrians' experiences, narration, and understandings of the unfolding events – this chapter proposes a different understanding of its causes, developments, and evolving definitions. Through such lenses, the temporality of the revolution is perceived in a *longue durée*, but also as an event belonging to and inscribing itself into a cyclical course, punctuated with repetitions and long-lasting legacies. Hence, despite its apparent defeat in the political field at the national level, the revolution was actually perceived by my interlocutors as already having an effect in the present at the local level (see Chapter 5).

Through my interlocutors' definitions of dignity in opposition to their current life under the Assads, as a life without humiliation, injustice, fear and corruption, one can see how the notions of 'justice, freedom, and dignity',[42] which became the main slogan and keywords of the revolution, are grounded in everyday and pragmatic experiences as well as local ideologies. Focusing on these notions, their roots and meanings, thus shows the specificities of the Syrian revolution and of the revolutionaries' motivations and demands, rather than reducing them to generic keywords '*legible* to a global audience' (Ghamari-Tabrizi 2016: 1, emphasis original). Reading the Arab revolutions within a global vocabulary of revolution or a Western-inspired and liberal agenda blurs their specificities, leading commentators, for instance, to analyse these revolutions as phenomena enabling the Arab world to catch up with universal history (Badiou 2011) placing them in a universal time oriented towards progress and liberal democracy (see Mazeau 2013). The turn to ethnographic attention characterising my approach therefore tends to contrast with 'the desire to turn Arabs into legible subjects of the March of History rather than making history the subject of their uprising' (Ghamari-Tabrizi 2016: 4). An ethnographic focus simultaneously pushes us to leave room for a redefinition of the term 'revolution', in order to avoid framing it in 'a conceptual and discursive universe with a written past and a known future direction' (Ghamari-Tabrizi 2016: 2). An ethnographic approach allows us to show that revolution is deeply understood in its local and regional history and within political traditions and legacies, making it appear in all its radicality and originality and going against the often simplistic understandings of Arab revolutions as appearing in an ideological and political vacuum and out of strictly economic, and sometimes ecological, circumstances (see Daoudy 2020).

Through my interlocutors' voices, the revolution appears as changing and evolving, as defeated and paused rather than failed or ended, calling for further investigation into its temporality, consequences and legacies.

The concept of *karama*, which appears so central to the 2011 revolution's inception, also constitutes one of the threads of this book: in Chapter 2 it appears as constitutive of Syrian revolutionary selves; in Chapter 3 as a condition of life and political claim in displacement and exile; and in Chapter 6 through the idiom of self-sacrifice. The evolution of Syrians' understanding of *al-thawra* is understood in spatial terms, as mainly happening inside (Chapter 2), as a temporal cycle that has to be repeated differently (Chapter 4) and, in Chapter 5, as shifting from the political to the social domain[43] as women rise against social and familial forms of *zulm*. In the next chapter I explore the spatial dimension of *al-thawra*, showing that rather than expressing itself through the downfall of the regime at the level of the state, *al-thawra* is enacted locally, both inside and outside Syria. *Al-thawra* thus appears through a series of spatial ruptures and disruptions rather than as a radical temporal rupture marked by a change of regime. Moreover, through these spatial phenomena and the movement they involve, new types of subjects are formed, transformed and cultivated.

## Notes

1 *Umm* means mother. Syrian women are usually called after their first son: mother of Ahmad, Mohammad and so on. It is a common sign of respect, as women's first names are rarely known outside the family and, when they are, are not publicly pronounced. Men are also called after their first sons (Abu Ahmad – father of Ahmad) especially when they reach their forties. See Khuri (1981) and Davies (1949) for more information on teknonymy in particular and on the use of kinship terms in Syria in general. This way of referring to each other also became an easy way to hide people's identity during the revolution, including those of young people (see more in Chapter 4).

2 Before Hafez al-Assad's coup and 'rectification movement', the Baath party had led a series of agrarian reforms that redistributed some of the land previously held by big landowners to farmers without lands (see Batatu 1999: 140–70).

3 See more on this point in Wedeen (2013: 842).

4 In the Egyptian dialect *'aysh* means both bread and life. The protestors on Tahrir were asking for *'aysh*, freedom, and social justice. *'aysh* was translated as bread (Mittermaier 2014: 54).

5 Bouthaina Sha'ban was the regime's spokeswoman. See also Ismael (2011) and Burgat and Paoli (2013a) for an analysis of the slogans of the uprising.

6 The Tunisian uprising started after Mohammad Bouazizi immolated himself. In Egypt, the demands to end police brutality were also central (see Ghannam 2013; Schielke 2015).

7 *Karama* was a notion not only mobilising non-violent protesters but also fighters, while crossing sectarian, social, political, and regional lines (see Harkin 2018).

8 Abu Leila did not have a son and was thus called after his eldest daughter.

9 My interlocutors usually had two meals a day: a breakfast composed of boiled eggs, vegetables, olive and za'atar before going to work, and a 'lunch' around four or when they come back from work at six.

10 See Schielke's analysis of the Egyptian revolutionary context (2015). He argues that Egyptians' demands for dignity means a 'humane life (*hayat bani adamin*)', that is, a life characterised by 'the modernist great promise of progress: the promise of social and personal advancement in the shape of education and cultivation, salaried work, and middle-class comfort and status' (2015: 173). Yet this perception of the good life also generated moral trouble and anger. Indeed, in order to attain such a life, Egyptians had to participate in a system they were simultaneously trying to eradicate by 'making money through illegal and immoral schemes, favouring their relatives, stealing and diverting public and private property' (Schielke 2015: 179).

11  See on this topic Aita 2007; Antoun 1991; Hinnebusch and Imady 2018a; Said 2018.

12  Engineers were mainly employed by the state in Syria and had increasingly low salaries with the liberalisation of the economy in the late 1990s and early 2000s, since their salaries were not readjusted.

13  See Longuenesse 1979, 1994, 1995 on social classes in Syria.

14  Wedeen notes that it was commonly said that Rami Makhlouf, Bashar al-Assad's cousin, owned 60 per cent of all investment deals in Syria (2013: 853). See also Anderson 2023.

15  There are many accounts of the formation of the regime around a close Alawi circle, a circle not only linked by a common religion but also by kinship ties, since the regime's inner circle and those who hold key posts in the regime came from Hafez al-Assad's native village and region (see Antoun 1991; Khuri 1991; Kienle 1991; Hinnebusch 1991; Seurat 1989). However, this circle was not homogeneous in terms of sect or class and rather appeared as a *jama'a* (small group) infused by a spirit of what Ibn Khaldun named *'asabbyia* (spirit of body) (Kienle 1991: 214; see also Seurat 1989).

16  See Abu-Lughod 2012: 25; Schielke 2015: 180 for a similar argument in the context of the Egyptian uprising.

17  This included leftist parties that recognised the Baath predominance in Syria's political life (Belhadj and Kienle 2007: 692).

18  See Al-Haj Saleh 2015; Karabet 2010; K. Khalifa 2006; M. Khalifa 2007; Yassin Hassan 2009.

19  This was the first of two riots in 2008 that are documented through former detainees' testimonies in a documentary: https://www.youtube.com/watch?v=8UlCXwtVFMg. The second riot was repressed bloodily with up to a hundred detainees being killed.

20  Syrians preparing to join or coming back from fighting the US troops in Iraq (see Chatty 2018).

21  This was done in response to the prison guards finding out that in one of the cell the detainees had managed to get some light – which was turned off at night as a form of punishment and humiliation – by taking electricity from the corridor's light.

22  The prisoners used to keep everything they could – small pieces of wood and iron – and make small knives or needles to pass the time and repair their belongings (see also M. Khalifa 2007).

23  There are three wings in Sednaya, each with four floors. The political prisoners occupy three floors and the military ones the basement. Each floor is divided in a right and left side occupied by cells and a corridor on each side. It is the median wall between the right and left cells and the wall between some of the cells and the corridors that were taken down with the help of heavy metal doors and smaller tools. Each floor also has two main doors leading to the centre of the building. Once the walls were taken down the prisoners designated a few men to take their demands to the administration. Meanwhile the prison wing was surrounded by military police and the detainees made their demands to the administration for better living conditions. The demands were that they stopped the systematic torture and that the jihadists of the second floor would receive the same treatment as the other floors. Thus far they had no light at night, poor food, and no visiting rights for their relatives.

24  See Mustafa Khalifa's *The Shell* (2007). This autobiographical novel gives a vivid account of the ways in which Muslim Brotherhood members and other political detainees were treated in Tadmor/Palmyra.

25  Different versions of this story circulate among former political detainees and on social media that, however all contain similar elements recounted in notes 21 and 23: (1) Some detainees managed to get light in their cells. (2) The administration decided to punish all the prisoners for this infraction. (3) The prisoners were heavily tortured in front of their cells. (4) The prisoners started to bang their doors and walls. (5) The prisoners attacked the guards and started to open doors and walls in the full wing (see for instance https://m.facebook.com/photo.php?fbid=567331226731 327&id=482323031898814&set=a.482363548561429&locale2=ar_AR&refid=13&__ tn__=%2B%3E and https://tinyurl.com/kvkxwjnx).

26  These include a range of approaches that present an economic explanation in terms of 'the haves and the have-nots' (cf. Wedeen 2013: 846); describe an event born only from the immediate context of the Arab Revolutions (Burgat and Paoli 2013b; Hinnebusch and Imady 2018b); or speak of sectarian conflict (Baczko et al. 2017; Sule 2017).

27  This reflection contributes to the emergent debate about the place of ideology in the Arab Revolutions, which have often been described as leaderless and without 'ideological scripts of the ideal society' (Haugbolle 2016: para. 1). However, although protesters were not driven by ideologies defined as 'elaborate strategies for a political order' (Haugbolle 2016: para. 1), different political ideas heavily influenced the Arab uprisings. If they were not driven by a

'bounded system of political thought' (Haugbolle and Bandak 2017: 197), ideology as thought-practices emerged in everyday routines and in the 'hopes, visions, and calculations' (Haugbolle 2016: para. 2) of revolutionaries. I argue that one also needs to pay close attention to the role of ideologies understood in a more classic sense (socialism, Islamism, baathism etc.) to understand the context prior to the uprising and of the relations between 'traditional' political activists, *shabab*, and *thuwwar*. Prior to 2011, Syrians lived in a society saturated by ideologies: the dying baathist ideology of Hafez al-Assad's regime and the novel 'neoliberal authoritarianism' promoted by his son (Wedeen 1998; 1999; 2013); leftist ideologies among which the most widespread were Nasserism and communism as presented by Riad al-Turk's political bureau; and different forms of political Islam from Salafism to the Muslim Brotherhood.

28   See Haugbolle 2016; Haugbolle and Bandak 2017; Wedeen 2013 on this topic.

29   My interlocutors refused to call the organisation by its official name: '*al dawleh al islamiyyh*' (the Islamic State). They framed this refusal as a political act; they did not want to give it the legitimacy of a state and did not want Syrians to get used to acknowledging it, even if just verbally, as a state. It was also a mockery since 'Daesh' is formed by translating the acronym ISIS to Arabic, although acronyms are not used in Arabic.

30   See the Caesar files, comprising over 55,000 pictures of 11,000 people killed under torture in Syrian regime jails (Le Caisne 2015; Human Rights Watch 2015).

31   I have described it in more detail elsewhere (Al-Khalili 2017b).

32   See Proudfoot (2022) on conspiracy theories in the Syrian uprising.

33   See Çifçi (2018) on the relations between the Kurds and Syrian revolutionaries.

34   Kurds were badly repressed by the nationalist Syrian Arab Republic of the Assads. They had, for instance, only partial access to citizenship. This led to a Kurdish revolt in 2005.

35   See Amnesty International (2015).

36   See Al-Om 2018; Brønd 2017.

37   See Dubois (2013) and Burgat et al. (2013) on the revolution's slogans and chants for more examples.

38   This was the case of the Syrian National Council established on 2 October 2011, and the National Coalition for Syrian Revolutionary and Opposition Forces (April 2013) (Bartolomei 2018).

39   See Al-Haj Saleh (2015) on the sociology of *shabbiha*.

40   See Ayalon (1987) on the ways in which the term *thawra* actually came to replace *fitna*, which was first used by Arabic observers in the eighteenth and nineteenth centuries to describe revolutions in France and elsewhere.

41   The short movie *The Shebabs of Yarmouk* (2013) illustrates Syrian youth's dream of leaving the country as they saw no future in it.

42   I argue that despite reflecting the influence of the Egyptian and Tunisian uprisings, as well as more broadly shared revolutionary ideals that could be understood as global humanitarian assumptions (see Fassin 2007; 2010; 2011; 2012; Ticktin 2014), these concepts express the specificities of the Syrian context (see for instance Harkin 2018 on dignity in the Syrian context; see also Ghamari-Tabrizi 2016).

43   See Saba Mahmood (2005) and Farha Ghannam (2002) on the definitions of the social and the political and their moving boundaries.

**Figure 2.1:** Road leading to the Syrian border. © Charlotte al-Khalili

## 2
## Revolutionary spaces and subjects: people of the 'inside', people of the 'outside'

> The Syrian revolution represents an extraordinary experience for hundreds of thousands of Syrians, as much a moral as a political trial, as much a renewal of the self as a social change. It is an insurrection against oneself and a revolution against what exists.
> (Yassin Al-Haj Saleh, 2016b: 39, author translation)

'The revolution happens *juwwa* (inside)', my friends and interlocutors often repeated. But *juwwa* meant different things: it was Syria as opposed to Turkey, liberated and besieged areas as opposed to regime-controlled ones, and the regime prisons as opposed to the exterior. The inside is a polysemic term that covered a variety of locations, as it was defined in opposition to a variety of outsides. *Juwwa* also designated *al-nas min juwwa* (the people from the inside) who were perceived as 'true' revolutionaries and heroes (*abtal*): it was they who were sacrificing everything to the revolution, particularly those living under siege or in prison – the places of ultimate sacrifice. Among my interlocutors, the 'inside' becomes the revolutionary space, the place where revolution happens and where real revolutionaries are. Yet, throughout my fieldwork, the inside increasingly became a war zone, and an inaccessible space for many because of the eruption of checkpoints from different factions and the regime, because of border closure and the besiegement of numerous liberated areas.

Displacement, whether internal or external, was one of the first and most important unforeseen and unintended consequences of the revolution, constituting a major spatial disruption. Syrians started to flee their homes in April 2011 as a result of the harsh repression of the revolution – districts and towns were shelled and besieged, and the enforced disappearances of protestors and inhabitants of revolutionary strongholds increased rapidly. By the beginning of 2015, 8 million Syrians had been displaced internally and abroad, and by March 2017 over half of Syria's 23 million inhabitants had been displaced: 7 million internally and 4.9 externally (Chatty 2018: 243).

All my interlocutors were forcibly displaced from Syria, although this displacement had different geographical origins, causes, duration and forms. Most of the revolutionary youths I lived with did not completely settle in Gaziantep until late 2015 or early 2016 – that is, after Turkey put an end to its open-door policy and as sieges were stiffening on revolutionary strongholds. Up until the Turkish border was permanently closed, my young, and here almost exclusively male, interlocutors were often going back and forth between Turkey and Syria as they continued their revolutionary activities within Syria's liberated and partly besieged areas. But with the intensification of the siege in *rif dimashq*, Homs, and East Aleppo, many fled to Gaziantep. The families I worked with also took refuge in Gaziantep at different times and came from various regions. Umm Khaled had fled to Lebanon with her daughter as her town came under heavy fire by the regime's army in 2012. She later returned secretly to Syria and travelled north to enter Turkey, joining her son through its open-border. Umm Yussef had fled Homs as her neighbourhood was about to be besieged, her son, Abu Zein, and his family choosing to stay behind. Her family members later joined her as they managed to escape the besieged city or as they were released from the Assad prisons. Umm Ahmad and her family fled *rif halab* in 2013 after Daesh took control of the village in which she had resettled from Aleppo's suburbs.

This chapter describes how the Syrian revolutionary struggle for dignity is transposed at the intimate scale as a logic of sacrifice among my interlocutors: *ya na'ish b-hurriyya; ya nmut b-karama* sang the protesters – either live in freedom or die in dignity. In processes of self-formation and cultivation, the call for dignity translates into a readiness to sacrifice one's present, time, and life, echoing the motto 'dignity or death' (see Chapter 6 on self-sacrifice and martyrdom). Moreover, the willingness to take risks, put oneself in danger, and face the repression of the regime – through detention, siege, and loss – established a hierarchy among the revolutionaries. It thus suggests that the rupture created by the revolution can also be located within Syrian selves; not only taking place at the historical and inter-subjective level, it also marked Syrians' inner worlds. Focusing on the notions of *sheghel b-l thawra* (revolutionary work), *wa'qef* (the pause) and *tadhiyeh* (sacrifice) of one's present and life; in this chapter, I show how revolutionary subjects emerge through the analysis of the inside/outside (*juwwa/barra*) dynamic dichotomy. This spatial approach to self-formation stands in stark contrast with the existing literature on revolutionary subjects, which describes self-formation in relation to time and more particularly to the 'event' conceived as a radical temporal rupture (see for instance Badiou 2003; Foucault 1994; Humphrey 2008; Robbins 2007). To explore spatial ruptures – the splitting of Syrian territory between rebel- and regime-controlled areas and mass displacement to Turkey – this chapter offers both a cartography of revolutionary Syria and an account of the ways in which revolutionary politics, praxes and selves are defined through relation to national space and forced displacement. I argue that the creation of revolutionary personhood happened through the creation of a specific relation to *juwwa* (inside) that appears as a space where the revolution is enacted. Once displaced, revolutionary subjects cultivate this identity through movement and the narration of these movements. Moreover, in the movement from *barra* (outside) to *juwwa* (inside), gender emerges as a major marker of revolutionariness and heroism since most of the technologies whereby one's revolutionary identity may be maintained through mobility are predominantly reserved for men.

## Revolutionary selves: asceticism and sacrifice

'If you had lived under siege you wouldn't complain about the food! At the end I used to eat grass and tree leaves', Abu Zein told his brother Ahmad, who complained about Umm Yussef, their mother, serving *mujaddara* (a simple but much appreciated dish made of rice or bulgur, lentils, and grilled onions, served with yogurt) for the third time in a row. Ahmad felt offended and a violent argument started between the two men. 'Do you think the food was better in prison?' Ahmad asked Abu Zein. 'We were eating rotten food when we had any at all', he continued. Ahmad turned to his mother and sisters: 'Do you think it's worse to live under siege or to be detained?' he asked, thus comparing two 'insides' and two different kinds of suffering and sacrifice. 'I had to sit like *this* for more than four months when I was in a solitary cell,' Ahmad said as he moved from his chair and sat on the floor, his legs pressed against his chest and his arms around them. 'Do you think it's better than living under siege?' he asked his female relatives gathered around Umm Yussef's dinner table. In this argument Abu Zein, who had lived under siege for two years, and Ahmad, who had been detained in security cells for a year, competed about who had suffered the most – and therefore made the greater sacrifice – during the revolution. The argument ended and the dinner resumed as the sisters and mother sided with Ahmad and agreed that there was nothing worse than being detained by the regime.[1]

In this argument, the two men deployed well-established hierarchies of sacrifice that made one a revolutionary and a revolutionary hero. The revolutionaries who lived under siege and/or were detained were seen as the most heroic for it was they who sacrificed the most. I was always told before being introduced to a new person about their revolutionary credentials: 'she was in detention for a year', 'he was under siege for three years', 'they've just arrived from inside (*juwwa*)', and so on. Someone's revolutionariness was thus assessed in terms of sacrifice and this sacrifice was intrinsically linked to inside as the examples above show. Moreover, a revolutionary was someone who had been through specific 'rites of passage' (Turner 1967; Van Genep 1961),[2] which included being wanted, injured, besieged, or detained by the regime. Someone who was *ndif* (literally clean, meaning ethical in this context) and had been ready to sacrifice herself and her everyday life, but who had not been arrested or besieged, would appear to be a revolutionary, but was not as revolutionary (that is, as heroic) as one who had been detained or lived under siege.

The revolutionary self was thus formed through the experience of violence and suffering that is framed in terms of spatially inscribed sacrifice by my friends and interlocutors.[3] But sacrificing oneself for the revolution also amounted to different forms of ascetic practices.

> You have to imagine that when one is inside one thinks one can die anytime. You are ready to die anytime and for that reason you cannot do things that would make you unready to die. Watching something *haram*[4] is a problem in such case. Because if you are killed suddenly just after, you wouldn't have time to purify yourself.

Manal told me before adding: 'There is only God and yourself inside … nothing else! Death is much closer when you are inside.' This idea that God (and death) is closer inside Syria was expressed in a conversation we had with her husband as we were discussing what movie to watch together that evening. This led them to discuss the kind of movies they used to see inside: movies containing nothing *haram*, because they had to be ready (and prepared) to die anytime and they did not want to be impure when they met death. In this discussion, being a revolutionary is presented as a readiness to sacrifice oneself (being inside means being ready to die anytime) that goes with a commitment to a form of asceticism (not doing anything *haram*).

This resonates with the words of Umm Khaled, a widow in her fifties from a small town that became a stronghold of the revolution, who laughed as she remembered how her daily life was affected by the revolution.

> After the revolution started I couldn't speak anymore with my husband! If I asked him what he wanted for dinner he would answer, 'How can you think of eating while there is a revolution going on?' But I still had to feed the kids! If I laughed when speaking to my sister on the phone he would say, 'How can you laugh when we have so many martyrs?' At night if I came close to him in the bed he would yell, 'What are you doing? Did you forget that we are in a revolution?' If he saw our sons sleeping he would wake them up, 'Why are you sleeping? You should be outside with the rest of us! Who is going to defend us?'

I often visited Umm Khaled throughout my fieldwork as she lived alone with her daughter and would invite me to drop in to drink coffee, share a lunch, or come with her on visits to friends or organisations where she sought aid. As we sat together at her place drinking coffee, she recalled how her late husband could not do, think, or speak about anything but the revolution.

These two stories call to mind Foucault's definition of 'becoming a subject' as an ascetic process (1994: 709)[5] and illustrate the 'holistic demands' of revolution on oneself (Holbraad 2014).[6] In the above description, all parts of life are affected, even the most intimate, from food to sexual activity. Meals, sleeping times, ways of communicating and the expression of desire all succumb to the effects of revolution. Here, being a revolutionary appears as a commitment to sacrifice oneself and one's present for the revolution's sake. This is accomplished either by death or radical transformation – that is, by becoming a 'New Man',[7] with a new subjectivity and consciousness that embody the 'revolutionary ethos' and 'enact the very revolutionary condition' (Yurchak 2003: 10).

Becoming a new man or dying for the revolution are thus two faces of the same reality (Holbraad 2014: 13). Revolutions, as socio-political transformations, presuppose personal transformation. This is comprehensively illustrated by the life stories of the Syrians I lived with, which underline their commitment to sacrificing their present and their lives to the revolution. The revolution was thus lived as a deep transformation of the self, leading to the emergence of revolutionary forms of personhood. Indeed, my interlocutors gave up their ways of life and their familial and social relations, and accepted being radically transformed and/or dying for the revolution.

Moreover, despite the absence of a codified 'New Man' initiative[8] – as in communist contexts, for instance (e.g. Cheng 2009; Holbraad 2014; Kharkhordin 1999) – and despite the fact that the emergence of revolutionary subjects was not linked to the establishment of a revolutionary state, it was, however, linked to seizing power in specific localities: the liberated areas. Hence, rather than looking at a planned transformation of the subject by revolutionary powers, I map out the ways in which revolution, as a transformational entity, has inflected Syrian selves, producing new kinds of subjects through the revolutionary process. In the Syrian context, the emergence of revolutionary subjects ready to sacrifice themselves and their present is intimately linked to being inside. Here 'inside' defines, first, the liberated areas as opposed to those controlled by the regime; these revolutionary and rebel-controlled spaces appeared in Syria with the beginning of the armed rebellion in the summer of 2012. But inside is also an indexical term, designating a revolutionary space (that is, where the revolution takes place and where revolutionaries are) and is the outside of other (smaller) insides: the besieged areas and the regime prisons. It is also part of a bigger inside: Syria – the horizon of the revolution.

## *Sheghel b-l thawra*: revolutionary work inside

> They [those from Damascus] didn't sacrifice anything! They just stayed in their homes and continued their studies and their work. … Inside [in the liberated areas] we were doing *everything* but it wasn't a job. I worked in *all* the fields: media, medical, military, civil society, education, humanitarian!

Tareq, a man in his mid-twenties who had lived under siege for nearly three years in a town of *rif dimashq*, described the life of the people inside, contrasting it to the life of those outside – the liberated but besieged areas as against the regime-controlled ones. I had been introduced to Tareq through his wife, Manal, who had fled their town a few months before him. He had been able to flee his town and join his wife by escaping clandestinely through an underground tunnel. He later hid in Damascus for several days until he could find an ID that would allow him to cross the checkpoints and reach liberated areas and later Turkey.[9] Tareq, the youngest of five children and the son of a shopkeeper, worked with his father before the revolution. His grandfather was a *fellah* (farmer) who used to own a middle-size farm before the land reforms. After most of the grandfather's land was seized by the regime, his sons started small businesses in the city employing their own sons. Tareq's father and his brothers were perceived as the primary caretakers of these business, in which they were employed and which they helped to establish. Higher education was therefore not deemed essential to enabling their sons to find work, establish themselves in life, and acquire a bride.[10] As a result Tareq did not go to university and was called for military service.

I spent a large amount of time with Tareq and Manal for several months after their arrival, as they were unemployed and had a lot of free time. We would usually meet with other friends who had also recently arrived from the inside (often besieged areas or prison) in cafés or in their homes at night to watch the latest released movies they had not had the chance to see inside, where there was no internet and a lot of restriction on films' content. When Manal found a job, I continued to meet Tareq regularly with another friend, Rasha, who had just arrived from Syria. The three of us enjoyed spending time chatting and drinking tea and eating *bizir* in parks. Rasha had been detained for a year and a half for her participation in non-violent protests and the distribution of aid to internally displaced people (IDP) but she would rarely speak about her time in jail when other people were present despite everyone knowing about her imprisonment.

In Tareq's, Rasha's, and most of my other interlocutors' stories, the inside (*juwwa*) was the definitional space of the revolution up until 2015. It was a space where everything was *de facto* revolutionary: the revolution was the inside and the inside was the revolution. Tareq's words highlight the synonymy of being inside and being revolutionary: even the most mundane practices became revolutionary *because* they happened inside. This definition of inside as a revolutionary space and outside as counter- or non-revolutionary space is explicit in Tareq's statement that the people inside were 'doing everything'. This meant that people living inside, and the activities taking place there, were the locus of the revolution, and most acutely in besieged areas. This idea was also expressed through the expression *sheghel b-l thawra* that Tareq contrasted with the salaried work of Syrians in regime areas and in exile. The inside was, however, not strictly cut off from all outsides. Until the summer 2015, Turkey's open-door policy meant that Syrian revolutionary youths present in Gaziantep were often going back and forth between the inside (the liberated areas) and the outside (Turkey), in an act similar to a revolutionary rite of passage.

Supplying civilians with electricity and water, providing medical care, delivering food, and managing schools inside – all activities that had been state-run in the past – were deemed revolutionary in liberated areas as they participated in the reshaping and the reappropriation of these activities and services. This collapse between everyday and revolutionary activities is actually linked to what can be named the heterotopic quality of the inside (*juwwa*). Heterotopias are 'real places' that 'are a kind of effectively enacted utopia in which all the other sites that can be found in a society, are simultaneously represented, contested, and inverted' (Foucault 1986: 24). The liberated areas were such places because revolutionaries had seized them from the regime, and aimed to govern them through the establishment of local councils that implemented new forms of self-governance and local democracy (Al-Khalili 2021; Munif 2020; Sakhi 2022). In the liberated areas, all activities supported the revolution by virtue of taking place in areas controlled by the opposition and because they were framed by revolutionary values. They could also be described as heterochronia – that is, the slices in time corresponding to heterotopic spaces. This temporal aspect of heterotopia has been aptly described by Syrian anarchist Omar Aziz (2013) as a collapse of the time of power (the temporality of the everyday, which is dominated by the regime) and of the time of the revolution (the exceptional time of revolutionary activities).[11]

The claim that one 'did everything inside (*juwwa*)', and that all the work there was revolutionary, has to be understood conjointly with another statement: 'There is no future in the besieged areas … You can't think of the future! There is no future for those living under siege.' Tareq told me this during one of our conversations as he tried to give me a sense of the difference between the life inside (*juwwa*) and outside (*barra*), here contrasting revolutionary Syria and Gaziantep. This absence of future and an orientation exclusively on the present recalls Amira Mittermaier's account of revolutionary organisation and action on Tahrir square in Cairo (2014). She shows how Tahrir is characterised by a similar mode of togetherness that she calls an ethics of immediacy: 'a range of embodied practices that revolve around attending to those in front of us, those around us' (2014: 55). The modes of sociality and being in the world that developed in such revolutionary spaces are 'radically oriented towards the present' (Mittermaier 2014: 55). Here one sees how there is an immanence between revolutionary work and the space defined as *juwwa*: in the liberated areas the revolutionaries were already experiencing in the present the society they aimed to establish in the future. Syrians enacted new modes of sociality and togetherness through what they called revolutionary work *(sheghel b-l thawra)*.

Tareq once explained that the work in education was thus marked by a spirit of anti-sectarianism: *shabab* or *nasheteen* ('activists', that is, active revolutionaries) tried to remove sectarian content from local schools' curricula. The work with the military followed the claim of justice: activists campaigned for the military not to detain anyone without fair trial. Activists' work in relief aimed to help people live in dignity by providing 'the people' *(al sha'b)* with food and other necessary goods. Through such 'work' *(sheghel b-l thawra)* the revolution was thus already happening inside and those inside were defined as the 'true' revolutionaries. Moreover, the fact that inside was totally immersed in the present and was characterised by an absence of future shaped Syrians' sense of self and their revolutionariness as a willingness to sacrifice their present and self.[12]

## Revolutionary-self, inside and decision-movement

Manal once told me when I visited her home:

> I have lived through everything in the last four years ... I can't even remember my life before these four years! But I don't regret anything despite the deaths and the pain. These four years changed many things for me; they changed the way I see things, the way I perceive the future ... I don't think in the same way anymore!

Like Manal, many of my interlocutors narrated how they had greatly transformed their lives and sacrificed their present – the way they used to live, their work, studies, and relations – when they became revolutionaries. In my interlocutors' narratives, the turning point in their lives was often linked to a spatial disruption: the decision to move to the liberated areas, arrest, being trapped under siege, and so on. Manal's father used to be a school-teacher in Syria before he migrated to Kuwait where he earned a higher salary. He left his wife and five children behind so they could live more comfortably with the money he sent and to ensure that his children received proper education and obtained university degrees. Manal, however, was left without a degree as she interrupted her studies to participate in the uprising. She joined the peaceful protests of 2011, then left her life and family behind to move to the liberated areas where she trained as a nurse to help remedy the lack of medical staff and the growing number of injured. After the FSA liberated wide areas of the country, many Syrians who had participated in the peaceful protests went to these opposition-controlled areas, where they did not fear arrest from the regime and could continue their revolutionary work. Manal later established a community centre in her neighbourhood in order to provide basic education and vocational training since all services had disappeared from the area as the regime withdrew from it. Tareq remembered how Manal blindly followed the call to join the opposition in the liberated areas and gave up her life and family to live and work there. Life-changing decisions that led Syrians to embrace the revolutionary cause further are described in terms of a sense of duty (*wajeb*), responsibility (*mas'uliyyeh*), and sacrifice (*tadhiyeh*).

Involvement in the revolution provoked a radical change in one's life, for it operated as a violent rupture with the past involving the adoption of new habits.[13] Such decisions have been described as a 'decision-event' in other contexts: a moment when 'the multiple strands of personhood achieve unity and singularity' (Humphrey 2008: 357).[14] In my interlocutors' cases, however, rather than being linked to historical events that are unique and out of the ordinary (often being reserved for heroes and historical figures – see Das 2018) the emergence of revolutionary subjects was instead linked to a decision-*movement* that had an impact on every aspect of their everyday lives. They became revolutionary subjects by moving to and being inside and through a multiplicity of everyday actions that constitute the revolutionary process, rather than a singular event.

Moreover, despite the fact that a revolution is a historical and rare event, the extraordinary circumstances of 2011 (state violent repression and revolutionary work) became increasingly ordinary for those who lived in liberated and besieged areas for years. The decision to sacrifice one's present – and potentially oneself – was thus intimately linked with staying in regime-controlled areas or moving to 'liberated' areas controlled by rebels.[15] In the latter case, my interlocutors explained how they 'went deeper' into the revolution as their entire life became dedicated to it. The everyday was totally transformed in the liberated areas: if one was a student, a civil servant, or a shopkeeper before joining the revolution, one became a nurse, a doctor, an educator, or a teacher in the liberated areas. Access to basic services was quickly restricted in the liberated areas where water and electricity were cut, and shortages of medicine and food were frequent. Residents thus had to adapt to a rougher everyday life without the services that they used to have under the regime; and this soon became their everyday normality in the midst of war and siege (see Al-Kateab 2019; Fayyad 2019).

Sacrificing the present and cutting oneself off from the past also affected Syrians' social and familial relations. Because they supported and participated in the revolution and often moved to or stayed in liberated areas, my interlocutors had to cut ties with relatives and friends. Umm Ahmad revealed that her entire family had stopped speaking to her as her neighbourhood became liberated and was controlled by the FSA. Her siblings and parents were in a neighbouring district that remained under the regime control and feared for their own safety if they kept in touch with her, since as an inhabitant of a liberated area she was de facto perceived as an opponent, or a 'terrorist' in the regime's terminology. This fear was accentuated by her sons' arrests and killing at the hands of the regime. This situation was very painful to Umm Ahmad, especially as she recalled a vibrant family life and close ties with her siblings before the uprising. But she also felt that it was the price to pay for fighting for the right cause, and regretted that her siblings could not recognise she and her children were right.

In fact, most of the Syrians I lived with pointed out that their entire social networks had been reshaped by the revolution and that the people with whom they currently socialised were people they had met in the revolution, who were, like them, 'working in the revolution' (*ishtighlu b-l thawra*). Involvement in the revolution thus often became synonymous with totally cutting ties with the past, family, and friends, and this reshaping of relations contributed to the transformation of my interlocutors' lives. These sacrifices did, however, create a dilemma for Syrian revolutionaries, especially when they were *barra* (outside). Some refused to keep their lives on hold, and decided to start families, get married, have children. Others migrated further to find a job, pursue their studies or obtain legal documents (see Chapter 3).

## Revolutionary vs family duties

Going deeper into the revolution also created tensions between competing duties and obligations such as family and personal goals, creating conflict between the desire to continue one's life, resume one's studies or professional career, and migration. The sacrifice of their present was signified by my interlocutors often saying that they had 'paused' (*wa'qef*) their lives, contrarily to those outside; their studies, work, everyday life, family, and social relations were put on hold in order to be fully involved in the revolution. This commitment to self-sacrifice was shown through their acute awareness of the risks they were taking and the likelihood of losing their lives. 'I am going back and I will fight until either Bashar dies or I am martyred,' Abu Zein told his mother on the day he arrived from Syria. He made it clear that his plan was to go back after he fully recovered from his injuries. He had been smuggled out of Homs's last besieged area as he required urgent medical treatment, being heavily injured in his left arm and eye. I was staying at Umm Yussef's for a few days at the moment of her son and his family's escape from al-Waer. The tension was very high as the family feared their arrest at the regime checkpoints.

The family had to pay a large amount of money and find IDs for Abu and Umm Zein in order for them to be able to cross the regime checkpoints. They also had to disguise themselves to look like ordinary civilians. It was harder for Abu Zein who was first rushed into a field hospital to attend his injuries and later had to fight the pain and cross the checkpoint without showing any sign that he had recently been injured. He recalled the deep pain he felt as he had to stand at the checkpoint. The family was later escorted by fellow FSA fighters until they reached the Turkish border, where only one of the fighters entered with them and joined us for the copious meal we had prepared to celebrate their arrival (see Chapter 3).

Abu Zein's insistence to go back to fight worried his wife and mother. Umm Yussef had had heated arguments with him, when he was still besieged, as she believed that his first duty was to protect his family and bring them to safety in Turkey. She knew from her daughter-in-law that the condition of those under siege was worsening quickly and their health deteriorating. A few days after Umm Zein escaped besiegement, we were preparing the evening meal together in Umm Yussef's kitchen. Her task was to make a traditional salad of cucumber, tomato and lettuce. As she cut the vegetables, Umm Zein remembered with emotion that at one point in the siege she had managed to get one tomato and one cucumber (in the region they are usually very small) and that she found herself wondering whether to cut them and make a very small salad to share between the four of them or cut them in halves to give to each of her sons, who had never seen and tasted these vegetables before. Indeed, as the siege stiffened in the old city,[16] no food or medicine was entering the neighbourhood and the shelling was becoming more intense.

Abu Zein was often described as a *batal* (hero): he participated in peaceful protests from the very start before joining the FSA to defend his neighbourhood when the repression escalated, and later remained there despite the siege and despite his parents and siblings leaving. Yet his mother and wife, although both strong supporters of the revolution, argued that he had sacrificed enough to the revolution and believed that he should now take care of his family, rather than going back to Syria to fight; in other words, be a good father rather than a hero or a martyr. As we sat in the kitchen, away from the men, where we cooked and ate with Umm Yussef and her daughters, Umm Zein explained that, unlike her husband, she had no plan or desire to go back to Syria. She had endured the siege and the shelling, but now that she had reached safety, she refused to return to a war-torn country. She believed that her family had sacrificed enough to the revolution and that it was now other people's turn. She was worried that her children had already paid too heavy a price, as they could not attend school – a favourite target of the regime forces – and they suffered from malnutrition and psychological trauma.

Umm Zein confided that although she was a fervent supporter of the revolution, family was even more important to her. Finally being safe and reunited with her in-laws brought intense nostalgia for her previous life. She had no support during the three years of siege where she had to care for her two young children while looking for food and other essentials in a place where very little was left, and where she regularly had to move flat to follow the fighters' progression. She explained that, although the revolution and struggle for freedom were necessary, the revolutionaries had not wanted the current situation;[17] they had not expected that their call for the regime's downfall and freedom would result in war and massive destruction of the country. 'We demonstrated against the regime to ask for its downfall, but it's a war now. We are fighting against air-jets now!' exclaimed Umm Zein. A very pious woman, Umm Zein framed the tension between the need to revolt against oppression and family obligations in religious terms. Discussing her husband's sacrifice to the revolution and readiness to die she said:

> He was telling me: 'God will not forget you! I am fighting and I will die in martyrdom.' I argued with him a lot! I was telling him, 'But if you are martyred what will happen to me and to the children?' And he kept saying: 'God will not forget you.' He wanted to go to Paradise, that's all! And he is right. But I think that those who have children and are married shouldn't fight for the revolution.

One can sense in Umm Zein's words the tension between the husband's desire to be elevated to the status of martyr (see Chapter 6), and his wife's asking him to be a dutiful father and husband. As Umm Zein explained to me, in her interpretation of religion, being a good husband and father brings one to Paradise as surely as martyrdom. Despite keeping to this line of argument with her husband she herself was shifting between revolutionary commitment and family duties.

Umm Zein deepened her understanding of family responsibilities and revolutionary duties by contrasting *al-nas min juwwa* and *al-nas min barra* (people of the inside and people of the outside). She often expressed her frustration with young men with no family responsibilities 'sitting' in Turkey; she believed they should be in Syria fighting the regime. She was also the first to censure anyone leaving for Europe, such as her brother, who was still in his early twenties, who left the country just after the uprising started. She condemned his behaviour; he should have been the one fighting, rather than her husband who was already a father, yet he was 'sitting and doing nothing outside'. She even claimed that she would have participated in protests and carried weapons herself (*ahmel slah*) if she had not been the mother of two young children.

Despite or maybe because of the all-encompassing demands of revolution on the self, revolutionaries cannot be reduced to their revolutionary identity. They do have conflicting commitments and duties, dreams and aspirations,[18] and their involvement in, and position towards the revolution evolved over time. Revolutionary subjects have to navigate between their revolutionary commitment, family obligations, religious duties and future dreams, among other competing horizons (see Schielke 2015). They also have different characters: some were scared to continue their work in the revolution, others were not ready to take certain risks, and not all were ready in the same way to sacrifice their family relations and former lives.

Rami, whom I introduced in Chapter 1, was the only male member of his family who did not join the armed rebellion after his town fell in the crossfire of regime and Hezbollah armies. This was partly linked to the fact that he had not been in his hometown when these events unfolded as he was studying in Egypt, but it was also linked to his own character and sensibility. He was later given the chance to join the armed factions his relatives had formed with fellow townsmen when they started to fight against the regime in liberated areas near the Turkish border. He, however, preferred to continue on his path as an engineering student and support the revolution in different ways. He did frequently go inside and visit his relatives but never agreed on joining the armed forces. Discussing his understanding of his own involvement in the revolution, he explained that he preferred contributing to it through other means, while recognising that had he been in his hometown when it fell under regime fire, he would have most probably join the rest of his family in the armed struggle. Some would say he was not brave or courageous enough to join the armed struggle; while others would praise his choice to work with peaceful means for the revolution and remaining outside.

## Going inside: revolutionary continuity and personal changes

The majority of my interlocutors had to flee their hometowns and find refuge in Turkey due to being wanted by the regime, the heavy bombing of their neighborhoods and towns, the constant fighting and later the besiegement of numerous liberated areas. This enforced displacement put them in a paradoxical position, for they were now outside while they defined the inside as the place of the revolution, and *being* inside, especially in revolutionary strongholds, as what makes one a revolutionary. In what follows, I examine how my interlocutors maintain their revolutionary self through movement as they seek to retain contact with inside, where the revolution *happens* and where the 'real' revolutionaries are. A gender and generational gap appears here, and a gendered definition of what it is to be revolutionary arises in an increasingly militarised context as the last part of this chapter, and Chapter 5, show.

Yassar, a young man who was living between Gaziantep and Syria's northern liberated areas, once told me, 'Going inside [in Syria's liberated areas] is a duty (*wajeb*) but it is also something personal.' When we met in October 2015, he was planning to go to liberated areas in the Idlib governorate and Aleppo city for two weeks, and he was trying to explain the compulsion he felt to go inside despite the obvious dangers.

> No work[19] can make you go to the most dangerous city in the world [Aleppo]! Only the cause and the sense of duty can … We started this revolution. Some people didn't even want the revolution! It is not fair to leave them in this situation [of war and humanitarian crisis].

Yassar did not know when he would be able to cross the border,[20] but he believed he would manage to do so in the coming days. The regions where he was going had been under intense shelling for the past weeks, which rendered his trip more perilous. He knew that he could die, and he added, 'You have to be prepared to die [when you go inside]; if you are not prepared to die you can't go there …'. Since he was travelling to the liberated areas of Aleppo that were thought to be on the point of being besieged by the regime forces, and from which people were desperately trying to flee, I asked him why he was going in the opposite direction to most people. 'I have to be *there* with the people. I cannot leave them in this situation … It's my duty, it's my country, it's what I have to do,' he answered calmly. Yassar, like many young people I met, presented going inside as a revolutionary duty and responsibility toward 'the people' (al sha'b). Like Yassar, many of the young used to move between inside and outside Syria so they could both cultivate and maintain their revolutionary identity and ethos by being in contact with inside and continuing their revolutionary work.

Here, self-cultivation appears as a malaka (habitus): one's ability to shape one's inner world (desire, will, and intellect) through outer (bodily) practices until one can regulate and govern one's behaviour (Mahmood 2001a: 216).[21] Yet, the bodily practices to which I refer are a series of movements, mainly across borders: self-cultivation through journeying, movement, and relation to space. I thus attempt to map out how (revolutionary) politics is cultivated at the level of the self through actions and bodily practices that, in this context, are mainly cross-border movements. Moreover, the particularity of the movement of Syrians between barra (Turkey) and juwwa (Syria's liberated areas) is that it was perceived as allowing revolutionaries to remain revolutionaries.[22] It was not a movement meant to generate a new identity but rather a movement that would lead one to remain the same – that is, a revolutionary. Or more precisely, moving appears as a deepening of a radical rupture, an apparently oppositional end-goal: it is about the cultivation and the deepening of a self born from a lived (spatial) rupture and disruption.[23] Here, being and going inside thus leads to the ontological transformation of the self, as it allows the self to be radically altered in order to maintain its revolutionary identity.

Thus, if going inside was meant to maintain one's revolutionary identity, it did so by paradoxically changing something within oneself. 'You cannot stay unchanged after you go inside. I don't know what will change inside of me this time but for sure something will change!' Yassar told me before travelling. Although he was going inside to keep in touch with 'the people', pursue his 'revolutionary work' (sheghel b-l thawra), and maintain his revolutionary identity, he also knew that his very self would be altered during this journey. This change reflected the rapidly evolving situation inside and the difference between outside (barra) and inside (juwwa). After being outside for a long time, going inside brought the necessary change that allowed the maintenance of one's revolutionary self; furthermore, for many, despite the strong chance of imminent transformation, the urge to go inside appeared to be a response to some sort of quasi-magical quality that they assigned to the inside.[24]

Young people, especially men, often told me that I would not be able to understand what life is like inside and how people feel when they go inside. Some of my interlocutors just went inside because they missed the *jawu* (the atmosphere). Yassar took advantage of a vacation from work to go inside and told me that he wanted to be *there* for the beginning of Ramadan to feel 'the atmosphere'. He explained that the atmosphere inside, especially during Ramadan, was something totally different because of the way the community came together, and he needed to have this experience of togetherness in order to 'reload his battery and get his energy back'. Yassar said that he had to walk in the streets of Syria, to smell its air, and to feel one with the people. Being inside Syria was presented as a way to revitalise and purify himself and return to his real self. 'I can think clearly when I'm there; I sleep like a baby! I even manage to write again …' In his case, the inside constituted a means to revert to his pure revolutionary self, as he would be cut off from the rest of the world and forced to go back to the essentials. Young men often commended the absence of electricity and other services, which obliged them to go back to themselves. There were no distractions: no internet, no telephone, no TV. They could, therefore, really be in touch with themselves and the people.

The inside's strong power of attraction for young men was illustrated by Umm Kamel, a policeman's widow from the northern countryside living with her four children, whom I met accompanying a friend on a visit to a *dar al aytam*, an orphanage for widows and their offspring. She told me how her 12-year-old son had once disappeared for several weeks and that she had learned from relatives who stayed in her native village that he had crossed to Syria. He had this urge, like so many other youngsters, to be *juwwa*. The power of inside was not only revealed by the urge to cross and be there, however, but also by the fact that, once inside, people found it hard to come back *barra* (outside). When young men left for the inside they would not reappear for long periods despite initial plans to return after a few days or weeks. This was, of course, sometimes linked to the situation at the borders as they could close for short periods of time (until the summer of 2015), but it was often independent of this pragmatic issue.

The contact with *juwwa* (inside) thus seems to maintain the Syrian revolutionary self. The different nature of the revolutionaries and their definition through their contact with the inside was echoed by the fact that people were classified in two categories: the people of the inside (*al-nas min juwwa*) and those on the outside (*al-nas min barra*). These designations were used to differentiate the revolutionaries who were still in Syria from the others, and were a shorthand way of classifying one's revolutionariness. Going inside was the most important technique Syrians developed to maintain their revolutionary identity as, by doing so, they would not only stay close to the revolution and the people, deepen their revolutionary selves, and reinforce their revolutionary commitment, they would also gain a *juwwa* quality through their contact with Syria.

Moreover, Syrian revolutionaries seemed deeply transformed by their embedded relations to and experiences of *juwwa*. Its transformational power was so radical that one could be strengthened by contact with it – thus becoming a *batal* (hero) – but one could also be burned by the intensity of such contact and run the risk of becoming *majnun* (crazy).[25] If Abu Zein was perceived as a hero for having stayed inside for so long, and Yassar for having been detained on several occasions and heavily injured in a protest (and yet continuing to go regularly inside), Amjad, a high-school student living inside and introduced in Chapter 1, was viewed quite differently. Amjad's strong attachment to the inside was often qualified in terms of craziness; he was described to me by his friends as having lost his mind, predicting his premature death because of his reckless willingness to stay inside: one of his favourite places was the front line, where he would stay chatting with friends in the armed factions. He thus seemed to be taking 'too many risks', to be putting his life in 'too much danger'.

The fine line between craziness and heroism is thus quite like that between suicide and martyrdom explored in the final chapter. What led some of his fellow comrades to consider him 'crazy' was perhaps the fact that he was perceived as being 'carefree': his cross-border movements were not as organised as Yassar's, for instance, nor his presence and revolutionary work perceived as necessary as Abu Zein's. Indeed, he did not have precise tasks or goals to carry on inside and his crossings of the border seemed to follow his own mood rather than specific duties. He once left the house where he was supposed to stay the night (a friends' place, where I was also staying), because other friends had told him of their attempt to cross the border at night. Everyone woke up, astonished at his departure and worried about him and what was perceived, also due to his young age, as an immature attitude. Hence, while the willingness to sacrifice oneself by staying or going inside was highly praised in terms of heroism (in the case of Abu Zein or Yassar for instance), it could also cause one to be regarded as mad if one's motives were not seen as genuine, were perceived as misplaced, or were understood as irresponsible and immature – as in Amjad's and Umm Kamel's son's case.

'We don't need more martyrs,' people would repeat to those who wanted to go inside without any greater goal than being inside. Going and being inside had to be motivated by perceptions of usefulness to the revolution. But not going inside could also be a cause of illness. Umm

Ahmad once said of her husband, 'He wants to go inside. He told me, "I need to smell the air of Syria, I need to touch Syria's ground, I need to grasp Syrian soil, I need to taste some of its fruits." So this year we went … Last time we did not go he fell ill and spent ten days in the hospital.' In this case, Abu Ahmad's intense and excruciating need to go inside was also linked to the need to be able to see and tend the graves of his three martyred sons, who had been buried in his village. The loss of five of his six sons had, indeed, deeply and durably affected Abu Ahmad's (mental) health as he remained muted and almost still in his bedroom since he had been forcibly displaced to Turkey.

## Going inside: revolutionariness and manhood

With the revolution turning into a fully fledged war, the definition of revolutionary identity through the medium of *juwwa* increasingly led to the equating of revolutionariness – defined through movement – and manhood. 'The way is too hard for women; you need to run for 10 to 15 minutes through mud and go down and up a deep trench,' Nour said, still covered in mud from the crossing. Nour, a man in his mid-twenties and my current flatmate's husband, was referring to the pass one had to follow when moving clandestinely between Syria and Turkey. He often crossed the border to go inside as he lived between the two borderlands and was only waiting for the Turks to open the border to move back inside with his wife. He would not take her by clandestine paths as he believed they were too hard for a woman. Negotiating the passage between the two countries was often narrated by those who had just arrived from inside and it was deemed harder than the journey from Turkey to Greece (see Al-Khalili 2017). One had to be a man, Nour believed, to be able to go inside; the fact that so few women seem to make the crossing confirmed this to my male interlocutors. Despite crossing becoming harder as the borders closed, women's movements were limited by Islamist factions controlling more checkpoints and imposing a male chaperone on them in the liberated areas they controlled. Moreover, women were also less likely to publicly speak about their underground movement.

Here, being a revolutionary can be understood in performative terms: it is only through specific actions that one is described and identified as a revolutionary, and for the male displaced revolutionary it is mainly through crossing to Syria. For men, reputation and status were mainly preserved through the repetition of this performance. Moreover, the way someone told his story and was capable of capturing his audience's attention and imagination was also central. One's identity was often fixed through a nickname, but one still had to perform the actions associated with the nickname in order to preserve it. In this context, going to Syria and recounting one's journey constitutes a heroic gesture: a performance that participates in the making of a 'true' revolutionary, or someone *min juwwa* (from the inside). Syrian men in their twenties and thirties entertained large groups of gathered friends and acquaintances with their latest *juwwa* stories. These stories would be repeated in different circles and widely commented upon and assessed by the audience as they circulated. Four male friends travelled together to Aleppo, split up to visit different places, then regrouped to return together to Gaziantep. They documented their trip by sending videos and pictures to WhatsApp and Facebook groups and were very excited when showing before a group of friends the video of their drive on the Castelado road:[26] 'the most dangerous road in the world' as they repeated. Nour, who was among the four friends, told the audience how he almost died during this last stay in Syria: 'I had just left the car when it exploded.' The stories of border crossings usually dominated the conversation for several days and were retold for each new guest, thus becoming a kind of heroic gesture.

Such performances were central to presenting the revolutionary self as well as vouching for the truth of the event related.[27] In addition, performing a story and sustaining the revolutionary self took place through the sharing of pictures as visual stories, which were sometimes presented as proof of their truth. Showing people in semi-private circles pictures of clandestine border crossings, often in a comic light, or publishing them on Facebook, were other ways of presenting oneself as a revolutionary and cultivating a revolutionary identity. The stories and pictures published on Facebook also reappeared annually on people's timelines on the date when they were initially posted, thus creating online 'memories' of detention, release from jail, or epic journeys to the inside, and occasions to recall these stories and reinforce a revolutionary identity.

The pictures were sometimes of torture and injuries, like those Umm Ahmad showed me of her son as she was recounting his story (see Chapter 6). Men were also not shy about showing me the marks that torture and injuries had left on their bodies, and sometimes videos that filmed the moments in which they happened.[28] These bodily signs and their representations participated in the performance and the truth of their stories. Outside, maintaining a revolutionary identity or self was thus very much a collective project and had to be connected to one's audience. An important proviso, however, is that such public display and story-telling was only heroic for men. For women, stories of detention

– which often meant sexual violence and rape (see Loiseau 2017; Yazbek 2018) – public humiliation, and physical violence were considered rather shameful and could lead to their social and familial exclusion (see Chapter 5). Moreover, by becoming a war zone, the inside became an increasingly hostile place for women.[29]

Consequently, the spatial definition of being and remaining a revolutionary through crossing to the inside has increasingly become a male prerogative after Syrians were forcefully displaced to Turkey. This highlights the difference between ideas of acceptable forms of revolutionary activities and forms of sacrifice for men and women (see Ghannam 2012; Peteet 1994; Winegar 2012). Indeed, 'while femininity is no more natural than masculinity, physical violence is not as central to its construction' (Peteet 1994: 44; see also Allen 2008). Syrian women were thus not expected to take up weapons and fight, nor were they commended for it or seen as heroes when they faced detention; indeed, they were sometimes perceived as crazy when they went back to the liberated areas. Women were rather praised for their *sumud* (resilience) which often meant staying put – whether inside or outside (see Buch 2010; Buch Segal 2016 ; Khalili 2006). Umm Zein was thus thought of as a revolutionary for staying inside, while Umm Yussef was considered one because she was waiting for her children and husband outside, enduring the hardships of a life under siege and in displacement with a scattered family. If women could cross checkpoints more easily and were less likely to be arrested in the early months of the uprising (see Chapter 5), with the situation turning into a fully fledged war, with the growing presence of Islamist factions, Daesh, and the multiplication of checkpoints, the journey became increasingly dangerous, especially so for women, leading many interlocutors and friends to flee to Gaziantep.

## Becoming revolutionaries through spatial ruptures

One morning in the autumn of 2015 I woke up to the voice of several men in the flat that I shared with Dina and Hanan. It led me to wonder what visitors were doing in our flat so early, especially men. I went to the living room to discover seven people sitting and drinking coffee. Dina introduced me to her family members – two brothers, two nephews, her eldest sister, and a female cousin. They had just arrived from Raqqa. They were exhausted, as they had spent two days on the way. The sister told us: 'We crossed all Syria to get here! Damas, Hama, Idleb, Aleppo, the Kurdish mountains … We entered through Antakya … We walked for 7 kilometres at night in the mountains, the road was like this [she makes a 60 degree angle with her hand]. There were families, children, pregnant women, old people, sick people …' The sister continued: 'At each checkpoint we came up with a new lie: we are going to visit relatives here, there, we are not leaving the country.' She sipped some of her coffee and resumed her story as we sat on the floor around her: 'the worse part was the crossing to Turkey … The Turkish police asked us for a lot of money so we could cross. The way was very muddy and hard: you need to cross a two-metre-deep trench …' she said while massaging her feet and ankles.

In this chapter, I argued that spatial disruption (the creation of *juwwa* and the displacement to *barra*) appears as engendering a specific kind of subject: the revolutionary self. I thus argue that revolutionary selves – defined by ascetic practices, the sacrifice of their present, and the willingness to give up one's own life – are formed by virtue of being inside, due to *juwwa*'s heterotopic qualities. In fact, despite the failure of the Syrian revolution to realise a political rupture at the level of the state, it has led to a series of spatial disruptions at local and regional scales.

Revolutionary selves are generated and cultivated through spatial disruption and relations with these insides, rather than through a temporal rupture and a specific event. The Syrian revolution hence appears as a spatial phenomenon, and is defined in terms of space. The revolution is what happens inside (in the liberated areas) and its horizon is the inside (Syria). Moreover, one becomes a revolutionary through rites of passage that are eminently spatial (being detained, besieged, going to liberated areas), and the revolutionaries are *al-nas min juwwa* (the people of the inside): those who live in liberated and besieged areas or are detained. Later, with enforced displacement to the outside (Turkey), the revolutionaries are those who go back inside: their identity is maintained through movement.

Such enquiry into the self-cultivation of revolutionary selves expands the theorisation of the formation and cultivation of pious selves through embodied practices by looking at the cultivation of revolutionary identity through (im)mobility and movement. Yet, revolutionary selves increasingly become synonyms for manhood, as going inside is mainly a male enterprise, pointing to the gendered aspect of the revolutionary. Although crossing to Syria is not uniquely a male practice, the experiences and discourses of going back and forth between Syria and Turkey were mostly marked by ideas and ideals of masculinity. As for the experience of physical violence and the readiness to sacrifice oneself, risk-taking and perilous actions seemed constitutive of a masculine revolutionary self rather than a feminine one (see Chapters 5 and 6).

By analysing relations between space and self-making, this chapter has similarly showed that Syrians transformed their identity through different types of mobility – expulsion, displacement, imprisonment and containment (that is, siege). In this context, *al-thawra* (the revolution) appears as a transformational entity operating at the scale of the self through spatial rupture and disruption. Up until the end of 2015, the revolution was thus defined as a predominantly spatial enterprise because it had locally succeeded in seizing power from the regime and was being enacted in these 'liberated' areas. This chapter also brings together displacement and revolution through the new cartographies and new subjectivities that emerge in the spatial ruptures at the heart of Syrian revolutionary experience. Here, the nexus between revolution and displacement that is central to this ethnography of Syrian revolutionaries in and through exile appears as generating selves.

## Notes

1  See Samira al-Khalil's comparison of besiegement and detention in her diaries (2016).
2  See also Armbrust (2019) on rites of passage in the Egyptian revolution.
3  A similar process of formation of the self through ritualised forms of violence has been described by Julie Peteet in the Palestinian context (1994). In that context, Peteet analyses the effects on Palestinian youths of ritualised beatings and detention by Israeli forces and shows how these forms of violence act as transformative experiences. Moreover, she argues that her interlocutors defined real men as those ready to sacrifice themselves for their family and the community and those resisting others' authority and control.
4  *Haram* refers to what is forbidden to believers (in an Islamic context). In this specific context it meant any movie with scenes including naked people or sexual content.
5  Interestingly, Foucault's concern with asceticism as a technique of self-formation and cultivation is intimately linked to his witnessing of the Iranian revolution (Ghamari-Tabrizi 2016). In his study of Foucault's writings on the Iranian revolution, Behrooz Ghamari-Tabrizi argues that Foucault's interest in ascetic techniques and the creation of new selves is linked to his witnessing the Iranian revolution, in which Shi'i rituals of penitence from the sixteenth century were given a new political meaning by Khomeini. Foucault was inspired by the ascetic rituals of self-flagellation and staged representations of Hussein's martyrdom in which the public took active part, seeing such rituals as practices that allowed believers to shape their thoughts to reach a 'certain state of perfection, of happiness, of purity, of supernatural power' (Foucault 1980: 162). Foucault argued that such public ritual practices of the self illustrated the intimate link between self-sacrifice and self-formation: one learns the truth about oneself by sacrificing oneself (1980: 80).
6  The all-encompassing claims of revolutionary action were vividly expressed by Sergey Nechayev, a nineteenth-century Russian revolutionary from the Nihilist movement, who wrote in his *Revolutionary Catechism* that 'the revolutionary is a doomed man … Everything in him is wholly absorbed in the single thought and the single passion for revolution' (1869).
7  Historically, revolutionary movements have been explicitly linked to projects involving the creation of a 'New Man' by their actors, theoreticians (such as Guevara and Castro 2009; Mao 1976; Nechayev 1869 and Trotsky 1957) and scholars alike (for instance Cheng 2009; Holbraad 2014; Kharkhordin 1999 and Yurchak 2003). Cheng (2009) shows that the correlation between the creation of a new political order and a new man appeared with the French revolution, inspired by the philosophers of the Enlightenment. The formation of a new subject that would support or fit a new political form of government was thus linked to the idea

of the Enlightenment thinkers in the field of education and their conception of the man and his mind as malleable (Cheng 2009: 8–12).

8   If there are no texts of reference discussing the New Man there are, however, local ideas and theories of self-formation. One example of this can be found in the Darayya *halaqa*, inspired by the thought of Abdelakram al-Saqqa and Jawdat Said (Al-Khalili 2021).

9   The difficulty and sometimes absurdity of crossing checkpoints from Damascus to Syria's north have been amazingly captured by Khaled Khalifa in his novel *Death is Hard Work* (2016), although it does not specifically focus on revolutionaries' crossing.

10  This is also described by Borneman in his book on Syrian men and masculinity in Aleppo (2007).

11  This collapse is described by Omar Aziz in the context of the establishment of the local councils (*al majales al mahaliyya*) in Syria's liberated areas. Local councils are administrative bodies that also deliver services to the population. They emerged after the regime's withdrawal when its provision of basic services (water, electricity, schools and so on) came to an end in Syria's liberated areas (Favier 2016; Al-Khalili 2017a; 2021; Munif 2020). They were a product of the local coordination groups that started to organise protests at the beginning of the revolution, appearing independently throughout the liberated areas and in very varied forms: some are elected bodies, others are nominated (Al-Khalili 2017a; 2021; Munif 2020).

12  I analytically use the term 'self' in reference to Foucault's 'technologies of the self' and, more precisely, to his concepts of self-formation and self-cultivation (1994; 1997). The technologies of the self are 'procedures ... proposed or prescribed to individuals to fix their identity, maintain, or transform it in pursuit of specific aims, thanks to relations of self-control and self-knowledge' (Foucault 1994: 213, my translation). Moreover, Foucault's concern with the self is linked to his analysis of biopower and governmentality (Michaud 2000; see also T. Mitchell 1990), for the self is shaped by relations of power; individuals are constituted as subjects through relations of power (Foucault 1997). This makes the notion particularly relevant for this chapter's argument, which presents the emergence of new subjects in relation to a specific political form: revolution. Indeed, what makes the concept of the technology of the self particularly appealing to the study of revolutionary selves is linked to the fact that one can understand revolution as a political project that presupposes a radical transformation of politics, society, and subjects (Holbraad 2014; Holbraad and Pedersen 2012).

13  Joel Robbins compares religious conversion to revolution (2007). See also Cherstich et al. (2020) on this notion and further ethnographic examples in Shah (2009) on Maoist revolutionaries in India.

14  In her work on the emergence of a subject – a 'singular acting person' – Caroline Humphrey argues that subject-formation happens in a 'situation of innovation and improvisation, of rupture with the past' (2008: 357). Embracing Badiou's (2003) definition of the event as a moment of definition of the subject, Humphrey looks into the relations between event and subject-making, noting: 'The troubled times in which anthropologists work require the conceptualisation of singular analytical subjects: individual actors who are constituted as subjects in particular circumstances' (Humphrey 2008: 357). While for Badiou the subject is 'one who recognizes the truth of a great historical event' (Humphrey 2008: 357), Humphrey, on the other hand, argues that anthropologists need a definition of the subject that is anchored in more ordinary circumstances. This is why she introduces the concept of 'decision-event' through which a person composes his singularity and becomes a new self in which former versions of his self no longer exist (Das 2018: 64). It is a 'decision to become this version of the self and not another' (Das 2018: 64).

15  I do not claim that all Syrians, whether in liberated or besieged areas, were there deliberately. Many did not have a choice to stay or leave. Yet, because of the heterotopic nature of the inside, their very presence inside made them part of the revolutionary project, although to a different degree than the activists (*nasheteen*).

16  They were initially besieged in the old city and later fled to al-Waer as the regime army advanced, where they were also besieged.

17  When we had this conversation in the early spring of 2015 she meant the war between revolutionaries and the regime.

18  The presence of competing duties and the shifting between different ethical horizons resonates with Samuli Schielke's analysis of competing horizons and obligations in terms of grand schemes (2010; 2015). He demonstrates that religious commitment enters into competition with romantic love, family obligations, and dreams of success in one's studies or work. People's lives are constituted of different worlds. Hence, life trajectories are rarely solely marked by a

unique and unconditional commitment to one grand scheme; rather, different competing and sometimes contradictory horizons orient people's lives.

19  Yassar referred to the fact that some non-governmental organisations employed Syrians who had to 'go *juwwa*' for their work – a form of work that, in this view, stands in stark contrast to revolutionary work.

20  Before 2015 the border was not permanently opened despite Turkey's 'open-door policy'.

21  In her seminal work on pious women's movements in Egypt, Saba Mahmood (2001a; 2001b; 2005) explores the cultivation of a pious self through the study of religious scriptures as well as social practices and bodily comportments (e.g. prayer, veiling). Mahmood inverts the Western understanding of the self as the agency that dictates the conduct of the body by claiming that it is through bodily actions that the self is trained and shaped. Mahmood also shows that the cultivation of pious selves is not an apolitical endeavour as its correlate is the transformation of social life.

22  Travel practices have long been an important element of life in the Arab and Muslim world, and they have historically been important means of shaping Muslim subjectivities (see Marsden 2011a; 2011b).

23  In a way these journeying practices recall those of Mongolia's Darhad nomads for whom movement is the attempt to reproduce the same (Pedersen 2016). In Pedersen's study, moving appears as a way to maintain the same – it is about continuity of the past and 'repetition of things' (Pedersen 2016: 220).

24  Similar feelings of compulsion have also been described in the context of trans-border travel and migration (see Elliot 2021; Marsden 2009a; 2009b; 2011a; Pandolfo 2007).

25  See Pandolfo (2007) on the dangers of crossing bordering lands and seas (in her case the Mediterranean), which she conceptualises as 'the burning', drawing on her interlocutors' term.

26  This was the only road linking the Turkish border to Aleppo city until it was taken back by the regime in 2015. Because of its strategic position it was often bombed by the regime when trying to besiege the eastern part of Aleppo, which was under rebel control.

27  Such storytelling echoes the practices described by Gilsenan in his study of narratives and violence in the Lebanese mountains, a society in which storytelling is central (1996: 57); see also Herzfeld (1989) on manhood in Crete.

28  This resonates with Peteet's description of Palestinian detainees displaying their injuries in public as a way to testify to their experience and assert their manhood (1994: 37).

29  This is not to say that no women were going inside and crossing the Syrian–Turkish border (see Al-Khalili 2017a; 2018).

Part 2
**End(ing)s outside**

**Figure 3.1:** Gaziantep. © Charlotte al-Khalili

# 3
# Of hospitality and displacement: life in a spatio-legal limbo

*Hospitality [is] the problem of how to deal with strangers*
(Pitt-Rivers 2012: 501)

'We are treated nothing like guests (*diyuf*) and you know that very well!' Umm Nidal told me during one of my visits to her poorly furnished apartment in Gaziantep old city. Umm Nidal was among the nearly two million Syrian 'guests' that Turkey counted in 2015, and which constituted 17 per cent of Gaziantep's population by 2017 (Carpi and Şenoğuz 2019: 126). She went on to expand on this:

> We are guests [*diyuf*] but now even with a *kimlik* [identification document[1]] we cannot travel without an authorisation from the *wali* [local administrative authority] to another city![2] Each time I want to go visit my relatives in Reyhanlı [a Turkish border-town located a three-hour drive from Gaziantep] I need to spend a day to get the travel authorisation [*ezen safar*]. You need to take the documents in the early morning to the *wali* and come back in the evening to get the authorisation. Each time you go you have to queue; I spend more time at the *wali* than on the way to Reyhanlı! And if you don't get this authorisation you can get arrested and sent back to Syria!

Umm Nidal often invited me to come by the house she shared with her sister and the latter's family in Gaziantep, where they found refuge in 2014. She always had stories to share and guests to introduce to me. She also took me to visit women to whom she delivered fabrics, colourful wool balls, and small accessories for their common embroidery work. Umm Nidal fled Syria when her town was retaken by regime forces after being briefly liberated by the Free Syrian Army (FSA). She had participated in women's protests, made scarves and small items decorated with the revolution's flag, and cooked for protesters and rebels. In a context in which peaceful protesters were violently repressed, jailed, tortured, and forcibly disappeared by the Assad regime, she feared for her safety in a town under its control. Umm Nidal often invited me to come to their house. We sat in her kitchen as she prepared coffee, lighting up a cigarette and slowly mixing the coffee powder into the pot of boiling water. As we continued to discuss the so-called guest status of Syrians in Turkey she said: 'You know how much I pay for this flat? 800 Turkish Liras [about US$200]. I pay twice the rent that my Turkish neighbours pay! And before we [Syrians] arrived, this same flat used to cost 200 Turkish Liras!'

The restriction on Syrians' internal movement within Turkey that Umm Nidal describes above became permanent in 2016, when Turkey signed a cooperation agreement with the EU, widely known as the 'EU–Turkey deal', that led to a crackdown on Syrians' movement. The deal aimed to prevent Syrians from entering Greece and the EU, and it allowed the EU to deport Syrians from Greece to Turkey. As these political developments took place, Syrians in Turkey became ever-more permanent guests of the Turkish state. As a result, there was a shift in the metaphor of Syrians as 'guests' (Arabic: *diyuf*; Turkish: *misafir*); it became a legal status that placed Syrians in limbo, rendering their everyday lives increasingly precarious and uncertain. Adding to displaced Syrians' difficulties, the issuance of kimliks had been inconsistent: despite being compulsory for Syrians from 2015 onward, they were issued to some but not to others in Gaziantep, as well as in other municipalities (Baban et al. 2017).

From 2015 onwards the question of Syrians' legal status and everyday life in Turkey became an increasingly central preoccupation for my interlocutors. This had led them to critique and challenge Turkish hospitality through a series of discourses and practices that guide my present reflections on hospitality's scalar nature. My attention was thus brought to *karam* (hospitality) by my interlocutors' insistence on designating their status in Turkey as one of guest, which became a powerful tool to denounce their precarious condition. Indeed, in the aftermaths of the Syrian revolution, *karam* turned into an acute political discourse about *karama* (dignity). Dignity (*karama*) and hospitality (*karam*) are both derived from the same Arabic root 'KRM', and respect and honour are notions central to both concepts, in addition to being deeply anchored in my interlocutors' revolutionary project.

## Scales, registers and scripts of hospitality

The Turkish state's policy towards displaced Syrians seems to be best understood as a series of scalar assemblages, or 'hospitality assemblages' – each composed by the different positioning of actors (the state, locals, Syrians), registers (moral, legal), scripts (historical, religious), and spatio-temporal frames (Shryock 2012). Moreover, processes of rescaling were central to performing, critiquing, and challenging hospitality. I thus focus on Syrians' everyday life in limbo, their experiences as 'guests' of the Turkish state in Gaziantep, and on their conceptualisations of locals' and the state's practice of hospitality.

Given that hospitality was both a state policy and a local practice, this chapter proposes a scalar examination of Syrians' daily encounters with the Turkish state, that is, their everyday interactions with state administrations and administrators (Gupta 1995), their dealing with their legal status, and their relations with their Turkish neighbours. I describe my Syrian interlocutors' lifeworlds in displacement; Syrians' interactions with the Turkish state and local Turks; and Syrian uses of scripts, registers, and spatio-temporal frames. In doing so, I show the various scalar assemblages at play in this context, allowing the reader to better grasp the evolving and shifting meanings of what it is to be a guest or a host and who can be guest or host in a given context. Moreover, with displacement becoming more permanent and uncertain, my interlocutors' spatio-temporal horizons shifted from a prompt return to Syria to a long displacement in Turkey and/or asylum in Europe.

Scales have been defined as framing (Caton 1987) and as stagecraft (Shryock 2012). Caton reveals the game of inclusion/exclusion at play in the shaping of hospitality: it can extend from an individual home to a village, and include or exclude different people from the practice of reciprocity. Shryock shows the importance of inequality between guests and their hosts – and the latter's sovereignty – since only designated areas of a house, for instance, are accessible to guests. In addition, according to Naor Ben-Yehoyada (2015: 186), 'acts of hospitality dramatize social relations by framing interaction between host and guest within temporal and spatial scales of inclusion and exclusion'.

The concept of scale, however, does not only encompass a geographical meaning: hospitality is a practice that cuts across different areas of inclusion and exclusion and defines them from the smaller to the larger. Scales have to be understood as both quantitative and qualitative: they comprise both spatio-temporal frames and jurisdictions (Valverde

2009). Bearing this in mind allows one to see how several (re)scalings can happen simultaneously and how they can overlap, creating several social, legal, and political differentiations, and shifting hospitable actors' roles. Such a plural understanding of scale shows how hospitable assemblages can be defined as scalar: they bring together different actors, scripts, and registers that refer to various spatio-temporalities, and they constantly redefine who are guests and hosts according to jurisdiction. This definition of hospitality as scalar reveals the failures and dangers of the state's use of the hospitality idiom. Indeed, for the state to capture the idiom of hospitality precludes reciprocity, since the host state and the Syrian guests belong to different scales. Furthermore, laws cannot force local hosts to be hospitable to unknown guests, since this imperative invokes different registers (legal/moral) and corresponds to another scale (national/local). As a result, hospitality fails and hostility prevails, not so much because hostility and hospitality are intimately linked (as Derrida proposed, 1997), but because the juxtaposition of scales confuses scripts and registers.

Hospitality is classically described as protecting a guest, providing refuge from the guest's enemies (Pitt-Rivers 2012; Shryock 2012). In a scalar shift, immigrants have been metaphorically presented as guests of the state they seek refuge in. Yet the law of hospitality is often presented as an ethical maxim and unwritten law, sharply opposed to the state's written laws. As Derrida (1997) points out, the state's rhetoric of hospitality paradoxically uses hospitality as a metaphor to speak of its guests' – the migrants' – obligation towards its hosts. What happens, then, when the guest (immigrant)–host (state) dynamic ceases to be metaphorical and becomes the legal language of the state? In the context of Syrians' displacement in Turkey, three hospitable assemblages, or spatio-temporal scales, mobilise different 'registers' and 'scripts' (Ben-Yehoyada 2015; see also Ben-Yehoyada 2014).

The first is the transnational space of the Umma, or community of Muslims, which presents co-religionists as 'brothers' and recalls the time of the Prophet. It includes the Turkish term *muhacir* (from the Arabic *muhajir*), which originally refers to those who followed the Prophet from Mecca to Medina when he fled the city, a journey known as the hijra. As muhacirs and Muslim brothers, Syrians were thus presented by Turkey's ruling Justice and Development Party (AKP) as oppressed Muslims in need of temporary refuge by drawing on a religious register and a Quranic script. The term muhacir historically refers to Balkan Muslims who were persecuted when the Ottoman Empire lost control of the western Balkans, and who fled back within its borders for refuge. This constitutes a second spatio-temporal scale drawing on a historical script and ethical register, one in which Syrian displacement echoes the Ottoman past. This is particularly resonant in Gaziantep, which for five centuries formed part of the Ottoman region of Aleppo before it was incorporated into the newly established Republic of Turkey in 1923. Since then, the country's national space has constituted a third hospitality assemblage that draws on a nationalist script and political register. In 2011 and 2012, most Syrians fleeing to Turkey stayed temporarily while their towns or villages were being shelled, and returned home when the attacks stopped (Chatty 2018). This was facilitated by Turkey's open-door policy, which was in place until May 2015 and prolonged the border opening established in 2007, which was associated with a free trade and visa-free travel agreement between the two countries. But as the Syrian regime's repression intensified, many Syrians were forced to flee and settle more permanently in Turkey.

In answer to Syrian mass displacement, a novel legal status was created: a 'temporary protection status' that defined Syrians as 'guests' rather than refugees or asylum seekers. In this assemblage, the state uses both a legal register and a nationalist script. By simultaneously mobilising these hospitable assemblages, the Turkish state blurred the ethical, religious, and legal registers, as well as the nationalist, historical, and Quranic scripts. Moreover, and more significantly, the mixing of scales confused Syrian guests and Turkish hosts about their roles in this unusual assemblage. Indeed, what happens when the state captures the language of hospitality, conflating the ethical and the legal? Furthermore, how can Syrians reciprocate state hospitality, and local Turks host the state's guests? In this chapter, I will show how my interlocutors challenge state hospitality by refusing its 'gifts' (cf. Alkan 2021) and how, by proposing concurrent rescalings, they create hospitable assemblages in which they claim to be legally refugees – which invokes the state's legal duties – while also claiming they should be guests of the local population, attributing to them ethical-religious duties.

This is thus an unusual situation, in which the language registers are somehow inverted: the state speaks the moral language of hospitality, while refugees and their defenders speak the language of international and state laws (cf. Derrida 1997; Rozakou 2012). But far from the dream of a state offering unconditional hospitality (Derrida 1997), which has been influential in the literature (Candea 2012; Candea and Da Col 2012), the state's use of hospitality's moral language shows the dangers conveyed by the state's capture of the idiom of hospitality.

## Of guests and refugees

When Umm Khaled visited the flat where I sublet a room from Dina they entered into a heated debate with each other about Syrians' situation in Turkey. Umm Khaled had fled her town in northern Syria with her daughter, leaving a martyred husband and son behind. Her two remaining sons eventually fled to Europe but she stayed in Turkey with her five-year-old. While Umm Khaled's daughter had a *kimlik* and went to a Turkish school, Dina's nephews had not managed to get this document from the local authorities and, as a result, had been out of school for over six months at the time of our conversation. There was indeed a gap between the law and its implementation: *kimliks*, despite being compulsory for Syrians, were not issued continuously.

As she served us coffee Dina asked Umm Khaled about her living conditions in Turkey. Umm Khaled answered that she felt that it was much better than in Lebanon, where she had briefly lived after fleeing Syria. To her, Turkey was the best place for Syrians to live at present. Dina was furious: Umm Khaled should not be satisfied with the way she was treated here: 'Turkey was not doing Syrians any favours'. Turkey was actually not fulfilling its obligations towards them, she argued. Invoking a different jurisdiction – the international – to critique the legal limbo the Turkish state had put them in, she said that Turkey had a duty to grant them refugee status and rights. For Dina, Syrians were refugees according to international law, and Turkey had the duty to grant them refugee status and rights. Although Dina agreed that the situation was worse in Lebanon and Jordan she refused to qualify the situation in Turkey as 'good' because of their precarious guest status. This feeling that Syrians are not guests in Turkey, despite being officially labelled as such, was widespread during my fieldwork. Some of my interlocutors, including Dina, hypothesised that the status of 'guest' was just a tool for the Turkish government to give them fewer rights than they would have if they were refugees.

Despite stating that life was better in Turkey than in Lebanon, Umm Khaled often expressed her feelings of being cheated by the Turkish government after the EU–Turkey deal came into effect, as she, like many other interlocutors, expected to receive material benefits from it. Rumour had it, among Syrians and Turks alike (see Dağtaş 2017), that the EU had given Turkey large amounts of money to alleviate the Syrians' situation.[3] Umm Khaled could hardly survive on the small remittances sent by her sons, who were refugees in Europe, but despite frequently queuing for hours, along with friends, at organisations and governmental bodies that were said to provide aid, she did not receive any support as she could not prove she really was a widow as the regime never issued a death certificate for her martyred husband.

The conversation between Umm Khaled and Dina gives a hint about the ambiguous legal situation of forcibly displaced Syrians in Turkey who have been named guests (*misafir*) by Turkish officials, administrative bodies, and in official circulars.[4] They legally became guests when they were granted 'temporary protection status', which corresponds to neither refugee nor asylum-seeker status. Refugee status has geographical and temporal restrictions in Turkey, where it can be granted to European citizens, while others are considered temporary asylum seekers before being resettled in a third country through the UNHCR (Toğral Koca 2016). Syrians have yet another status: labelled 'guests', they are granted temporary protection status that theoretically gives them limited access to healthcare and education. It means that they can stay in Turkey as long as the situation in Syria does not allow them to go back, conferring a status accompanied by three rules: an open-door policy (any Syrian can enter Turkey through the Syrian border); non-refoulement (Syrians cannot be sent back to Syria); and registration within Turkey (see Özden 2013). However, guest status is ambiguous and precarious, as it is mostly defined by administrative circulars rather than laws; furthermore, these three rules are not always followed, nor guest status always granted, as state circulars are not systematically applied at the regional and municipal levels, falling under the latter's jurisdiction.

In 2015 it became compulsory for Syrians living in Turkey to hold a *kimlik* in order to reside there legally and access healthcare and education. But since *kimlik*s were not continuously issued by the Turkish authorities, many Syrians were illegalised. Syrians could also apply for a residence permit (Arabic: *iqameh*; Turkish: *ikamet*) like any other foreigner. However, the *iqameh* must be renewed every one or two years on the basis of student, tourist or worker status, for instance, and it is therefore harder to obtain as there are income and insurance restrictions; a valid passport is also required, which was a luxury for many. Syrians were thus often put in a situation in which they were illegalised without the possibility of becoming legal; in other words, they were placed in a legal limbo. This fragile position in terms of the law was reinforced by constantly changing (and inconsistently applied) regulations and laws, as well as the near absence of rights and aid. In practice, this legal liminality affected Syrians' everyday life, access to schools, healthcare, accommodation, work, and the possibility of travelling both inside and outside Turkey. Syrians, as 'stranger-guests', in Pitt-Rivers's term, thus held a 'statusless status' and occupied a liminal position with respect to the law: they were neither fully inside (subject to laws and protected by rights) nor totally outside it (unprotected by rights nor subject to laws) (Pitt-Rivers 2012: 503).

## Hospitality's jurisdictions

Syrians' liminal position towards the law was particularly striking in the case of marriages, births, and the issue or renewal of passports. Officially recognised birth and marriage certificates, a family record book (*daftar 'ayileh*) and valid travel documents were necessary in order to go back to Syria, but also to apply for relocation or family reunification. Amal and Mohammad, two young activists who had graduated from a teaching institute in Aleppo, got married soon after their arrival in Gaziantep, but they felt that they 'were not really married' in the absence of a contract from Syria. In Syria, one can have such a contract established by a third party, so they paid someone to obtain it for them. Yet, as they were both wanted by the regime for their revolutionary activities, it was refused on the grounds that the groom had not completed his military service (which he actually had, before the revolution). After Amal gave birth, she felt the need to get their marriage registered even more urgently. She did not want her child to be stateless and born to an unmarried couple – as she would thus legally be born from an unknown father. In order to 'regulate' their situation, they decided to hire a lawyer to bring their case to court in Syria. This procedure was very costly as they had to pay several intermediaries; it was also very painful as they found their future, even though displaced, in the hands of the regime they had fought against and fled from. Eventually they succeeded in getting their marriage officially registered – a year of transactions with different fixers and hundreds of US dollars later.

In addition, as they were wanted by the regime, Amal and Mohammad were not issued passports[5] in Syria, and were now seeking to acquire them so they could obtain residence permits and apply for a 'proper' ID for their newborn baby. They faced two possible sources: the *Etilaf* (the National Coalition of Syrian Revolutionary and Opposition Forces, commonly known as the Coalition) or the Syrian consulate. Most people did not trust the passports issued by the coalition, fearing that their worth was only temporary. On the other hand, getting a passport from the regime meant going through a humiliating and pricy process as it costs at least US$800 for a passport that is only valid for two to six years.[6] Moreover, on various occasions regime officers claimed that a passport presented for identification was stolen, thus leading to the arrest of the holder and confiscation of the passport at a border control point. Yet the regime's passports are internationally recognised, and having proper documents was a major issue for the people with whom I lived. 'I will have no choice but to take a boat when my passport expires', I heard many times, as my Syrian interlocutors saw fleeing to Europe as a way to guarantee a clearer and more stable status by providing documents that would allow them to reside legally in a country.

Moreover, the possession or absence of documents such as travel documents, residency permits, passports, and marriage and birth certificates – and strategies for acquiring them – do indeed have direct effects on people's everyday lives.[7] It is a factor in creating (un)certainty and (in)stability, generating different future horizons, as well as strategies to meet them. In fact, legal status, processes, and situations create a specific 'texture of life' (Kelly 2006: 90): in the case of Syrians, this texture was precarious and uncertain because of the suspension of their 'ontological status as legal subjects' (Butler 2000: 81). Being 'guests' of the Turkish state, Syrians do not fall under international protection, yet they have to navigate a plurality of competing and juxtaposed jurisdictions.

On a legal and administrative level, Syrians displaced in Turkey must respect Turkish law while simultaneously navigating Syrian law. On the one hand, Syrian life in Turkey is subject to ever-changing – and not always respected – laws, and often decrees, when it comes to healthcare, schooling, housing, work, or travel regulations. On the other, when it comes to family law, renewal of passports, and issuing of marriage and birth certificates, Syrians must deal with newly established free Syrian institutions and/or those of the regime. They are thus dealing with the institutions of a 'wannabe state' (Navaro-Yashin 2012: 114), and/or with the institutions of a regime that does not recognise them as citizens, since most of my interlocutors were wanted by the Syrian regime for their or their relatives' revolutionary activities.

## Uncertain and precarious everyday: healthcare, education, work

Umm Khaled had lived in Turkey for a year and a half with her daughter and one of her sons when her sister, Umm Mohammad, fled Syria with her husband and four children. While Abu Mohammad and Umm Khaled's son embarked on the perilous journey to Europe at the end of the summer of 2015, the two sisters stayed behind with their children. Since Umm

Mohammad's family was waiting to be reunited in Europe, the two sisters and five children shared a tiny studio flat. It was always overcrowded, as Umm Mohammad's children had no *kimlik* and could not register for school.[8] During one of my visits, Umm Mohammad's six-year-old fell and cut his eyebrow while playing with his siblings. Umm Mohammad and her sister were scared to take him to the hospital without a *kimlik*. What if they got arrested and sent back to Syria? After visiting a nearby pharmacy and being told that the boy needed to get stitches, I accompanied Umm Khaled (who had a *kimlik*) to the hospital. In the first hospital, the staff refused to treat the boy. In the second, there were still translators available to assist Arabic speakers, one of whom found a doctor who agreed to put stitches on Mohammad's eyebrow; but the translator warned us that in two days a new regulation would forbid hospitals to treat Syrians without a *kimlik* for free, even in cases of emergency.[9] This meant that Syrians without a *kimlik* would have to visit private hospitals and pay large sums of money to be treated. The two women were shaken by the news: what would happen if Umm Mohammad or one of her children needed urgent medical treatment?

Umm Mohammad soon realised that she was stuck in an incongruous situation. When she tried to travel to Ankara to start the family reunification process with her husband in the winter of 2015, the family was not allowed to board their plane. They only had their Syrian IDs. These had allowed travel inside Turkey until a few months earlier, but an additional travel authorisation had become temporarily obligatory for any trip within Turkey during the general election period (summer 2015), and this had apparently become a permanent rule. The family's nightmare started when they realised that they needed a *kimlik* to get this authorisation, yet the municipality of Gaziantep no longer issued *kimliks*. They were caught in a vicious circle: they could not go to Ankara without a travel authorisation, but they needed a *kimlik* to get this authorisation; *kimliks*, however, were not issued in the city anymore, yet they could not go to another city to get one as travelling without a *kimlik* was not allowed. They eventually discovered that rules, regulations, and laws were not always followed when they boarded a bus whose driver agreed to overlook their absence of documents. The fact that laws and regulations change quite often and are not published in Arabic, and the fact that they are not always followed, gave my friends and interlocutors the feeling that they lived in a country without consistent laws, which contributed to the feeling that they were living in a state of constant uncertainty. They also felt that they were not treated with dignity and they yearned for a more stable and clear legal status, one that did not mirror hospitality and therefore did not contain the ambiguities and tensions of that status.

In addition, the opacity of administrative processes and laws led Syrians to rely on Turkish-speaking people – often Syrian Turkmen friends or neighbours, or Turks who worked in Iraq and the Gulf or had learned literary Arabic in religious classes. Everyone kept the phone number of a Turkish-speaking person with them at all times, as a precious resource. My interlocutors used to call them to deal with their landlords, help them find a flat, or come with them to local administrative offices to help with their applications. However, such transactions were not always free, since some people had started to conduct business on the back of the opaque legal and administrative systems.

After Umm Mohammad travelled to Ankara I was on the tram with her sister, on the way to visit mutual friends, when she explained what had happened to them. They had been asked by their neighbour, who had sworn he did not want anything from them, to pay him several hundred dollars for his help with some paperwork. She did not believe that he was now asking them for a sum of money they could not possibly have.

> He always said that he did not want anything and said that he was helping us for God's sake. I thought he was a generous man and a good believer … He came with Umm Mohammad twice to the administration office to give and take documents, and then he helped them travel to Ankara … Why would he do that to us?

The instability and unreliability of the law thus made my interlocutors feel unsafe, reminding them of the corruption and the quickly changing 'laws' at home. The lack of legal protections, the everyday precarity, and the general uncertainty – these all epitomise Syrians' guest status and its scalar implications. It creates jurisdictional conflicts between different authorities and legislation, as well as scalar conflicts between the state and the local population.

Here, the co-optation of the idiom of hospitality by the state thus puts Syrian guests in a legal and existential limbo, having to turn to various authorities to claim their individual rights. Moreover, Syrians' official guest status makes it impossible to apply for resettlement in a third country, or for permanent residency or citizenship in Turkey.[10] This pushed many of my interlocutors to try to reach another country where they would no longer be guests but refugees – a country where they would fall under a regime of law rather than one of favour; in other words, where they would have a 'good life' that is a 'dignified' life.

## Ambiguities and ambivalence of hospitality

'Did you hear about the little clay houses?' Leila asked me, as we met in a café. Leila, a woman in her early thirties whom I met through my volunteering work in a grassroots organisation, graduated in English literature just before the uprising started; she later fled to Turkey as she was increasingly at risk of arrest by Islamist factions in the liberated areas for organising civil disobedience campaigns against both the regime and the Islamists. After I told her that I had not heard the story, she said, 'Everyone is speaking about it! Turkey is building small clay houses on the [Syrian side of the] border and they are planning to send us all there.' As the campaign for the Turkish general election was raging in the summer of 2015, and as 'the Syrian issue' had become a major concern, this story forecasting the imminent return of all Syrians to Syria – in line with the rhetoric of several campaigning candidates – circulated quickly around the city.

This story gives a sense of the hostility perceived by my interlocutors that contrasts with the hospitality implied in the designations of 'guest' and 'brother' used by the Turkish government. It also gives a sense of the insecurity that they felt in Turkey, as they believed that they could be sent back to Syria at any moment. The story of the little clay houses also reveals that my interlocutors saw their life in Turkey as tied to the results of the general election; it also resonates with the fact that, with the closure of the borders and the de facto end of open-door and non-refoulement policies, Syrians who had entered Turkey clandestinely risked being sent back – and were effectively being sent back – to Syria.[11] Ultimately, this story demonstrates that the Turkish government's 'welcoming host' and 'brotherly guest' rhetoric had become one of 'hostile host' and 'dangerous outsider/guest-enemy'.

Yet, the hostility perceived by Syrians emanated not only from state officials and policies but also from the local population, through an increase in everyday discrimination and acts of violence. Around 9 p.m. one evening, as we were dining with a dozen friends at Leila's place, the police arrived and violently entered to inspect the flat, followed by angry neighbours. Leila got a Turkish-speaking friend on the phone and was told that the neighbours had complained about the noise we had made. This was surprising, since there was no music and we were rather quiet, as children were sleeping in the room where we had gathered. Although they could see that it was a simple dinner, the police decided to check the rental contract and the tenant's identification documents. Seeing her blue Syrian passport they threatened to take her to a nearby 'guest camp' if a similar incident happened again, although this was an illegal threat. A couple of days later, a group of young Syrians driving in the city, playing Arabic music with wide-open windows, were attacked by a group of Turkish men armed with wooden sticks. They went to the police to file a complaint but the policemen refused to do so, despite their bodies bearing marks of the attack. In the summer of 2015, social media was filled with reports of acts of violent hostility (Toğral Koca 2016),[12] which reinforced Syrians' feelings of being unwelcome and unsafe in Turkey. These situations reminded my interlocutors of their betwixt-and-between situation: owing to their guest status, they were subject to Turkish law and sovereignty, but they did not have rights within it. Moreover, these experiences show that the state's discourse of hospitality did not imply locals' hospitality.

By capturing hospitality's legal and ethical registers, the state did not leave any space for locals to participate in this hospitable assemblage. As Seçil Dağtaş (2017) shows in her study of hospitality in Antakya, locals felt that they had no place in the state's equation and claimed to apply hospitality on their own terms – following regional and religious practice. They refused, however, to be imposed on as the hosts of 'unknown' guests (Dağtaş 2017: 671). Moreover, by constantly emphasising the hospitality discourse and by publicly displaying its generosity toward Syrian guests, the Turkish state alienated its own population, prompting growing hostility toward Syrians (Carpi and Şenoğuz 2019; Dağtaş 2017). These situations are in fact a reminder of Syrians' betwixt-and-between situation in the law: although they were subject to Turkish law they did not have rights within it. The rhetoric around hospitality had shifted from the ethical-religious to the political, and later became a (geo)political bargaining chip.

Classic accounts of hospitality have shown that hospitality does not exist without ambiguities and dangers. Hospitality is an ambivalent offering, for the power relation at its heart puts the guest in a vulnerable position: she is always at the mercy of her host (Pitt-Rivers 2012).[13] Moreover, as revealed by Derrida's concept of 'hostipitality' (1997), which plays on the etymology of hospitality, there is tension at its heart. Benveniste (1969), whose analysis inspired Derrida, argues that hospitality is composed of the Latin *hostis* (foreigner, enemy) and the root *pet* (power, self-assertion). A guest is thus always a potentially dangerous Other, and is therefore never totally part of, nor totally outside, the community: neither hostile stranger nor community member. As underlined in the etymology of hospitality, the host–guest relation always threatens to collapse into enmity, constantly oscillating between suspicion and trust, and the guest can rapidly come to be perceived as an enemy or a spy. Hence, the status of guest is synonymous with the suspension of political and social rights.[14]

## The Syrianisation of Gaziantep

When my friend Amal had become pregnant, she said she '[didn't] trust Turkish doctors', and since she would have been required to supply her own translator when visiting the hospital in any case, she chose to visit a Syrian gynaecologist in an 'underground' practice instead. It was located in a recently built district mostly inhabited by Syrians, occupying the ground floor of a residential building that used to be a grocery shop. The glass doors had been covered with white paint and newspapers so that it looked empty from the outside. The waiting room was filled with a dozen plastic chairs, and a small school desk for the receptionist. As Amal knocked at the practice door, a little girl looked through the newspapers and turned towards someone inside to see what she should do. Amal pressed her to open the door: 'Yalla! ftahi al-bab!' (Go on! Open the door!). The little girl finally turned the key and we entered the waiting room, where a receptionist asked Amal for her card, a makeshift thing with a number and the patient's name. There was a pile of business cards and a blue box being used as a till on the desk where the receptionist sat, whenever she was not running to open the door for patients and then quickly locking it behind them. When Amal gave the receptionist her card, she was asked for 10TL (US$2.50). Amal explained that when she comes for a follow-up visit she only pays 10TL, but when she comes for a general one it is 25TL (US$6.25).

The doctor's room was small but seemed to have all the equipment a gynaecologist usually has, except for that necessary to take samples. The doctor asked us to sit in front of her large desk and looked for Amal's file in a wide notebook where she kept a double page to write notes on each patient. The desk was separated by a wooden screen from the medical chair and the ultrasound device. After repeating 'Bismillah' (in the name of God) in a low voice a couple of times, the doctor turned on the ultrasound screen and showed us a small black outline around a tiny white spot that we could see moving regularly – a small heart beating. She praised God (Alhamdulillah) as she explained that we were seeing a small embryo. As the examination ended, the doctor prescribed a blood test and some medicine for Amal. She wrote the name of the medicines on a small piece of paper that she signed as if it were an official prescription, and listed the blood tests to be run on another paper; however, neither could be used in a pharmacy or a non-Syrian practice. Moreover, one of the medicines she wanted to prescribe was nowhere to be found in Turkey or in Aleppo. She explained that she had got it from Aleppo until recently but that it was no longer available there. 'I tried to get it from Damascus but I was told that no one could find it there either,' she added. Amal insisted on having the name of the medicine as she could ask some friends to bring it from Lebanon. Like most of my interlocutors, she preferred medicine from Syrian sources, because she trusted them and because their exact equivalent could not always be found in Turkey.

As we left the practice, Amal called the specialist whom her gynaecologist had recommended for the blood tests. As his 'practice' was quite hard to find, he agreed to meet us in front of a shop where he came to pick us up, and then walked us to his practice located in a basement, a former warehouse. It was very dark and not as clean as the one we just left, and contained a couple of seats facing a desk, as there was no place for a waiting room. On one side there was a bigger chair where Amal sat for the blood sample to be taken. I waited in the same room. After the nurse had taken the necessary samples, the doctor told Amal that she would shortly receive the results via Whatsapp.

To explain her visits to these underground and unusual practices, rather than to public hospitals, Amal repeatedly said 'I don't trust Turkish doctors'. This seemed to be quite a widespread feeling among my interlocutors, who preferred to depend on the Syrian network of healthcare facilities. Syrian medical practices, which are not legal but are tolerated by the authorities as long as they only serve Syrian patients, have increasingly appeared in Gaziantep. This also illustrates Syrians' refusal of Turkish hospitality, here of free healthcare for *kimlik* holders. Ironically, free access to healthcare was actually a main point of contention among the Turkish locals and a source of growing tension with displaced Syrians, as it seemed that some locals were unhappy with the state dispensing free healthcare to Syrian guests (Dağtaş 2017). Moreover, the avoidance of Turkish healthcare facilities through the use of their own underground and illegalised practices demonstrates Syrians' ability to reject their state-imposed guest status, thereby violating hospitality's rules as well as Turkish sovereignty. My interlocutors' subversion of their guest status – and of their lives in a legal limbo – was made clear by the emergence of 'Syrian alternatives' not only in the field of healthcare but also of employment and food consumption.

Since hospitality has to be a reciprocal practice to exist, Syrians could challenge state hospitality by refusing its gifts and favours. Moreover, given hospitality's scalar nature, my interlocutors found ways to play with and subvert their condition of guest by a series of rescalings, or scaling through different scripts and registers.[15] The inversion of power relations between guest and host, and the creation of a Syrian city within Gaziantep, led to its Syrianisation, to borrow Syrian intellectual Yassin al-Haj Saleh's term (2016a; 2017a).[16] Syrians have imported practices and goods to the city, but they have also, to some extent, inverted power relations between themselves and their hosts, positing the latter as their guests. My interlocutors not only refuse to be Turkified (most visibly by refusing to learn Turkish), but they also Syrianise their Turkish hosts. I found that a similar form of inversion was happening on the scale of the city of Gaziantep. The Syrianisation of the city enables understanding of how Syrians subvert their status of guest and transform themselves into (potential) hosts. By playing on different historical scripts and geographical scales, Syrians reclaim Gaziantep as part of Syria and present themselves as native inhabitants of the city.

The horizontal expansion of Syrians' presence within their host's space was also visible through the increasing prevalence of Arabic script, Syrian shops, restaurants, organisations, private schools, and cultural centres, along with grassroots and civil society organisations, governmental bodies, and opposition institutions. With this complex network Syrians made it possible to navigate Gaziantep without speaking Turkish by working in Syrian businesses or organisations and practically only consuming Syrian goods. This was reinforced by the informal renaming of Gaziantep's main landmarks among the Syrian community. A square always crowded with pigeons was, for instance, renamed *sahet al hamamat* (the square of pigeons) and a street full of sweet shops became *shara' al-baqlawa* (the street of baklava). Through such practices, Syrians propose another form of stagecraft that enters into competition with Turkish sovereignty.

The challenge to Turkish hospitality was salient in the consumption of Syrian food. Offering food is one of the hosts' primary obligations, but Syrians circumvented it by bringing their own with them. Before the border was sealed, my interlocutors would regularly bring food from the inside. As I met with friends at one of our frequent evening gatherings, one of them told us that a Syrian man entering Turkey with 30 kilos of meat had been arrested at the border. This caused much laughter at our table as my friends imagined the surprise of the border guards, but it did not seem weird to them, as they remembered food made in Syria with intense nostalgia. I was often told that Turkish and Syrian food had nothing in common, and people often made negative comments about Turkish food, which is quite ironic given that Gaziantep is famous all over Turkey for having the country's best cuisine. Hanan, the woman with whom I lived, explained that the taste of Syrian food was irreplaceable as she struggled for several weeks to get some olive oil from her parents' village on the other side of the border. When I was invited for a meal, the products from Syria were always pointed out, for me to taste first. I quickly noticed that families' fridges were filled with Syrian food. In our home, I heard endless discussions about how to get olive oil, olives or *za'atar* from Syria. Bringing and consuming their own food are common among immigrant communities. But it is not only that Syrians preferred to eat their own cuisine, here, but were also bringing fruits, olive oil or meat – raw produce rather than cooked food – from a war zone into a borderland city, even though there was no climate difference, for instance, that would make it impossible to find similar fruits, vegetables and meat in Gaziantep.

These practices illustrate the questioning and the subversion of the guest–host dynamics defined by the state, as well as the Syrianisation of Gaziantep as Syrians refuse Turkish hospitality. This rejection of state-led hospitality is due to the impossibility of Syrians' reciprocating hospitality, because the host and guests are not on the same scale. In addition, this refusal of state hospitality was linked to my interlocutors' rejection of their infralegal position and their replacing a logic of favour with a legal one. But this is also intimately connected to the desire to be in the host position, since this position is associated with honour, prestige, and power, whereas guests fall under hosts' sovereignty (Dağtaş 2017; Shryock 2012).

On the scale of local population encounters, my interlocutors challenged their status as guests, contributing to the inversion of the guest–host paradigm. They repositioned themselves as the hosts by offering food to their Turkish hosts, as one of the guest's duties is to eat her host's food (Herzfeld 1987).[17] My interlocutors stressed local people's lack of hospitality and visible hostility. Indeed, since hospitality is a constant negotiation and (re)definition of assemblages, Syrians challenged and subverted their condition by creating new hospitality assemblages – playing on scales, registers, and scripts to redefine who is host and who is guest.

## Syrians as hosts

> There was this newly married woman who had just arrived in our village. Her husband told her to go visit the neighbours and to come back immediately after she drank coffee. But he insisted that she should wait until she drinks coffee. So she went to her neighbours and they served her tea, maté, then fruits. Then it was time for lunch, then dinner, but by night-time had still not drunk coffee. Only the next morning at breakfast was she served coffee. So she left very quickly and came back home. Her husband asked, 'Where were you all this time?' and she answered, 'They just served the coffee now!'

Umm Khaled recounted this tale about hospitality on one of our visits to Umm Zayd, her friend and former neighbour, and they both laughed loudly as she finished it. They had fled from the regime army together with their children when their town fell under its heavy fire. Umm Zayd's sons and husband had left for Europe and she was now waiting with her 18-year-old daughter for family reunification. As we arrived at her place and were invited to drink maté,[18] Umm Khaled humorously pointed out the peculiar customs of their area, in which coffee, as in other parts of Syria, remained the symbol and cornerstone of *karam* (hospitality), as it had in all of the visits I have described thus far.[19]

During my fieldwork I heard many stories praising Syrian hospitality, challenging the idea that Syrians were guests in Turkey, and simultaneously implying that their Turkish hosts were bad hosts. Most of these stories furnished a standpoint from which to criticise Turkish hospitality and added to direct complaints about their hosts' hostility.[20] When I visited a nearby city and stayed with Umm Riyad, whom I introduced in Chapter 1, her son complained about the way Syrians were treated in Turkey. As he depicted his Turkish hosts as bad, he remembered how he had himself been a good host in Syria:

> When the Lebanese fled and came to Syria we gave them everything they needed. I was volunteering with the Red Crescent and, believe me, the camp they stayed in had nothing to do with the camps Syrians are put in here! They had everything they needed. We were bringing them the food from the best restaurants, and from our mothers' kitchens! When we asked them if they needed something they asked for hair gel and *arguileh*! Why? Because they had all the rest!

His mother added: 'In the South [of Syria] they didn't even stay in camps; we hosted them in our own houses.' The example of Iraqi refugees was also presented as another token of Syrians' exemplary hospitality. As Umm Nidal complained about her rent increase, she gave the attitude of Syrians towards Iraqis as an example of good hosts' behaviour. 'When the Iraqis came, we left our homes to them and went to rent worse ones.' This was not a view shared by everyone. A friend of her son, Saleh, a Palestinian-Syrian (a Palestinian refugee in Syria)[21] intervened and argued that Syrians had also taken advantage of Iraqis by subletting their houses for a higher price. As in Turkey, this had caused problems for the locals in Syria, since rents had increased for them too. Umm Nidal disagreed. 'They had a lot of money and they agreed to rent our houses at such a price, which created problems for the rest of us!' Saleh drew to her attention that this was exactly what the Turks were saying about Syrians and added: 'The Iraqis left with all the money they had, and so did we. They didn't have the luxury to bargain over their rent, and we don't either.'

Through such stories, hospitality was framed as a Syrian virtue in opposition to that offered by their 'bad Turkish host'. This idea was supported by videos and articles that created a buzz on social media when the 'refugee crisis' peaked in the summer of 2015. They showed how Greeks had been welcomed by Syrians when they fled their homes during World War II, and how this hospitality had to be reciprocated now that Syrians were seeking refuge. This made Syrians wonder if Turks realised that, in other circumstances, *they* could have been seeking refuge, and that they could be asking for hospitality in the future. On the other hand, Turks had symmetrically reversed stories that depicted Syrians as bad guests: stories of Syrians eating in restaurants without paying, and sometimes beating up the owner, were widespread on the street and in Turkish newspapers (Dağtaş 2017). Such stories lead me to interrogate the discourses around bad guests and bad hosts as moral tales and narratives about ethical duties rather than recalling real events. They show that 'hospitality more often than not seems to be a common language in which to argue and disagree, a language of accusation and disappointed hopes, a language of insult and wounded pride. Hospitality, it seems, is 'schismogenetic' (Candea 2012a: 46). Indeed, critique of hosts by guests is a widespread phenomenon; hospitality is often thought to be better elsewhere, whether in the distant past or in different geographical locations (see Shryock 2008: 406).

In addition to this oral challenge, Turkish hospitality was subverted by the inversion of Syrians' guest position. Despite being defined as guests, Syrians became hosts themselves to different types of guests: the anthropologist, relatives and friends arriving from Syria, Syrian friends and acquaintances on social occasions, and even their Turkish hosts. Like any anthropologist, I became the guest of my interlocutors, hospitality being 'the unavoidable condition of possibility of ethnography' (Candea and Da Col 2012: 3). My Syrian hosts showed their hospitality by offering me coffee, large amounts of food, and welcoming me with endless pronouncements of '*ahlan wa sahlan*' (welcome) and '*beit beitek*' (my house is yours).[22] I became the guest of Syrians who were themselves guests in Turkey. This paradoxical situation was pushed to its extreme when, arriving from a besieged area with only a few bags, Umm Zein, finding me at her mother-in-law's place, greeted me with a small gift: a tiny bottle of perfume she had brought all the way from Syria. Newly arrived Syrians were also hosted by friends and relatives. After they arrived in Gaziantep, they would often live in their relatives' or friends' homes until they could find their own place, often nearby and through the same local networks. Some buildings and neighbourhoods thereby became mostly inhabited by Syrians. With time Syrians started to move to other neighbourhoods, often to bigger and more comfortable flats, as they were more familiar with the way things worked. Yet, even when they lived in, or moved to, predominantly Turkish buildings and neighbourhoods, the relations between the two populations were often tense in my interlocutors' narratives. This seemed to be linked to the language barrier, but also to mutual hostility (Dağtaş 2017; Carpi and Şenoğuz 2019). However, in the flat I shared with Dina and Hanan in a building otherwise inhabited only by Turks, some of our female neighbours started to visit regularly, albeit sitting silently and communicating through gestures, serving coffee and smoking cigarettes.[23]

Syrians' hosts were thus also treated as their guests. This inversion of guest–host relation is inscribed in Syria's history as a place of refuge,[24] and it shows that hospitality can be turned into a game of power and sovereignty (Shryock 2012: 20). Here, it was used to invert power relations between hosts and guests, Turks and Syrians. As Dina, the woman with whom I lived at the time, hosted our Turkish neighbours, she was excited to tell me as we prepared plates of fruit in the kitchen that our guests were very impressed that 'although [they] fled their country, [they] were able to serve them such nice fruit'. She was proud to be able to impress her guests and, by doing so, challenge Turks' views on Syrians. This was also true on a larger scale, as Syrian businesses and organisations became an attractive source of employment for Turks, who had started to seek jobs with Syrian organisations and organisations working with

Syrians. This pushed the inversion of power relations further as Syrian organisations started to employ Turks.

By playing with the registers of hospitality, and by using different historical scripts, my interlocutors thus shift their position from that of guest to host, challenging Turkish sovereignty at the scale of the state and of the local population. Eventually, these rescalings point to Turks' and Syrians' exhaustion with the overwhelming duties that hospitality imposes on both hosts and guests, and the impossible situation Syrians and Turks are put in by a state that captures the hospitality idiom, exacerbating tensions between the two populations. Indeed, in co-opting hospitality as an ethical-religious register, the state pushes Syrians to dream of a land where hospitality is not 'duty-based' but effectively 'rights-based' (Chatty 2017); where, in other words, they could be extracted from the burden of hospitality's reciprocity and duties – where they would be refugees rather than guests.

## Hostile refuge and migratory horizons

'The life of Syrians in Turkey is becoming exactly like their lives in Lebanon, and maybe even worse! All Erdogan's statements about Syrians aren't worth a Syrian cent!' This was written on her Facebook page by Zeina, a friend in her mid-20s, who had been living in Turkey for two years after living in Lebanon for a further two. Appearing in the spring of 2017, it reveals the degrading situation of Syrians in Turkey, the increasing uncertainty, and the ever-growing feeling of being unwelcome and unsafe. After two years in Lebanon, the young woman came with her mother to Turkey as she explained that she could not afford to live in Beirut any longer, as life was becoming more expensive and they could not secure a proper legal status. After two years in Turkey, however, she found herself in a similar situation: working was made harder by new regulations and a crackdown on organisations, and this time Zeina wondered where she would go next. 'I fled from Syria to Lebanon, then when the situation got worse I came here. And now what? I have already started my life all over again twice, I don't want to have to start all over again for the third time!' As the situation was going from bad to worse, Zeina, who was planning to get married and start a family, could not help asking: 'Why would we get married? Do we even have a future in this country?'

When I returned to Gaziantep in March 2017, where I settled for nearly two years and wrote my PhD thesis, the legal status of Syrians had also changed quite dramatically. On the one hand, those who held work permits and university degrees were now being given the opportunity to apply for citizenship. On the other, Syrians working without a permit, or with a permit issued in another city, lived with the constant risk of being sent back to Syria or deported to Sudan – the only country where Syrians could enter and remain without a visa in 2017. This risk pushed Syrians who could do so to work from home to reduce the risk of arrest and deportation, which, in turn, led to the loss of job opportunities as employers feared being harassed by the police. Moreover, the Turkish government had imposed a quota system to increase the number of Turkish citizens working in Syrian organisations and businesses. This novel configuration seems, however, to be symptomatic of the temporary protection status, which, due to its lack of clarity and weakness, leads to ambiguities and renders Syrians' positions uncertain and precarious. Although a minority of Syrians were able to access a work permit, and potentially citizenship, as a result of the temporariness and uncertainty of these new statuses their guest position still loomed. This situation is emblematic of the state's conflation of hospitality's ethical and legal registers, and it was intensified with the deportation of Syrians back to northern Syria in the wake of the ruling AKP party's defeat of the opposing Republican People's Party in the 2019 Istanbul mayoral election (Al-Mehdi 2019). In this context, as in those of the 2015 general election and the 2017 constitutional referendum, Syrian guests clearly become a political bargaining chip as opposing political parties promised their bases that, once in office, they will deport Syrians.

By focusing on Syrians' forced displacement in Turkey, this chapter has suggested new ways of looking at hospitality, conceiving it as a series of concurrent scalar assemblages in which guests and hosts exchange positions through a series of legal and ethical registers, historical and religious scripts, and everyday practices. Hospitality fails because the state captures it, and by doing so it turns the ethical into the legal, and alienates both the Turkish and Syrian populations. Hospitality thus appears as a scalar assemblage that can be rescaled by guests and hosts alike, creating new assemblages that bring together different registers and scripts. My interlocutors rescale Turkish state hospitality through their claim to international jurisdiction, as well as through their reorganisation of Gaziantep's cityscape. Hospitality is therefore reframed through different spatio-temporalities and by various social groups. It also engenders new groups and spatio-temporal horizons. But hospitality is also something that Syrians tried to escape by claiming international protection under the rule of law, for instance.

As Zeina's concluding story shows, the impossibility to have a permanent and stable status (in other words, a dignified life) in Turkey due to the temporariness of guesthood, as well as the growing tensions between both Turkish and Syrian populations, appeared during my fieldwork as one of the main factors for Syrians to contemplate a future in Europe, where a more certain and less precarious life is imagined. The emergence of novel migratory paths and aspirations interestingly resonates with current debates about grand schemes and horizons in the context of migration (Graw and Schielke 2012a; 2012b; Schielke and Debevec 2012; Schielke 2020), describing how, in the midst of an uncertain and precarious present, Europe is constituted as a desired future horizon.

With the never-ending war, mass displacement and tremendous destruction, the possibility of return to Syria has definitively faded away. Instead, the precarious lives of Syrians in Turkey, which are being exacerbated by hardening political repression in the country, have meant Europe is increasingly being idealised as a place that both answers past revolutionary claims of justice, freedom and dignity, and palliates a precarious and uncertain present, thereby broadening horizons for the future. In the aftermath of the Syrian revolution and its defeat, my interlocutors imagined three futures for themselves: going back to Syria, staying in Turkey or crossing the Mediterranean. Yet, at the moment of finishing this book and ten years after the beginning of the uprising, Syrian future horizons and dreams have been profoundly reshaped, as Syria and Turkey are no longer desired places to live in the present, or to build a future.

This idealisation of Europe is based on my interlocutors' aspirations for a good life, one in which they are treated with dignity (in this context, ruled by just and stable laws) – a life they could not achieve through revolution in Syria, and which state hospitality and guest status have denied them in Turkey. Syrians' statusless status and life in a legal and spatial limbo have thus been a major motivation to attempt crossing the Turkish–Greek border in hopes of finding a more certain status and a good (dignified) life in the EU, as well as definitively escaping the moral and existential weight of hospitality and gaining a status falling under international jurisdiction as asylum seekers and/or refugees. This ultimately suggests how, in the aftermath of a defeated revolution and in the midst of precarious displacement, new migratory dreams and horizons have emerged. Syrians seek *karama* (dignity) rather than *karam* (hospitality/generosity). By claiming a dignified life, my Syrian interlocutors aspire to be subjects of law rather than religious piety and moral duties. Ultimately, through their use of the idiom of hospitality, my interlocutors draw a definition of what a dignified life in exile should look like. Tracing a continuous line between the fight for dignity at home and in displacement calls for closer attention to the nexus between revolution and migration.

## Notes

1  *Kimlik* is the Turkish word for 'identification'. In this context it refers specifically to the identity document given by the Turkish authorities to Syrians displaced in Turkey.
2  This situation started in the late summer of 2015 at the time of the parliamentary elections and the EU–Turkey deal.
3  As part of the EU–Turkey deal, the EU agreed to provide 3 billion euros to Turkey (Smeets and Beach 220: 158).
4  See Cavidan 2012; Özden 2013; Toğral Koca 2016.
5  Most Syrians only hold national identity cards, as passports were only used by a minority of people wealthy enough to travel abroad before the revolution. Yet, with mass displacement, getting a passport became a crucial issue.
6  Males older than 11 who did not do their military service (apart from those exempted for medical reasons, or as the only son, or who paid bribes) were given a two-year passport until 2019, then two years six months; all others can get a six-year passport. But the men who left Syria without getting their passports stamped (that is, those who fled from liberated areas) are also issued only with two-year passports.
7  See in the context of Palestinians in the West Bank (Kelly 2006) and Turkish-Cypriots in Northern Cyprus (Navaro-Yashin 2012).
8  Even a *kimlik*, however, did not assure Syrian children's access to schools, since their registration could be refused by the school management and many could not afford the cost of transportation or taking their children out of work (Baban et al. 2017).
9  This incident happened in the autumn of 2015.
10  As addressed in conclusion, the situation has evolved over the years. The UNHCR is, for instance, allowed to resettle specific numbers and categories of Syrians, and Syrians can also apply for Turkish citizenship following specific criteria. However, these two options only concern a small minority of Syrians. Moreover, even when successful in obtaining resettlement in a third country, Syrians still need an exit visa from the Turkish government that is hard to obtain for those who did not hold *kimliks*.
11  This concerned Syrians who had just crossed the border and were immediately returned to Syria, but could also concern Syrians living in border areas without a *kimlik*, because a stamp on one's document – a sign that the border had been crossed in a legal way – was now needed to obtain this document.
12  For more details see Toğral Koca 2016.
13  In the framing of the Balga Bedouins, hospitality is a synonym for warfare and a question of sovereignty (Shryock 2004: 52). See also Fausto (2012) on hospitality and enmity among the Arawete, and Marsden (2012) on hospitality's dangers among Afghan traders.
14  Candea and Da Col 2012: 5; Pitt-Rivers 2012.
15  In his work on unauthorised migrations in the central Mediterranean and the interception of migrants by Sicilian fishermen and Italian authorities, Naor Ben Yehoyada suggests rescaling the concept of hospitality in order to understand these transnational processes (2011; 2014; 2015). He analyses hospitality as operating in different domains – the moral and the political – and on different spatio-temporal scales: the present in Sicily and a common Mediterranean past, as well as in relation to regional, local, and European authorities. It is the combination of these domains and scales that determines action, responsibility, and sovereignty (2015: 183).
16  According to Yassin al-Haj Saleh, the globe has been Syrianised: the 'Syrian question' has contaminated the entire world rather than being contained within the country (2016a). Instead of an end to the conflict and the start of a democratisation process in Syria, the world is moving in the same direction, becoming more chaotic, more fascist, and suffering from similar forms of violence (2016a).

17  See also on this topic in other contexts Humphrey 2012; Shryock 2008; 2009; 2012.
18  Maté is a drink originally from South America consumed in great quantity in some parts of Syria.
19  This is also common among the Balga Bedouin of Jordan (Shryock 2004: 135; 2008) and in Cretan coffee houses (Herzfeld 1987).
20  Herzfeld 1987; Pitt-Rivers 2012; Shryock 2012.
21  Interestingly, Palestinians in Syria had the same rights as Syrians apart from political rights, which is an exception for Palestinians in the Arab world.
22  See in the Cretan and Jordanian contexts Herzfeld 1987: 77 and Shryock 2003: 24 respectively.
23  Some Turkish activists and organisations also started projects to bring together Syrians and Turks.
24  See Chatty 2018; Zaman 2016.

**Figure 4.1:**    Waiting and hoping. © Zouhir al-Shimale

# 4
# Temporality of the defeat: waiting in limbo

Reflecting on the 1948 Nakba ('the catastrophe', referring to Palestinian forced displacement), Palestinian historian Elias Sanbar equates spatial with temporal displacement: living in limbo entails a redefinition of duration since time can no longer be the same when dealing with enforced displacement:

> By departing from space, the Palestinians ... also departed from time. Their history and their past were denied. Their aspirations and their future were forbidden. Hence they found themselves trapped in an ephemeral dimension, and for half a century they would live in limbo, achieving a very special relationship with the concept of duration. Since the present was forbidden to them, they would occupy a temporal space made up of both a past preserved by a memory afflicted by madness and a dreamt-of future which aspired to restore time. (Sanbar 2001: 90)

The idea that by departing from one's homeland one loses a sense of time, captures quite vividly my Syrian interlocutors' experience of time in displacement. It also echoes their own comparison of their situation with that of Palestinians. Living in limbo meant the Syrians I lived with found themselves in a state of constant waiting: waiting to be reunified with vanished or scattered relatives, waiting to start their lives again, waiting for their revolution to succeed and the war to end, and often waiting to migrate further. They were waiting for news and relatives from Syria, for administrative travel documents, for the border with Syria to open, and for a way towards Europe to open up.

Exploring the consequences of a thwarted revolution on perceptions of time, I argue that waiting for the revolution to repeat itself makes Syrians' present 'unliveable',[1] because the hope they invest in the past and the uncertainty of their future leads to a suspension of their present. Waiting has become the temporality of displacement and of the aftermath of a defeated revolution, a temporality oriented towards the paused revolution and Syrians' recent revolutionary past. Waiting for revolutionary action to resume inside Syria, and for the revolution to succeed in the near future, my interlocutors seem inhabited by a paradoxical hope for the past, an inversion of Piot's 'nostalgia for the future' (2010), which becomes a hope directed at the past, or an inward hope.[2] The Syrians I lived with long for a heroic and utopian past to replace a disenchanted and uncertain future. Yet it is not the repetition of an idealised past that they hoped for, which would give rise to unalloyed nostalgia, but a different repetition that one can only grasp if one understands time as duration.

## Displacement and permanent temporariness: unhomely and uncanny homes

> I haven't been able to buy anything for my flat ... when I do the laundry and think that I need a drying rack I immediately remember: why should I buy anything for this house? I'm not here for long, I want to go back (*bidi arja'*) ... We are like the Palestinians now! We are waiting to go back home, but who knows when it will happen!

Nura, a woman in her thirties from a town in north-west Syria, had to flee to Turkey in the spring of 2016 after she became wanted by an Islamist group newly controlling her town. In Syria she lived with her parents and worked as a teacher. Her hometown had previously been liberated by the FSA in 2012, but then retaken by the regime. She had remained there throughout, pursuing her revolutionary work (*sheghel b-l thawra*) focused on bringing aid to IDPs and continuing her training of young women and men on civil disobedience and local governance. She was forced to flee only after her work became known by the Islamist factions that subsequently took control of her town.

Being obliged to live in Gaziantep was very painful for her as she had refused to leave her town even when it was retaken by the regime, although it put her at great risk as she had actively participated in the revolution. She did not expect that she would have to flee her home after her town was taken from the regime by rebel groups – but this time (2015) it was dominated by Islamist factions. It was all the more painful to see young men, with whom she had demonstrated 'shoulder to shoulder', joining these groups and imposing their rules – including the interdiction to exhibit the revolution's flag – and an ideology that, to her, sharply contradicted the revolution's values. Nura had been in Turkey for a few months when she expressed to me her feelings about being stuck in a temporary state: she could neither settle in Turkey nor go back to her home. She knew that, like the Palestinian refugees scattered through the Middle East, to whom she compared herself, she would probably not be able to go back home any time soon. Yet, at the same time, she could not give up hoping to go back soon and could not turn what she saw as her provisional house into a more permanent home. Doing so would mean accepting that she was no longer waiting to return home and that her temporary displacement had turned, *de facto*, into a permanent state.

This impossibility to transform a house into a home is linked to an 'unhomely' feeling that led my interlocutors to feel that they could not dwell in temporary accommodation (see Navaro-Yashin 2012: 181; see also Bryant 2014 and 2016 on uncanny time temporality and the unhomely). Moreover, such a form of waiting also resonates with the permanent temporariness of Palestinians displaced to Lebanon to whom many of my interlocutors compared themselves (see Allan 2014; Peteet 1991; Salih 2016; Sanyal 2011; Sayigh 1995; 2005).[3] Gaziantep thus appeared as a betwixt-and-between space *and* time, a liminal space (Turner 1969; see also Rundell 2009).

## Active waiting and resilience

'This is the key to our home in *rif dimashq* [Damascus suburbs]', Mustafa told me with emotion as he took a bunch of keys out of the backpack he had just put on the floor. 'I keep it with me all the time. Do you know why? Because we are going back! As soon as my town is liberated, I will be on my way!' Mustafa is a man in his early twenties, someone I regularly meet in my flat as he likes to spend time with my host's nephews. He fled his home near the capital with his parents as the fighting intensified, and first took refuge in his parents' hometown near the Turkish border before they were forced to flee again as it was taken by Daesh. As we sat together in the living room looking after the kids and drinking warm tea, I asked him about his story and his situation in Gaziantep. His reaching for his backpack embodies Syrians' hopes to return home, and its necessary correlate for revolutionaries – the success of the revolution.[4] Like most of my interlocutors at the beginning of my fieldwork and up until the summer of 2015, Mustafa was confident that he would go home in the near future, thus envisioning Gaziantep as only a temporary stop. The references to Daesh and Islamist groups in Nura's and Mustafa's accounts index the turn to the beginning of the 'two revolutions' (see Introduction) against both the Islamists and the regime, which also marked, for many of my interlocutors, the impossibility of remaining inside Syria, and a larger sense of defeat as the situation in Syria increasingly slipped out of their hands.

'As soon as we [the revolutionaries] retake our town from Daesh, I will go back to my family place [near the border], and someday I will go back home [near Damascus]. I know I will go back home soon', Mustafa continued with confidence. These are not only emphatic words that demonstrate his commitment to the revolution and his faith that the regime and Daesh will be defeated; they were also embodied in different actions. My interlocutors always kept an eye on developments inside the country, whether on TV or on social media. I rarely visited a house in which the TV was not showing the latest news from Syria, nor did I have many conversations without my interlocutors constantly checking their phones to read the latest updates on the situation inside and see the latest developments of such and such a battle. Moreover, the permanent readiness to leave Gaziantep and go home was vividly illustrated by my interlocutors preparing to return, and effectively returning, to Aleppo, as its liberation by the rebels seemed imminent in the early summer of 2015. The Syrians I lived with who were from Aleppo, located about a hundred kilometres from Gaziantep, were very excited by the prospect of their city's liberation. Knowing that my fieldwork would last another eight months they kept teasing me, 'We're going back! We're not staying here! We're going as soon as Aleppo is liberated! You can come with us or stay here alone ...'

I regularly met with a group of friends in the evening, but our usually noisy meetings, dominated by laughter, loud voices telling stories and jokes, and communal singing of revolutionary songs, turned silent. No one really spoke to one another any longer; everyone was fixated on their phones, waiting for updates on Aleppo's situation. The young revolutionaries with whom I had first worked when I came to Gaziantep, when I volunteered in one of their organisations, were trying to evaluate when they should be ready to go back and help to prepare its future self-organisation. With excitement and certainty of the city's imminent liberation growing, many of them returned to Aleppo to help 'prepare its liberation' in the summer of 2015. Most of them were back in Gaziantep after a couple of months however, when hope had faded following the Russian intervention. Others instead were trapped under siege and only came back in the winter of 2016. Aleppo's fate became worse as revolutionaries saw the part of the city they had liberated come under siege by Syrian and Russian forces. Syrian waiting thus became indefinite as it was appended to a situation over which they had no power. This led to their displacement transforming from temporary to a state of permanent temporariness.

Indeed, in Turkey, my interlocutors were waiting for state apparatuses to release detainees, for administrations to deliver documents, for embassies to provide visas, for governments to open borders, and for international conflict to end. In other words, they had little leverage on their waiting and its outcome. In fact, their waiting was shaped by states for whom it is a political tool (Hage 2009a: 3).[5] In such a context, waiting amounts to a test of resilience and steadfastness (*sumud*) rather than patience,[6] which could be described in terms of 'waiting for' – when one is stuck in a situation and cannot do much about it – and 'waiting on' – an active decision (Schwartz 1975).[7] For instance, the fact that Nura oriented her waiting towards returning home, rather than migrating to Europe or actively settling in Turkey, was a personal choice that can be understood as a political form of resilience. Waiting was a way of continuing the political struggle, of not abandoning their lands, of marking that Syria was still theirs, and showing that they were not planning to leave it to the Assad regime. Refusing to settle permanently in Turkey and treating it as a temporary stop was thus a way to mark their commitment to, and hopes for, the revolution. Yet the temporariness of displacement was not linked to waiting to return home for everyone; it was, for some, entangled with their waiting to flee to Europe in search of a better, that is, more dignified, life.

## Spatio-temporal limbo: waiting as erasure of the present

'No one knows what will happen to us in Turkey but in Europe there are laws. We know what will happen and, as everyone says, it is better for our children's future,' Umm Mohammad told her sister, Umm Khaled, as she tried to convince her to flee to Europe. Umm Mohammad was waiting with her children to be reunified with her husband, who had taken the sea route to Europe. Like many of my interlocutors, she did not envisage staying in Gaziantep as she saw no future in Turkey. '*Ma fi mustaqbal hun*' (there is no future here), my interlocutors often said, and many were looking at all kinds of ways to leave the country. The uncertainty of the future in Turkey was rendered more acute and was given a sense of urgency with the increasing pressure on Syrians there, the deteriorating situation in Syria, and the opening of the Balkan route into Europe in the summer of 2015 (see Conclusion). Therefore, not only was the present of my interlocutors precarious and hostile but their future was increasingly uncertain: no one knew what tomorrow would bring.

'I don't think of the future! Never! I only think a couple of hours ahead, that's all!' Umm Yazan told me as we were on a bus to her place. She made this point as we were discussing her current situation in Turkey. Her words underline the unpredictability of Syrians' future in the country. A 50-year-old housewife living alone with three of her children, Umm Yazan would often tell me that living in Turkey was the best for the present moment but not an option in the future. She was thus looking for ways to send her children abroad while she herself either returned to Syria or joined them in Europe. In order to explain her decision to leave Turkey, she stressed the poor education system, the increasingly religious orientation of the curriculum, the growing authoritarianism, and the lack of affordable medical treatment. Another reason that pushed her to want to leave was the extreme instability of her situation in Turkey: she had just lost her job, her children were unable to find employment, and she was about to be evicted from her flat (see Conclusion).

For the Syrians I lived among, migration seemed the main way to live in the present and to have a future.[8] Yet, for my interlocutors, migrating did not automatically mean the end of waiting; many found themselves stuck in refugee camps in Europe, and many were still waiting (elsewhere) to be able to go back home.[9] Thus, spatial movement was not always an answer to temporal immobility. Ultimately, if displacement means being outside of space, waiting is experienced as being 'outside of time' (Rundell 2009: 50). In other words, revolutionaries in Gaziantep lived in a temporal limbo: they were stuck between the past and the future but without a present.[10] Yet what does it mean in concrete terms to have no present? What happens to time when waiting is oriented and directed to the past?

## Living in a suspended present

> I feel like I'm in a big prison here! I don't go out, I don't know anyone ... this is not a life! We have no life here: we don't know anyone! There [in Syria] we used to visit people all the time. We used to host people all the time ...

Umm Zayd was lamenting to her friend Umm Khaled as we spent the day at her house. The life she speaks about here is her 'social life'. The two 50-year-old housewives used to be neighbours in Syria, where they both took part in the revolution along with their male relatives. Now, they still regularly visited one another despite living on opposite sides of Gaziantep. As Umm Zayd spoke, two small glasses of maté were going around the circle formed on the floor of her living room with her daughter and Umm Khaled. Her daughter and I sipped our maté silently through the small metallic straw before giving the glasses back to Umm Zayd who added more maté, sugar, and ginger powder, topped it up with boiling water, and gave it to the next person in the circle.

In this discussion, describing her life as empty and boring, Umm Zayd stressed the loss of the Syrian life they used to know and the impossibility of reconstructing a 'normal' social life in Turkey; in other words, the loss of their present in exile. Indeed, 'one explanation of waiting ... could be that it entails loss of the notion of the "present"' (Malik 2009: 64). She seemed to be only killing time while waiting for reunification with the rest of her family in Europe. When I met Umm Zayd and her daughter, they had been separated from Abu Zayd and their three sons for over a year. The men had crossed the Mediterranean one after the other, hoping to start a new life on the other shore. Umm Zayd was waiting for the Belgian embassy finally to give them an appointment and hoped to receive a visa to be reunited with Abu Zayd. She spoke with her husband daily to hear the latest information about their case, but neither the embassy in Ankara nor the Belgian administration would provide any certain news. They kept telling them to wait until the end of the month, repeating the same advice every month. After a year of waiting, Umm Zayd expected to have to wait for another two or three months. 'These last months will be the hardest!' she concluded.

As the two small maté glasses kept going around our circle in a strictly defined order, Umm Zayd's daughter described how her own life had been paused since her family fled Syria. She had finished high school just before they were forced to leave so she had not had a chance to register and continue her studies. Her family had first fled to Lebanon, where she thought she could register for university, but she had to postpone her plans as her family started to speak about going to Turkey. She then imagined that she would start learning Turkish and enrol in a university in Gaziantep, but her brothers left for Europe and after her father joined them it was clear that they would not be staying in Turkey either. Once again she had to postpone her plans to study and was now waiting for her life to finally begin after she joined her father. 'It has been three years now and I haven't started university yet!' she said bitterly. She now spent her time waiting, helping her mother around the house, and watching Turkish soap operas.

In addition to the disruption of everyday and social life, ritual life was also dramatically affected by waiting. 'There is no 'eid for Syrians as long as there are still people in jails. Haven't you heard that from the Palestinians? They won't have 'eid until they return home! Well, we are the same now!' Umm Yazan responded when I asked about her 'eid plans, as the last days of Ramadan were approaching. 'eid al Fitr and 'eid al Kbir, which respectively mark the end of the month of Ramadan and of the pilgrimage to Mecca, were normally moments of happiness and the occasion of great festivities. Yet they were neither sources of joy nor marked by any big celebrations for the families waiting for detainees or who had family members in besieged areas, and more generally for those supporting the revolution, as summarised by the phrase, Ma fi 'eid wa al balad shaheed ('there is no 'eid when the country is martyred'). As the two of us sat one night on her balcony enjoying a late cup of coffee and the breeze after a long, hot day of fasting, Umm Yazan concluded with a series of rhetorical questions:

> Isn't what is happening to Syrians haram? Why is this happening to us? Why do we have to be suffering at home and outside home? Why do we have to live in exile? Why do we have to be separated from our loved ones? Why do we have to send our children through the seas and risk their lives?

Syrians' present was thus transformed by and through waiting: the tempo, rhythm, and texture of waiting changed the experience of the present. Moreover, waiting radically altered my interlocutors' everyday, social, and ritual life: their 'normal life' (hayat 'adiyyeh) seemed suspended in displacement. But this pausing of my interlocutors' present is very different from that explored in Chapter 2, which was a voluntary pause to take part in the revolution; in Gaziantep, the suspension of their everyday life was involuntary and linked to their position in limbo described in Chapter 3. It was not a voluntary sacrifice of their present for a higher purpose, but an unexpected and unwanted consequence of the revolution's repression and defeat – forced displacement. Yet, although it put their present in brackets, waiting was not inactive and passive: despite my interlocutors' 'normal life' being suspended and despite their claims of not doing anything apart from waiting, their everyday life was not empty.[11] Their active waiting was confirmed by their performance of everyday house chores, their attending language courses and knitting or cooking workshops, queuing to get aid, constantly dealing with administrative procedures, and investing time in diverse transactions that aimed to put an end to their waiting.

## The temporality of active waiting: punctuated time

As I walked into Umm Ahmad's living room, she greeted me and, as soon as I was seated, she asked me, 'Do you have any news about Abu Moatassem [the detained father of a close friend]?' I answered in the negative before telling her that I had been advised to meet with a detainee, freed a couple of weeks earlier, who had just arrived in town. I was often told that meeting with freshly released prisoners offers the best chance of hearing about missing relatives. Former detainees who became my acquaintances and friends explained that they memorised each other's phone numbers as they were about to be released in order to call and give their co-detainees' relatives news of them. They also memorised the names of those who had been killed under torture, the date and circumstances of death.[12]

I asked Umm Ahmad if she wanted me to ask this particular ex-detainee if he knew anything about her sons' fates. She agreed and told her daughter to bring paper, pen, and the pile of precious family photographs she kept in a folded plastic bag placed in her handbag. Alongside her sons' names and dates of birth, as well as her own and her husband's, she wrote the dates and places of their disappearance. As I knew that I would be asked by recently released prisoners whether her sons had been seen in any security branches or prisons since their arrests I asked Umm Ahmad about it. She made an upward movement with her eyes and eyebrows, meaning no. She then offered to give me pictures of her sons so they could be physically identified. Before I could answer, she started to show me the photographs, commenting on the date, place, and occasion on which each had been taken. As always when speaking about her detained and martyred sons, she became very emotional. She started to cry when she showed me the picture of her youngest son and told me the story of his abduction and death under torture in a regime jail. Three of Umm Ahmad's sons were martyred in protests and detention and two were still missing after they had been arrested by the regime. The family now consisted of Abu Ahmad – whose losses had deeply affected his mental health – a son, the son's wife and their child, and an unmarried daughter. The daughter selected a couple of pictures that she photographed with her phone and sent to my Whatsapp account.

Meeting former detainees occupied a large part of my fieldwork and I was often introduced to people who had just been released, as my interlocutors knew it could help to locate the missing relatives of some of the families with whom I worked. Each time I met a former detainee, I would ask about Abu Moatassem, a friend's father, and about Umm Ahmad's sons. For detainees' relatives, searching for a detainee and trying to get him released was a complicated, costly, and time-consuming task that included finding middlemen who could pay someone in the regime to get information and broker a deal: first to get him[13] transferred to a civil prison, or to arrange a visit, and then to get him out of jail. It was a risky transaction as one could lose a huge amount of money if cheated by the intermediary. The transaction was thus usually twofold and involved a third person, with payment being made in two instalments, often remaining with the third person until the detainee was visited or released. This quest could also include trying to get a detainee's name on a prisoner exchange list and the constant search for a better, more trustworthy and efficient intermediary. The whole process of searching for relatives and attempting to negotiate their release periodically turned into a flurry of daily activity.

Abu Moatassem, for example, had been detained for three years; his family had made many attempts to have him released when the middleman called his son Moatassem and announced that his father would be freed in a week's time. Moatassem immediately started to think of ways to get his father out of the country quickly after his release, since staying in Syria could mean his being arrested again. He had to find a safe way for the old man to cross the entire country and be smuggled into Turkey, and worried about whether his health would allow it after being detained for so long in horrific conditions. Moatassem began to contact friends and acquaintances to find out about the newest roads and get tips; he also had to arrange a money transfer to pay the middleman, so he made a series of phone calls to see who was still doing this and how much it would cost him. As the day of release approached, Moatassem became more and more tense and, on the day itself, life seemed to pause and time stop; Moatassem could not eat or work, and was annoyed when I tried to open a conversation. Time passed slowly, becoming sticky, dense, and heavy, as he spent his day staring at his phone, watching the time pass, expecting his father's release at any moment.

In the past, every couple of months the middleman had called and announced a release that never actually happened, so hope decreased as the day advanced. Periodically, Moatassem contacted his family and the middleman to be updated on the situation, but no one knew what was happening and Moatassem was left waiting in front of his phone. Abu Moatassem could be released any time between 12 noon and 4 p.m. but, as the end of the working day approached, Moatassem started to lose hope that it would take place. Although, by 4 p.m., it was very improbable that his father would be freed, Moatassem was still hoping that it might happen at an unusual time. As on previous occasions when he had been told that his father's release was imminent, Moatassem continued to wait for another couple of days, unable to resume his 'normal life' and focus on his work, as he kept calling his family and the middleman, hoping for a satisfactory resolution. The middleman would always come up with an excuse as to why the release had failed and would then disappear until he announced Abu Moatassem's imminent release again, a process that was usually repeated every two months or so. After these intense upheavals everything seemed to go back to 'normal' waiting, until the middleman got in contact to ask for some money, or tell Moatassem about some paperwork that needed to be done, or to announce another release date.

In such a situation, my interlocutors' paused and suspended present appears as time 'punctuated' (Guyer 2007):[14] a time regularly interrupted by various events linked to their waiting for things to happen in the near future. If there is a 'lack of progression of time' similar to the one experienced by Palestinian wives of detainees, such a contraction does not 'restrict their lives to the present' (Buch Segal 2013: 125) as there is no resolution of the situation for Syrian detainees and their relatives, and one has to prepare for new upheavals. There is no formal procedure that one can follow to get a relative released from jail, or to arrange a visit, so the present of Syrian detainees' relatives is not routinised and structured by administrative procedures.[15] In fact, the present for relatives of Syrian detainees is punctuated instead by outbursts of intense activity that momentarily interrupt its normally suspended state.[16]

Syrian detainees' relatives – as Moatassem's story shows – would suddenly engage in a flurry of activity in the search for the detainees' whereabouts and for solutions to get them out and, after encountering dead ends, would briefly pause their search until they found another option. Such effervescence was often linked to the news of a collective release from the regime's jails – people were feverish to see if their relatives were among those freed – or to the contents of a list of detainees to be exchanged between two factions, or to the announcement by a middleman of the detainee's imminent release. Syrians' waiting – for news of missing relatives – was thus punctuated by periods of intense activity that brought them back to a present that otherwise seemed paused and suspended.

## Waiting as hoping: the temporality of the aftermaths?

Syrians' experience of time in displacement has been marked by the tragic unfolding of their revolution, as Islamist groups increasingly took over rebel groups and the FSA in liberated areas, as the regime besieged and retook liberated territories, and as the revolutionary war of liberation turned into a proxy war. During the revolution and the first years of displacement, the time of struggle and planning was the near future: of the success of the revolution, of a new Syria, of return home, of detainees' liberation. With the revolution's defeat becoming clearer, however, it seems that the near future has been evacuated, yet this period is central to revolutionary action, for it is the time of 'the reach of thought and imagination, of planning and hoping' (Guyer 2007: 409).[17] Moreover, the revolution's defeat also leads to a shift in temporal horizons from the near future to a present consisting of waiting and a long-term horizon of the revolution's successful return and its afterlife. In the aftermath of the defeated revolution, the near past and distant future appear as the main horizons of the revolutionary project and action, and are invested with hope, whereas the near future is a time of uncertainty that seems an extension of my interlocutors' indefinite waiting in the present.[18]

> After Umm Najem's husband was arrested in Idlib by the regime forces, she did not hear of him for nine months despite her attempts to discover his whereabouts. When the security forces sent his belongings to her home – his watch, his ID card, and other things he had with him when he was arrested – they announced that he was dead ['killed under torture' as Nura translated it for me]. She had four small children, and she was living in her in-laws' home. After her husband was martyred, and after the four-month mourning period, she married his brother so she could keep living with her

children at her in-laws. It had then been over a year since her husband disappeared, and she had lost hope that he was still alive. A year after she married her brother-in-law, her husband was released from jail and he came home to find that his wife had married his brother and was pregnant by him … Can you imagine these people's situation?! This is why people never give up hope and, unless they see their relatives' bodies, never accept they are dead.

I first heard the above story from Nura, whose own husband was martyred in the early days of the revolution. I interpret this story as a moral parable of hope, and an injunction to resilience and patience, as well as testifying to arbitrary arrests, indefinite waiting, and uncertain temporality, and their effects on kinship and gendered relations. I heard different versions of it from women waiting for relatives detained in the regime's jails and, despite some variations in names, locations, and other details, the tale always included the same narrative elements: 1) the arbitrary arrest of the husband; 2) the belief that he is dead because his belongings have been returned; 3) the wife's marriage to her brother-in-law; and 4) the return of the detained husband.

As Nura compared the incomparable – the martyrdom or detention of a relative – she used this story to contrast waiting for a detainee with her own situation. She had nothing to wait for anymore, no hope that her husband would ever come back, and no hope for a future together. On the other hand, if he had been detained there would still be a slight hope that he would come back, she explained.[19] Yet waiting for a victim of enforced disappearance in a country known for its arbitrary arrests, and for torture on an industrial scale,[20] is an indefinite and uncertain process. Waiting for detainees is an unlimited process – especially for those of whom no one has heard anything since their abduction, and those still detained in security branches, meaning that they are not allowed visits and do not have a 'judgment' or a release date. The discovery of a crematorium in Sednaya prison (see Weizmal 2019), as well as the leak of 50,000 pictures of 11,000 detainees killed under torture in 2013, known as the Caesar file (see Le Caisne 2015), confirm that Syrians are potentially waiting for something that will never happen.

Waiting, as the parable shows, thus belongs to an economy of hope.[21] Hope becomes a specific temporal orientation and social practice when people continue to hope to be reunited with their relatives despite the circumstances and the slim likelihood that such a thing could happen, and despite the repeated failure of things to work as planned. The 'work of hope' (Pedersen 2012) is apparent in Moatassem's renewed hope each time he heard from his middleman. Each time, although this process had been going on for over a year, he hoped that his father would finally be released. The temporality created by this work of hope is one in which the future has an effect on people's actions in the present. Hope modifies the articulation between future and present tenses, for it is not defined as the imagination of the future in the present but rather as the future becoming a model for actions in the present (Miyazaki 2006: 157).[22] The fact that hope is a process explains why my interlocutors' repeatedly unsuccessful attempts to release their relatives from regime prisons did not halt their continued efforts for their release. This creates a 'radical certainty' among Syrians waiting for their detained relatives, a certainty that is not supported by predicting the future but rather by abstaining from doing so (see Pedersen 2012: 148).

How did the future impact on my interlocutors' present – or was it, rather, *made* present? On an individual scale, their orientation towards the future through hope has direct effects on their present, and it is one of the temporal modalities that explains the evacuation of the present and its replacement by a pre-experience of the future. The modalities of hope among my interlocutors show that living in the moment does not necessarily mean living in a present without a past and future.[23] This thought of the future that is yet unknown suggests the idea of a pre-experience of the future that does not correspond to a clear image of it, as it is still unknown. Ultimately, the future is not the actualisation of the present or its prolongation into the future as it becomes future; rather, it is the 'uncertain actualization of virtualities' (Grosz 1999: 28, quoted in Pedersen 2012: 145). On an individual scale, my interlocutors' persistent hope against all odds, especially for the release of detainees who may have been dead for years, and in the success of their revolution – and the actions that sustain these hopes (working for one's relatives' release and for the revolution) – can only be explained by seeing that the future (the success of these actions) is pre-experienced in the present. Umm Ahmad, who had two detained sons, refused to go through the pictures of detainees killed under torture made public in the Caesar file, for she argued that she would only believe her sons were dead if she was brought their bodies. Here, the temporality of having relatives detained appears as twofold: it leads to a pre-experience of the future, and to a re-experience of the past, in the present.

## Past re-experienced in the present

> When your son is martyred, you can find some peace because you know he is with God. He is in Paradise. But when your son is detained, you can't be at peace. If you eat you think: did he eat today? If you're cold you think: is he cold now? If you take a shower you think: did he have a shower today? Each time you do something you think of him and wonder what is happening with him …

Umm Ahmad, who said this to me, had not heard from her two detained sons since they were arrested four years earlier, and a further three of her sons had been martyred. Most people who knew her and her sons (such as Umm Nidal) thought that there was very little chance of any of them being alive. Yet Umm Ahmad was still waiting for her sons and still searching for signs of life from them. Her life, as well as those of her husband and family, was greatly affected by this waiting. Umm Ahmad's story shows how the past is re-experienced in the present through narratives, conversations, actions, activities, and gestures. In this family the most striking evidence of the past being re-experienced in the present was the naming of Umm Ahmad's grandchildren after her martyred or missing sons. Traditionally, grandchildren are named after their grandparents, especially grandsons.[24] It was expected that Umm Ahmad's first grandson would be named after her husband (his grandfather). Following such practice, the son virtually becomes the father of his father: Rashid was expected to name his son Hussein after his father, thus becoming Abu Hussein, literally the father of Hussein. But he called his son Ahmad (after his brother), becoming Abu Ahmad like his father – something very unusual – thus seemingly reproducing the past in the present. It is as if his martyred brother was born again. This was reinforced, Umm Ahmad explained, by the fact that he had chosen the name of his son after meeting him for the first time, for he saw a strong resemblance with his brother Ahmad, which made him choose that name rather than that of another of his martyred brothers.

During my weekly visits to Umm Ahmad, a ubiquitous topic of discussion was her disappeared and martyred sons. She told me about their childhood, their education, their characters, their involvement in the revolution, their disappearance and tragic deaths. Her stories were never univocal, as her daughter and daughter-in-law, who were always present in the room, not only constituted an audience but also contributed to the stories with small anecdotes. Umm Ahmad would often illustrate her stories by showing me pictures of her sons. She had also kept all their diplomas, certificates, transcripts, and a few notebooks from their time in school. These items were wrapped in a small plastic bag placed in a handbag she had taken with her when she fled. She was proud that her sons had been *shater* (brilliant students), and these documents seemed to be among her most precious belongings. In fact, even more than illustrating her stories about her sons, the artefacts seemed to be an embodied synecdoche of her sons: these material artefacts became a part of her sons that preserved them with her in the present.[25] The stories that acted as subtitles for the pictures and diplomas were often repeated, as well as the ritual of carefully passing the pictures and diplomas from hand to hand around the room. The daughter would hand one to her mother, who sat next to me and talked me through it, pointing at the name, grades, and levels and recalling anecdotes about each of the sons. As she recalled these stories her voice would break and she often burst into tears. Seeing her grandson walking around the room, she recalled with emotion how her son Ahmad and his younger siblings sang Marcel Khalife's '*Wa ana amshi*' ('And I Walk')[26] on the balcony of their house. This memory seemed to be sparked by the fact that her grandson, like her son that day interpreting the song, was wearing blue jeans and a red shirt.

As she described in the extract above, Umm Ahmad's life was structured around and by her sons' absence. The absence of Umm Ahmad's sons could be described as their phantom presence. Like phantom pain,[27] their absence is present and has effects on social life and relations in a similar way as a missing limb seems present to the body that lost it, since phantom pain is still felt even in the limb's absence.[28] Moreover, it indexes the sensory absence of those materially absent (Bille et al. 2010b: 3), thus making apparent the presence of the absent, and the strong effects of her absent sons on her life because of their absence. As well as making her sons present through shared memories and producing their phantom presence through artefacts such as their material belongings, along with one son's metaphoric embodiment in her grandson, Umm Ahmad's constant thinking and talking about them could be described as inducing their haunting presence.

In that sense, the 'presence' of the absent collapses past and present on the one hand, and inside (*juwwa*) and outside (*barra*) on the other. The effect on her husband of their sons' disappearance and of waiting was even more dramatic, as he was the victim of regular panic attacks that made him unable to work or to have any kind of social life. I never met Abu Ahmad over the years that I knew his family, though he was always sitting in the room next door, only separated by a glass door from the room where his sons were embodied through discourse and artefacts. Through the account of Umm Ahmad's life, one can see the deep impact of the permanent or momentary absence of relatives on Syrians' lives. My interlocutors' past, the revolution, and the memory of revolutionaries are present in people's everyday lives, and are also re-enacted through performances.

## Repeating the past to create difference

The re-experience of the past in the present was further engineered through different public and semi-public performances: in protests, but also at dinners and wedding parties, the singing of revolutionary songs and the performance of *dabkeh* (traditional Syrian dance) evoked what had happened during the first protests of 2011. My interlocutors thus refused to relinquish the revolutionary past, re-actualising it in the present. In wedding and birthday parties, one of the attendees would suddenly begin a revolutionary melody and would be followed by the rest. The rest would rapidly form a circle, burst into anti-regime slogans, and perform a *dabkeh,* or just jump to form a circle and hold one another by the shoulders, following the patterns of the early protests in Syria. These performances were much more intense at weddings, where they had the proper space to happen. Traditional wedding songs would suddenly be interrupted and the wedding-hall turn into a protest area as young people formed circles and started to sing.

Actual protests were re-performed weekly on a larger scale in Gaziantep's main squares until they were forbidden by the local authorities, whereupon they shifted to parks and smaller squares before they were scattered by the police. During one of these protests, I saw Umm Khaled spontaneously join the large circle of protesters as she heard the revolutionary slogans and saw the revolution's flags from the playground across the road where she had taken her daughter to play. She joined the circle and started singing along, tears slowly rolling down her cheeks. I approached her and she told me that she felt she was reliving the first protests in her hometown. It was a very emotional moment for her to re-experience the early days, when hope in the revolution was still high, before losing her husband and one of her sons. On another occasion, former detainees organised a protest on Gaziantep's main square in support of detainees in regime jails. The protest organised by former detainees took the form of a cathartic recreation of prison scenes with some of the protestors making up an audience as they stood in a half-circle that formed a stage for other protestors to act as detainees. They sat next to each other, blindfolded, handcuffed, and tied to one another. Others nearby re-enacted scenes of torture. A female ex-detainee instructed two protestors on how to stage the beating and torture of detainees; they had brought tires to remind the audience of *dula*, an infamous torture method,[29] and rubber rope, which those acting as guards held in their hands.

These outcroppings of the past in the present re-performed the first days of the revolution, not only as a form of remembering it, but also as a reactivation of hope and a repetition of the revolution itself. The repetition of a defining past event (the revolution) in the present resonates with the temporality of the Nakba that Anja Kublitz describes as 'a kind of mythical time that conjoins past and present' (2013: 108). Similarly to the repetitions of Syrian protests that are supposed to lead to another outcome and open up a different future, the repetition of the Palestinian past is not identical: 'repetition in a Deleuzian sense should not be understood as repetition of the same, but as repetition of that which differs-from-itself' (Kublitz 2013: 117). The Palestinian temporality of the Nakba is an effort to make a difference, that is, to break away from the circularity and repetitiveness in which Palestinians are fixed. Moreover, the re-enactment of al-Nakba points at a different future: each Nakba aims to create a better future for the Palestinian collective (Kublitz 2013).

Here too, Syrian performances link the past directly to the future: through the repetition of the past, they hope to change the future. The repetition is therefore the future tense: the past is meant to be repeated (though differently) in the future. This creates a time that is non-linear and non-progressive. The ideas of a non-linear and a non-chronological time grasped by the Deleuzian concept of duration[30] are central to understanding displaced Syrians' time wherein pasts are in the present, but futures remain without presents. This describes the paradoxical movement from past(s) to future(s) without a present, a time in which the present is evacuated. Moreover, not only does the time go from past to future, but the future also appears as a repetition of the past. The present disappears through waiting and through hoping that the past will be realised in the future. In the Syrian context, however, it is not the present that is reimagined from the perspective of the future but rather the future that is reimagined from the perspective of the past. This creates an inward sense of hope as Syrians hope for the past to be repeated in the future, and are longing for this repetition. Yet, as the re-enactment of the revolution's early protests illustrates, there is not only one past: there is the heroic revolutionary past and there is also the tragic ending of the revolution. Doubts are thus multiplying about the collective future: would it be a successful repetition of the heroic past or an apocalyptic version of its tragic ending?

## Of near and distant futures: hoping for the past to come back

Abu Zein and I were drinking coffee in the late summer of 2015. His family was about to embark on the perilous journey to Europe; they had lost hope in the imminent success of the revolution. Abu Zein, on the other hand, refused to flee as he waited for the revolutionary cycle to repeat itself, yet successfully. As he told me:

> What I really hope for is that now the cycle of anger will start again. You know, now we are waiting for a second revolution! We are preparing to be ready this time. But maybe the second revolution will never come. Maybe we won't see anything; maybe only the generation of our children will see it.

The kind of repetition to which Abu Zein alludes here is thus quite different from the classic definitions offered by anthropologists.[31] The kind of repetition at stake here, a repetition with difference, rather resonates with Bergson and Deleuze's idea of duration and Deleuze's concept of 'different/ciation'. The concept of a nonlinear and virtual time and the correlated idea of a different repetition are indeed central to my understanding of my interlocutors' sense of time in the revolution's aftermath. By collapsing the tripartition of time, the concept of duration helps make sense of their past-oriented hope for a different repetition of their revolutionary past in the future. If my interlocutors' waiting seems reversed – directed to the past and awaiting a different repetition of the past – it is because the temporality of displacement is simultaneously a temporality of the aftermath.

My argument is thus twofold: to show that waiting corresponds to a temporal limbo or permanent temporariness, suspends my interlocutors' present, and disrupts their sense of time; and to demonstrate that the disruption of displaced Syrians' experience of time has created a temporality of displacement that is simultaneously a 'temporality of the aftermaths of political catastrophe' (Scott 2014: 2). Indeed, what is peculiar about my interlocutors' sense or experience of time is that it is marked by the tragic consequences of their defeated revolution. It is the temporality of immobility, a non-heroic or even anti-heroic temporality that contrasts with the temporality of revolutionary action.

My interlocutors' tragic temporality thus leads to a reconfiguration of time itself: it is not only the experience and relation between past, present, and future that is changed; rather, the very definitions of past, present, and future are radically transformed. My interlocutors thus lived between a heroic (revolutionary) past and a disenchanted near future, in a dystopian or tragic present. Such a relation to time can be defined as the Syrian temporality of the aftermath: the relation between past–present–future is redefined in the aftermath of revolutionary action, which creates the feeling of being suspended or stuck in the moment as my interlocutors wait for the past to be re-actualised in the future.

## Experiencing a time out of joint

I propose to understand the relation to time entailed through, and by, waiting as a suspension of the present, and a hope that the past – the time of the defeated revolution – will be repeated, but successfully, in the distant future.[32] In the aftermath of a revolution whose successful outcome is suspended and which seems to be slowly disappearing due to its defeat, the present is tragic – the revolution cannot happen now – and the near future is a disenchanted time marked by hopelessness and apocalypse. In this moment of revolutionary defeat and political and humanitarian catastrophe, a sense of out-of-jointness emerges as 'time is no longer assimilable by history' (Scott 2014: 9). This 'disjointed' time or 'time out of joint' is a time of 'loss of the old metaphysical security of futures to come' and the experience of the present as 'ruined time' (Scott 2014: 10; see also Derrida 1995).

In the aftermath of the Syrian revolution, time was no longer linear or progressive for my interlocutors. Contrary to revolutionary temporality – usually understood as one of 'progress' (the past must be overthrown and the present sacrificed for the sake of a utopian future), for them the utopia belongs to a finished past and an unreachable inside (see Chapter 2), the present is tragic and defined by unlimited waiting, and the future is uncertain. Moreover, waiting has often been framed as waiting for a better future, by a progression from worse to better, or as a temporal quality of a present spent hoping for the future and remembering the past. But what happens when hope is turned towards the past rather than the future? When one waits for the past to be repeated in the future, and when this waiting is disenchanted?

In my interlocutors' case, the near past is heroic: the revolutionary project, action, and hope belong to the past. The present is tragic, marking the end or the ending of a heroic and utopian time. The near future is endowed with a sense of disenchantment and disbelief as the repetition of the past is uncertain. The aftermath of the Syrian revolution is thus characterised by a sense of inward hope: a hope directed to the past. This inward sense of hope differs, however, from the nostalgia that has been described by Ghassan Hage in the context of migrants waiting to return home, as 'waiting for the past-to-come' (2018: 207). Whereas such nostalgic waiting is defined by the longing for a 'lost plenitude' (Hage 2018: 207), my interlocutors never reached this lost Eden, nor do they aspire to return to a perfect (and idealised) past. On the contrary, the Syrians I lived with hope for a different rendition of the revolution, as the one they experienced could not fulfil its aims. This is a paradoxical sense of hope only if the past is seen as abolished by a present that is marching towards a better or utopian future, but the paradox evaporates if the past is understood as what is meant for the future, or, rather, the future is meant to repeat the past but make it last. However, it should not be a repetition without difference; in the future the revolution should not end tragically.

Thus, my interlocutors' time did not consist of a nostalgic past, a utopian future, and an absent present. The Syrians I lived with were rather living in a tragic (and suspended) present, between a better past and a disenchanted future. Moreover, the revolutionaries had become more modest in their claims and hopes as they faced the destruction of their country and the loss of many lives. One could argue that the present is dystopian – in the sense that it has annihilated and reversed all the revolutionary hopes – and the future tragic, because it will never be able to attain the past. My interlocutors lost their sense of present not because they found pleasure in past memories and hope in the future – they were scared of such mental projections – but, rather, as they re-performed/ pre-performed the past/future in the present.

This sense of tragedy is very well grasped in Syrian playwriter Mohammad al-Attar's work, in which Syrian refugee women are re-interpreting and re-staging classic Greek tragedies. In his *Antigone of Shatila*, the female narrator addresses the public, stating the resemblances between Antigone's fate and their own experiences. She says: 'the feeling of injustice is the thing we share the most acutely'. In the play, Syrian women re-enact the classic tragedy, through their own testimonies of life in revolution, war and displacement, creating a polyphonic effect as they act as the classic characters by telling their own stories, creating parallels and resonances between the two. Ultimately, as in Greek tragedies, the unfolding of tragic events can only be made sense of in light of a higher causation or a divine transcendence. The distant future becomes the moment of the revolution's true outcome and it is also the moment of divine justice. The meaning of the present as the revolution's defeat, the finished revolutionary past, and the uncertain future is supposed to be understood not only by the return of the revolution but also in the afterlife on Judgement Day. I come back to the temporality of the revolution's aftermath in my final chapter and deepen its analysis as I examine the understanding of the tragic outcomes of the revolution through Islamic cosmology. In this understanding, the revolution's temporality is thus embedded in a wider temporal frame: a cosmological time that reframes and stretches the revolutionary temporality as it is understood in relation to Judgement Day and the afterlife.

## Notes

1  I borrow this term, and draw inspiration from, Nadeem Malik's study of Pakistani waiting and the absence of the present in the midst of economic crisis and religio-historical waiting for the Messiah (2009).

2  In his study of Togolese life in the midst of political and economic crisis, Charles Piot describes this paradoxical nostalgia directed towards the future rather than the past as 'Togolese longing for a future that replaces untoward pasts, both political and cultural' (2010: 20).

3  This relation between spatial and temporal limbo has also been explored in the context of asylum seekers' detention, likewise a situation of liminal spaces (for instance Agier 2002; Rotter 2016; Turnbull 2016; Whyte 2011) and has also been described as a 'spatial quality of temporality' or 'spatially qualified time' (Navaro-Yashin 2012: 7).

4  Keeping one's home keys despite displacement also echoed Palestinians' conservation and exhibition of home keys in exile, even decades after fleeing (see Sayigh 2005: 21; Khalili 2004).

5  See also Auyero 2011; Buch Segal 2013; Lakha 2009; Minnegal 2009.

6  See Janeja and Bandak 2018: 8; see also Khalili 2006.

7  Appadurai (2002; 2013) frames this difference as 'waiting for' and 'waiting to' and defines a 'politics of patience' that marks the shift between a passive waiting and a politically organised one (see Janeja and Bandak 2018: 8–9).

8  See the discussion on Iranian youth's migratory aspirations in Khosravi (2017).

9  See Agier 2002; Fassin 2013; Rotter 2016.

10  See Malik (2009) on temporal limbo.

11  Similarly Rebecca Rotter describes, in her work with detained asylum seekers in Australia, how her informants spoke of their experience of waiting as passive, saying that they spent their time doing nothing (2016: 80). In light of her ethnographic material, however, Rotter argues that although the asylum seekers described their present as a 'stagnant time', they were actually active and even productive (2016: 80). Countering the idea that waiting creates a spatio-temporal limbo – materialised in detention – that equates to passivity, Rotter writes that 'more [is] maybe taking place during seemingly uneventful periods of waiting' (2016: 84).

12  Such memorisation techniques have also been described by Mustafa Khalifa in his novel *The Shell* (2007) where he describes his experience in Tadmor Prison in the 1980s.

13  Although there are many female detainees in Syrian regime prisons (see Coquio et al. 2022; Loiseau 2017; Yazbek 2018), and I met many former female detainees, the families I worked with happened only to have male relatives detained. This is why I use the masculine pronoun here.

14  A punctuated time is a time in which intrusions are 'qualitatively different rather than quantitatively cumulative' (Guyer 2007: 416).

15  Syrians are in this sense quite unlike Palestinian detainees' wives, who constantly engage in administrative procedures so they can visit their husbands and thus become 'captives of the immediate present, a present that can never become a future because, as soon as the women's practices are completed, they must be repeated, thereby engendering a sort of temporal contraction' (Buch Segal 2013: 122).

16  In her ethnography of Moroccan women waiting to join their spouses in Europe, Alice Elliot describes how the women's lives are punctuated by similar outbursts of action (2021; see also Vigh 2009; Graw and Schielke 2012a on waiting in migratory contexts).

17  Guyer describes how structural adjustment created a long-term economic horizon and an 'enforced presentism' in Nigeria under military rule (2007: 410).

18  Here my argument differs from Guyer's description of a 'shift in temporal framing' (2007: 410) that evacuates both near past and future.

19  This resonates with Adam Reed's study of Bomana prison in Papua New Guinea, in which the detainees on remand 'wait for' (they still have hope of a positive outcome), whereas convicted detainees 'wait out' (they are hopeless and are no longer waiting for anything in particular) (2011; also see Hage 2009a).

20  For instance, the Caesar files compiles over 55,000 pictures of people killed under torture in Syrian regime jails (Le Caisne 2015).

21  See Crapanzano 2003; Hage 2009b; Miyazaki 2004; 2006; Pedersen 2012; Reed 2011.

22  In fact, one's 'apparently irrational optimism' can be explained by 'reimagin[ing] the present from the perspective of the end' (Miyazaki 2006: 157; see also Nielsen 2011: 398).

23  See Pedersen's description in the context of young Mongolians navigating post-Socialist uncertainty (2012), in which he argues that the present of marginalised people – described as living in the moment – is not an 'atemporal' present that has no link with the past and the future (Day et al. 1999: 21). Indeed, by differentiating 'living in the present' and 'living for the moment' one can perceive different forms of presentism (Pedersen 2012: 143). The moment thus contains 'the thought of the future' as its duration is 'a dynamic field of potential relations without beginning or end, from which the present is actualized' (Pedersen 2012: 144).

24  This is also indicated by the use of descent terms between parents and children and grandparents and children: a father calls his children baba (father) and a mother her children mama (mother). The same happens between grandchildren and children and for uncles and aunts with their nephews and nieces (see Khuri 1981: 360; see also Davies 1949: 251).

25  This is quite alike the photographs of deceased relatives exhibited in homes (Parrott 2010).

26  'Wa ana amshi' is a revolutionary song by the Lebanese singer-composer Marcel Khalife.

27  Comparing the absence of people and things to a missing limb, the editors of An Anthropology of Absence argue that in fact, one's absence is present and can still be felt as the absence of a limb and this absence is felt through phantom pain. The absence can become the 'constitution of [one's] social relations and actions' (Bille, Hastrup and Sørensen 2010b: 5).

28  French-Algerian artist Kader Attia has explored the relation between individual and social bodies and their missing limbs in terms of phantom pain and traumatic absence, drawing parallels between amputees and the colonial past in an artwork titled Réfléchir la mémoire (2016).

29  These torture methods have been described in detail in Mustafa Khalifa's literary account of his decade in Tadmor prison (2007).

30  For Deleuze, inspired by Bergson (1908), la durée is composed of qualitative multiplicities, a flux that is non-chronological and creates qualitative differentiation that constitutes time (Hodges 2008: 409). The concept of durée leads to a different understanding of time from the linear, for its logic implies a different relation between virtual and possible as well as between present and future. Indeed, the future is not bound to the present, as the possible only exists in retrospect (Hodges 2008: 410); rather, duration creates a 'living present' through the continuous 'different/ciation' (in Deleuze's terminology) of multiplicities, thus bringing together a succession of instants that are commonly thought of as past and future. Ultimately, it is the tripartition of time into past, present, and future, and the idea of living in a present that becomes past as the future replaces the present, that disappears with Deleuze's conception of duration.

31  It is not the religious idea that collapses the two aspects of time that Edmund Leach discusses (first, the repetition of certain natural phenomena, and second, the irreversibility of life-changes and the inevitability of death for organisms) that leads to the conclusion that human beings are immortal because time repeats itself (Gell 1992: 30). It is neither repetitive time in

the sense of cyclical or periodic time (see Barnes 1974), nor Leach's notion of alternating time (1950). Nor does it correspond to Leach's suggestion that 'sacred' time – the time of rituals – goes backwards (Gell 1992: 32). Looking at the temporality of ritual practices based on Van Gennep's studies of rituals' three stages, Leach argues that the liminal phase of ritual – between separation and reaggregation – is characterised by time going backwards to where rebirth happens: death becomes birth (Gell 1992).

32  In his work on post-revolutionary Iran, Shahram Khosravi describes the waiting of his informants as leading to two opposing attitudes towards time: some youth 'seek pleasure in the present with no concern about the past or the future', others express 'a deep estrangement from the present, seeking refuge in a nostalgic past or an expectant future' (2017: 89). The one I suggest here is a third kind of waiting.

Part 3
**Afterlives of defeat**

**Figure 5.1:**   Women Protest. © Manal Shakhashirou

# 5
# From the political to the social: the speed and depth of revolutionary transformations

'How long did it take for the French revolution to succeed? A hundred years?' I was often asked rhetorically, before my interlocutor concluded, 'We still have a long way ahead of us!', referring to the four years that had passed since the beginning of the Syrian revolution. The possible success of the revolution was thus located in a distant future that will be a different repetition of the past. However, I was also often given the example of liberated areas that had rejected the *zulm* (oppression/injustice) of Islamist groups that had gained control over them. Nura described how people had refused to submit to these rules whereby women's dress must be modified, men were forbidden to smoke in public, and revolutionary emblems were banned in her city (Al-Khalili 2017b; 2018). According to her and other interlocutors, such actions, as well as renewed protests inside Syria, exemplified the revolution's legacy and the continued presence of the spirit of the revolution inside (*juwwa*). The areas where it happened had first been liberated by the FSA and had witnessed the involvement of communities in local bodies of administration and governance after the revolution. Nura, among other interlocutors, explained that after these localities were liberated by the FSA, women started to participate in public and political life, increased their mobility, and became breadwinners, getting new opportunities to work outside their homes in community centres and newly established institutions (Al-Khalili 2018). They thus saw the revolution's enduring spirit in the fact that after being taken over by Islamist groups, women organised protests against restrictions imposed by these groups.

The possibility for the revolution's future success was thus linked by my interlocutors to 'irreversible' (*ghir rdud*) changes in the social fabric and in people's 'mentality' ('aqliyyeh), that were already happening in the present. This was stressed by the fact that the revolution became increasingly called 'al thawra al mustamera' (the permanent revolution) stressing its long-lasting and constant effect. Despite political change at nation-state level becoming a more distant horizon, my interlocutors thus argued that permanent social transformations were taking place in the present at the local level. These in-depth transformations were believed to enable a political revolution in the long term. To my interlocutors, this widespread spirit of defiance was proof of the success of revolutionary transformation on the social level; such changes gave them hope that what Abu Zein called 'cycle of anger'[1] would start again. This led my young interlocutors in particular to believe that even in the regions retaken by the Assad regime, people would eventually start a more radical revolution, even if it took a generation.

If the renewed protests happening inside Syria's liberated areas were interpreted as a renewed struggle that replicated the 2011 uprising – they similarly opposed zulm (oppression/injustice) and illegitimate authority inside Syria – such struggle was also located outside, where it was similarly directed against traditional and usually taken-for-granted forms of authority. These acts of 'everyday resistance'[2] (maqawameh yawmiyyeh) index in particular Syrian women's questioning of gender ideology and socio-religious conservatism, as pointed out by Nura for instance. Here, the term 'resistance'[3] has to be understood as an ethnographic concept that signifies a struggle against all kinds of oppressive authority. Resistance literally translates as maqawameh but it was most often expressed by my interlocutors in terms of struggle against authority (sulta) and oppression (zulm). By taking seriously my interlocutors' claims, and their understanding of continuities between their political struggles and the transformations of their social and intimate lives, I propose to make sense of their questioning of the dominant gender ideology in (pre-)revolutionary Syria (see Peteet 1991). My aim is not to describe these processes in terms of 'emancipation' or 'empowerment', which would risk imposing a white Western feminist gaze that universalises a historically bounded situation (see hooks 1984; Ghamari-Tabrizi 2016).[4] On the contrary – inspired by bell hooks's feminist writings and building on Julie Peteet's work on Palestinian women in the resistance – I aim to draw out processes of transformation of gender structures and meanings rather than analyse the situation in terms of liberation versus subordination (Peteet 1991: 5).

This chapter thus focuses on the discontinuities perceived by women within the beit – which encompasses the material house, the home, and the family lineage (see Kastrinou 2016; Sanyal 2011; Sayigh 2005) – in gendered relations, roles, norms and practices, despite numerous continuities also existing. Discussing their involvement in the revolution and its impact on their lives, my female interlocutors often brought together their struggle against two kinds of authority: political (the regime) and familial (*beit*). Yet this is not to say that all my interlocutors saw such continuity. Some rather framed it in terms of causality. Moreover, showing the continuity of their struggles in the streets and in their homes, as well as inside Syria and in displacement, my interlocutors challenge Syrian women's image as passive victims of war, as they are often described in the mass media, or as refugees who are 'powerless' and 'victims' of their male relatives' actions (Alhayek 2015: 698). The women I lived with described themselves as powerful political actors and agents of social change. If they were not necessarily political actors in the classic sense of the term – political activists (*nasheteen*) – since their actions blurred the boundary between the political and the personal, making the personal political, they did, however, refer to themselves as *hara'ir* (free women)[5] or *thuwwar* (revolutionaries) and were actors of political and social changes at the level of the house.

The focus on ruptures rather than continuities is an emic perspective emerging from my interlocutors' perception of their situation as having dramatically changed. Discussing their involvement in the revolution and its impact on their lives, the women I lived with often brought together their struggle against two kinds of authority: the political and the familial. They conceived these two fights in terms of struggle against authority (*sulta*) and oppression/injustice (*zulm*). However, continuities exist too, especially among older women: during one of our conversations Umm Khaled laughingly and kindly reminded me that 'the man is the head of the house but the woman is the neck' and she spelled it out for me: 'you see, the man might be the head who takes the decisions but it is the woman that makes him turn, like a neck, in the direction she wants him to go' thus showing that women have always had ways to make men go in the direction *they* wanted them to follow.

Focusing on the ways in which these changes mainly affected women allows us to see an often overlooked dimension of revolution and its often invisibilised actors (Winegar 2012; see Abu-Lughod 1990; 2012; Wilson 2016). But it simultaneously offers a counterpart to Chapter 2, which examined revolution as an increasingly male endeavour *juwwa*. Here, the outside appears as a rather female space, as it was marked for my interlocutors by the absence of male relatives: some detained, others martyred, some inside working or fighting, others already in Europe applying for family reunification.

## Women in revolution: women's revolution?

'If we get rid of Assad we would still have to get rid of all the tyrants in our houses', Mariam – a 30-year-old teacher who had recently arrived in Turkey with her two young children and husband – told me as we were discussing the future of the revolution. Developing her thought, Mariam explained that not only the regime's authority in Syria but also men's authority within the home – mainly that of the father – should be dismantled. I first thought that such discourse would be restricted to the circles of 'activists' (*nasheteen*), who, in Gaziantep, often consisted of young, lower-middle and middle class women such as Mariam. I later discovered, however, that the idea that for women the struggle against the regime and its defeat would be incomplete without a struggle against what Mariam described as oppression within Syrian homes, was much more widespread than I had first assumed. This sentence was echoed by Umm Zein, who was perceived as a rather conservative person, socially and religiously, although the chronology she posited between the downfall of the state and of patriarchal authority within the home were not the same as Mariam's.

> I want to fight for freedom (*hurriyya*) within my own home first: I want freedom from my husband first! We have to fight for the freedom of women from men. I need my freedom from my husband before getting my freedom from Bashar!

Umm Zein, a mother of two and a housewife in her mid-twenties, said this as we sat in her mother-in-law's kitchen discussing her own and her husband's involvement in the revolution while rolling small pieces of dough in our hands for the *kebbeh b-l laban* (a dish of bulgar and meat balls simmered in yogurt) that we were preparing. Umm Zein was engaged to Abu Zein when she was 15 and they married two years later. She remembered that her mother decided to marry her off because she was 'not good in school'. Marriage had at first been presented as a threat, but later her mother followed through on it as her grades did not improve. Umm Zein recalled being quite happy about the prospect of leaving school and starting marital life, especially after she was introduced to her future fiancé, whom she found handsome. She gave birth to their first child a few years after their marriage and to a second one as the first protests started in their city. Umm Zein said that this was the reason why she did not participate in the protests. Nonetheless, despite not participating in street protests, she saw herself as a freedom fighter for challenging her husband's authority at home, and for fighting for her rights within the household.

Umm Zein's and Mariam's words stress that, for women, the political revolution against the regime had to translate into a social one within their homes.[6] Moreover, as depicted throughout the book, Syrian women participated, and played an important role, from the inception of the peaceful struggle against the Syrian regime. Women had a wide variety of roles and tasks: they took part in protests (both women-only and mixed ones), designed and prepared banners, sang and addressed the protesters, participated in peaceful sit-ins, cooked and knitted for protesters and fighters, participated in cleaning campaigns, reported human rights violations, became citizen journalists, worked in field hospitals, volunteered in aid and relief for internally displaced people, and a few became fighters. Women's role in the revolution was thus not only a hidden one, and did not only take place within their homes. My female interlocutors attended protests and they were sometimes the only ones able to carry out specific tasks. In a context in which women were traditionally perceived as belonging in the private sphere of the home (see Bourdieu 1972; Elliot 2016b; Ghannam 2002; 2011), they were not primary suspects when it came to cracking down on revolutionary activities. This was especially true in the uprising's first phase when women were not yet as targeted as men by the regime and could more easily protest, for instance, the siege in Deraa and demand food. My female interlocutors reportedly played on regime's (and community's) stereotypes of women to pass through regime's checkpoints wearing niqab and *habayas* under which they transported medicines and food for the protestors and besieged (see below). These new kinds of practices led to the emergence of new forms of sociality and social relations.[7] Moreover, these changes affecting the Syrian social fabric were considered, by my interlocutors, as irreversible (*ghir rdud*) and permanent (*da'am*).

In addition, these transformations affected a wider circle than the young (middle-class) activists who took part in direct revolutionary action. Indeed, revolutions happening in emblematic squares can only be turned into a real transformation of social relations if it is also mirrored within people's homes (see Winegar 2012).[8] It is thus not only by protesting in the streets and taking part in political action that women challenged their relations with patriarchal authority. One thus has to trace the changes inflected by revolution within the private sphere of the *beit*. In Umm Zein and Mariam's words, *zulm* (injustice/oppression) characterised Syrian political and social life, and revolution was thus seen by women as having to happen both in the streets and their homes, an idea shared by many women I met. The social rupture was thus not necessarily seen as something that should happen first and prior to the uprising against the regime, but rather as a simultaneous or consecutive struggle, translated into very pragmatic and everyday issues. Soon after she arrived in Turkey, Umm Zein started to go outside her home by herself, switched her *khimar* (a full face veil that differs from *niqab* by virtue of an extra black veil that covers women's eyes) for a black hijab and *manto*,[9] and started to travel unaccompanied, for instance on trips to visit her mother, who lived in a nearby city. All of these practices would have been impossible before the revolution, as she explained.

## Revolution, repression and reorganisation of the *beit*

> What a life! Even if I make it to Europe none of us [her relatives] will live in the same country. And now Raya [her elder daughter] is asking for resettlement in the US with her husband and son ... We will not get our life back in Europe!

Umm Yazan said this to me on one occasion as we discussed the subject of her family reunification. Like Umm Yazan's family, all the families I lived among were affected in one way or another by their involvement in the revolution, its repression, and their subsequent displacement. In such a context, the patriarchal authority and patrilineal organisation of the *beit* – that is the material house, the home and the family lineage – had first been shaken by women's participation in the revolution and repression, and had later been reinforced by displacement. The dismemberment of Syrian families was essentially marked by the absence of male relatives. This led to dramatic transformations within the *beit*'s organisation and relations and gave my female interlocutors new roles and responsibilities: they became more mobile, looked for work outside the home, and became figures of authority and decision makers. This is particularly well illustrated by Umm Yazan's family story.

Umm Yazan, a mother of six, used to be a housewife before the revolution. She described her everyday life, before 2011, as mainly dedicated to her children, grandchildren, and her household. Her children were aged from 8 to 24 at the beginning of the uprising and she had five grandchildren from her two married daughters. Her parents, married children, and in-laws all lived within walking distance of her house so they visited one another on a daily basis, and her (social) life was organised around these visits. Her married daughters recounted how they visited Umm Yazan, their mother, several times a week and how they organised outdoor activities (*meshwar*) on weekends with the entire family. Umm Yazan rarely spoke of the past and of her life before the revolution as it caused her intense sadness; however, as her son was about to cross the Mediterranean, she reminisced to me about her home, her life before the revolution, and her children's childhood. She drew an idyllic picture of pre-revolutionary life as she described the beauty of her house and garden, her good relations with her neighbours, how her children would help her to prepare coffee and welcome her guests, and how quiet and well behaved they always were, with the older offspring taking care of the younger when their mother was busy. She was deeply nostalgic about this time of her life, when she had all her children living around her.[10]

The repression of the revolution and subsequent forced displacement affected Umm Yazan's family greatly, beginning with two of her daughters, Raya and Sara, who fled to Homs in the early months of the revolution after it became too dangerous to participate in demonstrations. They were then involved in a network that recorded human rights violations but, as the army advanced on Homs, they moved to Damascus to hide and pursue their work. Soon after they reached the capital, they were arrested. Their father, Abu Yazan, moved to Damascus to negotiate their release while Umm Yazan stayed in Hama with her three youngest children; her daughter Nour followed her husband when he joined the armed rebellion. Soon after her husband's departure, Umm Yazan sent her two youngest children to a relative in Lebanon as the army started to bomb their town, and she went with her older son to Damascus, where her husband had been arrested while negotiating his daughters' release. Abu Yazan was quickly released from jail, but it took several months to free their daughters. After their release, the two young women left the country as they feared for their safety. Sara had to seek medical treatment, the result of being severely tortured. Umm Yazan brought her younger daughters back from Lebanon and settled in Damascus with other internally displaced families from her town, as she found it to be a safer place. A few months later, Umm Yazan's son was arrested in Damascus for delivering medicines to besieged areas. Fearing further arrests in the family, Umm Yazan fled to Turkey with her two younger daughters, where she was reunited with Raya and Sara. Abu Yazan stayed behind to arrange their son's release.

When I met her in January 2015 Umm Yazan was living with her two younger daughters, her husband was still in Damascus, her son was still in jail, while Nour was besieged with her family in Homs old city. Raya had just got married in Gaziantep and Sara, also recently re-married, had fled to Europe with her new husband (see below) . Two months after I met Umm Yazan, her son was released from jail and came to live with her, only to flee to Europe in the summer of 2015. A month after her son arrived, it was the turn of Nour and her family to escape their besieged neighbourhood and reach Turkey, but they could not settle in Gaziantep as Nour's husband was unable to secure employment, so they moved to İzmir where he set himself up as a smuggler (İzmir was one of the main locations from which Syrians crossed the Mediterranean) with former fellow fighters. Umm Yazan's family story exemplifies many that were scattered by the revolution's repression, particularly in terms of its largely female composition. Through the description of Umm Yazan's *beit* one sees that she lost not only her home's material building and its familiar surroundings, but also her family life, and the relations with her extended family and neighbours usually associated with the home, which were disrupted by her children's involvement in the revolution, the repression of the revolutionaries, and their forced displacement.

I argue that one of the revolution's consequences is the dramatic disruption and the radical reorganisation of the patriarchal and patrilocal organisation of the *beit*. The Syrian, like the Arabic *beit* more broadly, is usually organised following a patrilocal logic: the sons bring their wives into their family, which in Syria often meant that they moved into the same home, built an extra floor on the top of their parents' home, or, alternatively, took a house nearby (Joseph 1999c: 186; Kastrinou 2016). The *beit* is structured according to a 'patrilineal logic',[11] and the relations one observes in the *beit* can be described as 'patriarchal connectivity':[12] a system in which the family and the individual are extensions of each other (Joseph 1999a). Yet, one can wonder about the ways in which this patriarchal logic was inflected by the fact that most of the families with whom I lived, as Umm Yazan's family story illustrates, were undergoing the temporary or permanent absence of male relatives as a result of revolution and displacement. Moreover, one can question how the pre-revolutionary *beit* (family relations, sociality and power relations within the home) has been dramatically transformed through revolution and displacement.

The literature shows that the absence of male relatives, by disrupting the household dramatically, changes women's roles and status, whether it is linked to migration or displacement (for instance see Abu Nahleh 2006; Brink 1991; De Haas and Van Rooij 2010; Elliot 2021). Through the detailed description of Umm Yazan's family during the revolution, one also starts to perceive how women's participation in the revolution restructured the *beit* (see Aretxaga 1998; Buch 2010; Jean-Klein 2000; 2003).[13] Indeed, my female interlocutors began to challenge their understandings of their roles as mother, wife and daughter through their actions in the revolution. If these roles seemed taken for granted by most of my female interlocutors before the revolution, gender inequalities started to be increasingly read in political terms throughout and after it. In other words, it is through revolution that 'gender relations came to appear as susceptible to transformation as were other social relations' (Aretxaga 1998: 78).

## Reshaping the *beit*: women's roles and responsibilities

Before the revolution Umm Khaled, a widow and mother of martyrs in her fifties from a small town in northern Syria, led a life that mainly took place within the private sphere of her home and in women-only spaces. Her husband and sons took care of most things that had to be done outside the home – from work to shopping – while she took care of everything inside it (see Bourdieu 1972; Vom Bruck 1997a). Umm Khaled also remembered with humour that, during the first ten years of her marriage, her husband also used to choose her clothes for her. 'He would never pick what I liked!' When she finally convinced him to let her buy the clothes she wanted, she did not go herself to the market of the nearby city, as she was constantly busy with her children and the housework. 'I would describe exactly what I wanted but he always made mistakes!' Umm Khaled's mobility was thus limited to her immediate neighbourhood, where she visited her female neighbours every morning before her husband and sons came back from work and school. By that time she would have prepared lunch and done most of the household chores. In the afternoon, she usually helped her husband in the fields or took care of her children and finished the housework. At the beginning of the uprising, Umm Khaled secretly joined women's protests in an act of defiance against the regime's authoritarianism; it was a gesture which also seemed to challenge patriarchal authority, as she had told her husband and sons that if they did not join the protests she would.

She was later forced to escape the town with her youngest child, while the men stayed behind to defend it against the regime army and militias. Soon after, Umm Khaled learned that her husband and one of her sons had been martyred. Her town was retaken by the regime and the rebels were on the run so she had to flee further before being reunited with her sons. She had very bad memories of these times and of the humiliation inflicted on her at the regime checkpoints when soldiers discovered on her ID where she was from. Her town had become synonymous with rebellion, as most of the men had taken up the weapons that many of them already had and used to protect themselves against wild animals when they worked in the fields, and for wedding and other celebrations. Umm Khaled had no safe place to go to in Syria and, as her sons were on the run, she had to cross clandestinely into Lebanon. It was the first time she had left Syria and travelled by herself, she remembered with emotion. Her sons later found employment in Gaziantep where she joined them and took charge of making the money last as long as possible.

Whereas she recounted a life mostly confined to her home and its surroundings in Syria, Umm Khaled now spent most of her mornings running all over the city to find the cheapest deals to feed her family. She regularly left her flat before 6 a.m. to go to the *suq al irani* (the Iranian market) where she found the cheapest meat; she also had to go to faraway neighbourhoods to find the organisations that were said to provide aid and help widows reunite with family members in Europe. After spending several months in Gaziantep with her two sons, Umm Khaled was left alone with her daughter when they fled to Europe, where they hoped to apply for family reunification. She also started to work in the kitchen of the Syrian *dur al aytam* (houses for widows and their children) when they received funds from the Gulf during Ramadan. When her sister came to live with her, her brother-in-law gave her the money he had put aside for his wife and their children, showing that she had gained a different status by living on her own without male relatives.

Umm Khaled's biography and story show how transformations operated in women's mobility, the division between private and public spheres, sex-segregated spaces and sociality, access to work in displacement, and the effect of all these on women's roles and statuses. Through her story, displacement seems to operate as an 'incubator for transformations' and as an intensifier of social change (Wilson 2016: 10).[14] But here, life in displacement also appears to enhance revolutionary change.

The changes in Umm Khaled's status were not only linked to the absence of her husband but also to her becoming the wife and mother of martyrs. Because of this status, people listened to her, she could voice her opinion in public, and she was well respected in the community. She often told me about entering into arguments on political issues – mainly concerned with the righteousness of the revolution(aries) and the need for the regime to fall – with female neighbours and women queuing at the offices of aid organisations, using her status as the widow and mother of martyrs to support her statements. This echoes Lotte Buch's description of the effects on their wives of the absence of Palestinian men in the West Bank; she writes of the 'honourable social presence' wives of martyrs gain, as the permanent absence of their husbands allows them to start a new life: find a job, get some education, and so on (Buch 2010: 5).[15] This status can be contrasted with that of detainees' wives, whose social standing and presence become ambiguous as a result of the temporary absence of their husbands: they are watched by the community and their relatives, and do not gain as much mobility and independence as martyrs' wives (Buch 2010).

Yet it was not only Umm Khaled's status as the widow and mother of martyrs but also the fact that she had herself taken part in the revolution that assigned her the new role and its responsibilities, a role in which she asserted the strength and decision-making skills gained through her political involvement. Moreover, after having fled within Syria and crossed into Lebanon and later Turkey on her own she had proven her ability to navigate inhospitable spaces without the protection or supervision of male kin. In fact, among the Syrians in Gaziantep, not only widows but also women whose husbands and sons were temporarily absent saw an increase in their mobility and a change in their roles and responsibilities. One of the reasons for this was that by creating anonymity, displacement to Gaziantep allowed women to escape such control and to move and act more freely; in an anonymous environment, the pressure to conform to social norms diminished greatly. This stands in stark contrast with life under the Assad regime where the private and public spaces often had very blurred boundaries, since as the saying goes 'walls have ears' and, as reported by my interlocutors, the community's control over women's morals, especially in suburban and rural areas, was often tight.

But Umm Khaled's status, and new relation to the inside and outside, is also linked to a broader understanding of kinship and class. As Farha Ghannam's study of working-class families relocated from Bulaq to al-Zawiya in Cairo shows (2002; 2011), the classical understanding of the relations between gender and movement through different kinds of spaces is enriched by adding the concepts of kinship and class (see also Elliot 2021; 2016b; Göle 2002; Vom Bruck 1997a; 1997b). Indeed, various factors – age, marital status, economic need, number of children (Ghannam 2002: 101) – determine women's access to public places. For instance, in the Egyptian communities that Ghannam studied it was accepted that women should ideally not work outside their homes once they are married, but this also depended on the household's income: if the husband's income could not sustain the household, it was accepted that women must do so (Ghannam 2002: 105). Similar attitudes prevailed among my interlocutors.

Hence, in order to complement her husband's meagre civil servant's salary, Umm Khaled also worked in the fields near her house, which made it possible for her family to have extra vegetables and fruit. On the other hand, Umm Ahmad, a working-class housewife in her mid-forties from the Aleppo suburbs, had never worked outside her home and thus had moved and socialised almost exclusively in female spaces until she was displaced to Gaziantep. This was also due to her family being very conservative religiously and socially: women were, for instance, not allowed to leave the house without a male relative. Having lost three of her sons, and with another two missing and her husband sick, it was now she and her daughter who were in charge of working and collecting aid to sustain their precarious lives, a hard task that they did not see as emancipatory.

Women's mobility was also limited by religious and social conservatism. Umm Yazan belonged to a lower-middle-class urban family, and despite her wish to work as a schoolteacher – a profession she had trained for and practised before getting married – she had not been allowed by her husband and his family to continue her professional activity after marriage. They were in favour of a strict separation of female and male spheres, spaces and activities. This was not solely motivated by their more comfortable revenues, since Umm Yazan also mentioned financial difficulties, but rather because her husband and his family were in favour of a strict division of spaces and roles. For instance, her husband had their two eldest daughters removed from school at 14, but she was able to impose her will for Raya and Maya to continue their studies until 18.

However, in the revolutionary effervescence of 2011–12, Umm Yazan and Umm Khaled challenged their restricted mobility, whereas Umm Ahmad helped revolutionaries from home. At the beginning of the uprising, Umm Khaled secretly joined the first women's protests in her hometown, covering herself with a *niqab* so she would not be recognised. Umm Yazan's movements outside the domestic space also began to increase during the revolution. She collected money for and distributed goods to internally displaced families, women being then less suspected and targeted. She recalled crossing checkpoints with her *niqab* filled with medical supplies without attracting the soldiers' attention. As in other militarised contexts, such as in Northern Ireland in the 1970s, women used their gender identity and perceptions of them as victims of war to circumvent the army and security forces (Aretxaga 1998: 66). In the Syrian case, my interlocutors reported using their wide *manto* (a long coat falling to one's feet) to smuggle medicines and other goods to liberated and sometimes besieged neighbourhoods, or using a *niqab* or a *khimar* in order to circulate more freely with anonymity (see also Bhabha 1994 and Fanon 1967 on Algeria).

Ultimately, the revolution did not increase the mobility of older women only, something that would be in line with Suad Joseph's analysis of 'patriarchal connectivity', wherein women, as they become older and closer to the menopause, take on a larger role in the *beit* and their mobility increases accordingly (1999a). Younger women also challenged patriarchal and patrilineal logics in the revolution. For example, Umm Yazan's daughters Sara and Raya fled Syria because they had been arrested, and were still wanted by the regime for their active participation in the revolution. They had to flee to Turkey alone as their parents were caring for siblings and relatives remaining in Syria. They thus started to live without any (male) relatives in Gaziantep at a time when the Syrian presence in the city was still low-key, and Syrians did not yet inhabit entire buildings or neighbourhoods, which later enabled the reproduction of social dynamics resembling those in Syrian towns and neighbourhoods.[16] In Turkey they found their first jobs and started to socialise in non-sex-segregated spaces.[17] This represented an important change, one clearly compelled by the revolutionary developments in Syria, as they had previously only been allowed to go out or travel between cities with a male relative, and they would never have been allowed to spend a night outside their family home. Although they were not safe in Syria anymore, they had to make their way to Turkey alone because their relatives would have been at risk if they had accompanied them into liberated areas and to Turkey before returning to a town under regime control. This was also linked to the fact that Sara and Raya had asserted themselves as independent political actors and subjects by participating in the revolution. They had joined the protests in their town and became involved with activist networks unbeknown to their parents and relatives.

Sara, for instance, was married and a mother of three in 2011. While living in exile in Gaziantep, she confided to me that back then she had joined the protests despite her husband's support of the regime. When the security services started an arrest campaign targeting protestors and activists, she fled her city with her sister without informing their family. As many activists in the revolution, they had to cut their ties with family and friends and continue their activities underground in order not to endanger them (see Chapter 2). Soon after, Sara was arrested by the regime and detained for several months in appalling conditions. After her release from jail she refused to go back to her married life, and asked her husband for a divorce settlement. She had been married to him without her consent when she was 16 and had never liked him, she said. Moreover, after her active participation in the revolution she felt that it would be impossible to live with him because of his support for the very regime that she had fought against, and that had detained and tortured her. Since neither her husband nor her family agreed to or supported the divorce, Sara had no choice but to leave her three children in their father's custody.[18]

Losing her children rendered her separation from her husband particularly painful, a separation already hard given its impact on her relationship with her relatives, who considered it a brutal rupture of Syrian social and marital orders.[19] Sara then fled to Turkey with her sister Raya to avoid being re-arrested. Participating in the revolution thus had the potential to dramatically reorganise family relations, increase women's mobility, and give them new roles.

## Marriages as loci of political and intimate struggles

Umm Yazan had married off her daughters Sara and Nour before the revolution, when they were respectively 16 and 17, to men that she and her husband had chosen. When I asked about the circumstances of their engagements and marriages, Umm Yazan gave me a vague answer; she cited her husband's poor health and her fear of becoming a widow to justify marrying her daughters at that age, as she herself had been married in her twenties after she had finished her studies, and had had her say in choosing her husband. It seemed, however, that arranged marriage at a younger age was a tradition in her husband's family, as her daughter Nour explained, remembering that her sister Sara had not even been given the chance to refuse her husband. Umm Yazan chose these men for her daughters because she knew their families, who were neighbours and belonged to the familiarity of the *beit*'s surroundings (see Goody 1990; Khuri 2004; Mundy 1995). In addition to coming from known and respectable families, the men had homes, stable jobs, and were pious and moral subjects. This presented a variation of marriage between first cousins (FBS–FBD, or marriage between father's brother's son and father's brother's daughter), which was widely followed a generation earlier in the region. When they did not follow this endogamous pattern, marriages were still 'arranged between allies, friends, and kin' (Abu-Lughod 1990: 44), as my interlocutors' stories illustrate.

Umm Yazan had two other daughters, aged 20 (Maya) and 23 (Raya) in 2015, who did not marry before the revolution and were the only ones to finish high school. When I met Umm Yazan, Raya had married a man of her own choice a few months earlier, someone her mother did not like.

When I questioned the striking difference between her daughters' marriages before and after the revolution, Umm Yazan explained that she could trust Raya, who knew what she wanted, so she did not have to interfere with her life. She described Raya as a strong, smart, highly capable woman who she admired for her involvement in the revolution. It seemed that Umm Yazan had resisted marrying Raya off before the revolution, despite the tradition in her husband's family for daughters to be married before turning eighteen, as Raya reminded her of her younger self: she had participated in the 1982 uprising as a teenager alongside the Muslim Brotherhood. Yet there was more to it than Raya's character, since Maya also married according to the same logic of political endogamy – alliances based on revolutionary rather than family affiliation – despite her mother's observing that she was rather weak and had not participated in the revolution.

Raya had met her husband at a meeting with a group of revolutionary friends. When Omar introduced himself, Raya was shocked as she was very familiar with his name, one she remembered seeing carved into a wall of the one-square-metre cell in which she had been detained for several months in Damascus; Omar had been detained in the same solitary cell a few months earlier. She told him that she knew him already, better than he could imagine, before revealing what they had in common. Several months after this first encounter they decided to get engaged and got married later the same year. Their marriage faced resistance from both families, which did not know one another or come from the same city or social background. Moreover, whereas Raya's family was socially and religiously conservative and lower-middle class, Omar's was rather liberal and upper-middle class. Raya explained her parents' opposition by saying, 'It is harder to marry a man from Homs [for a woman coming from the nearby city of Hama] than a foreigner' (see Kastrinou 2016: 98). Umm Yazan was particularly dissatisfied with this marriage, but Raya went ahead with her decision and her mother did not try to prevent it. Abu Yazan seemed to have played no part in the arrangement since he was still inside and thus had to rely on his wife to make the decision.

The fact that Raya had been active in the revolution inside, and was still outside, and that she had lived on her own with her sister for a year before her mother joined them, made it difficult for her mother to assert authority over her. She had managed to find employment and accommodation, and had lived without male relatives in a foreign city, breaking numerous taboos and living an independent life; she was thus not willing to re-submit herself to her parents' authority. This was not an isolated case as women, once involved in politics and public life, started to build new networks of sociality, meeting the men they married through their involvement in political life, rather than through their families.[20] Wartime and times of crisis are actually periods of 'cultural ambiguity', when women find themselves engaged in activities and duties that are outside the field of their expected behaviour (Peteet 1991: 7; see also Aretxaga 1998; Elshtain 1987; Ridd and Callaway 1986). I argue that one of the most striking changes can be located in new forms of marriage.[21]

Umm Yazan's 'standards' had been changed by the revolution, by her own admission. The shifts in kinship relations and marriage patterns can be described as a social change that amounted to revolutionary transformation, for it was linked to the fact that Raya had participated in the revolution, had helped her family to resettle outside Syria, and had been living independently. But it was also due to Umm Yazan's understanding that things could not be as they used to be. Marriage practices indexed the socio-political transformations that the revolution had initiated in this new socio-political configuration, and now the most important criterion was that her daughter's husband be a trusted and ethical (*ndif*) revolutionary and had a diploma rather than a house and a good job. For instance, Maya had not been directly involved in the revolution for she was sixteen when it began and still in high school; her mobility and participation were more limited than Raya's. When Umm Yazan started to mention her wish that Maya would marry, citing economic pressure and the desire to find a way for her daughter to start a new life in Europe, Maya proposed the man with whom she was in love as her future husband. Maya met Ali through her sisters at a gathering with friends who were part of a network established in their town during the revolution. He was a trusted revolutionary, and an acquaintance of her sisters. The two young people started to meet, alone and in secret, something that could have never happened before the revolution, when Maya had not been allowed out of the house by herself. These meetings were facilitated by Umm Yazan's absence from home and the absence of male relatives in general. When Umm Yazan discovered that her daughter was regularly meeting a man unaccompanied, she was furious; her daughter should be engaged to a man before being alone with him. Umm Yazan also found it a warning sign that Ali did not come and ask for her daughter's hand, and she was worried about his intentions and morals.

Pressured by Umm Yazan, Ali arranged a meeting to ask for Maya's hand, but Maya was certain that his proposal would not even be considered by her mother: he did not come from the same community – he belonged to the Ismaili minority – despite coming from the same city; their families did not know one another; he did not study and did not have a well-paid job; nor did he have plans to go to Europe any time soon, as he did not have the money to pay for the crossing and his family could not support him financially. Moreover, he asked for Maya's hand in a rather heterodox way, as he was not accompanied by a family member to support his demand (cf. Kastrinou 2016: 101). His proposal was met with suspicion and without joy by Umm Yazan, who hoped to marry her daughter to the son of a family she knew well, who was educated, planning to cross to Europe, and could afford it. More than wealth, what seemed to matter the most in displacement was education, as it was the only thing on which people could still rely.[22] Yet eventually, after Umm Yazan had sent relatives to enquire about Ali's family in their hometown, she agreed to Maya and Ali's engagement[23] for two reasons: first, he had participated in the revolution and had good revolutionary ethics and, second, he had eventually agreed to travel to Europe in order that Maya and he could pursue their studies.

Through Umm Yazan's marriage strategies for her daughters and their resistance to (and subversion of) them, one can get a glimpse of larger transformations: daughters gained control over their marriage options, unsettled patriarchal relations, and imposed a new form of marriage through their involvement in the revolution.[24] Here, women clearly appear as agents of social change and of family remodelling. Moreover, there has been a shift from marriages based on kin and community ties to those based on political affiliations as a locus of social rupture. Indeed, my female interlocutors refused these forms of endogamous marriages after the revolution, when new forms of alliance appeared: 'politically endogamous marriages' (Peteet 1991: 181).[25] These changes in marriage patterns, more than merely a consequence of displacement, were a revolutionary rupture, for alliances were redrawn on the basis of revolutionary affiliations, ethos, and actions rather than traditional endogamous logic.

## Revolutionary marriages

The political endogamy that characterises revolutionary marriages allowed cross-class and cross-sect marriages, as sectarian and class differences were partially erased by revolutionary dynamics. Although cross-sectarian marriages existed prior to this, they were rare and mainly restricted to marriages between different branches of Islam or between different Christian denominations.[26] For example, some of my interlocutors contracted Sunni-Ismaeli and Sunni-Shia marriages before the revolution; Sunni-Alawi and Sunni-Christian marriages were much rarer, although not uncommon in its aftermath. Yet these marriages, although more frequent after the revolution, were not always readily accepted by the families. A friend who was Alawi had to flee Syria with her Sunni fiancé in order to get married. Not only was he Sunni but he had also participated in the revolution, and my friend's family had sided with the regime and saw their community at risk of a Sunni uprising, in line with the regime's sectarian propaganda. Moreover, it was always easier for a woman from a non-Sunni background to marry a Sunni man, while a Sunni woman marrying a Christian or Alawi man was rather rare and most often not accepted by her family. It is accepted in practice that Sunni Islam allows men to marry women from monotheistic religions but not women to marry non-Sunni men, as the understanding is that a man will make his wife become Sunni over time.

Furthermore, it was not only the shape of marriage itself but its celebration that was transformed in the aftermath of the revolution.[27] Some transformations have to be attributed to the effects of displacement; before the revolution, my interlocutors remembered how they used to have sizeable parties bringing together their extended families. In Turkey this was no longer possible. Not only were families scattered but most people could not afford such celebrations. Some of my friends and interlocutors even got married online as they could not be in the same place to celebrate their marriage. With the groom already in Turkey or in Europe, the bride would organise a women's party by herself in Syria or Turkey before joining her spouse. Other transformations were clearly linked to a revolutionary ethos. For instance, my interlocutors often thought it inappropriate to invest large sums of money in marriage ceremonies in the current context of loss, dispossession, and ongoing war. Meanwhile, ceremonies that were held often had a revolutionary dimension: a friend chose to celebrate her marriage in an orphanage in order to spend the money on impoverished children and their mothers rather than on her guests, a token of solidarity and a political statement that she was not forgetting the orphans and widows of the revolution. Marriage ceremonies also made space for new symbols. During marriage parties and ceremonies, revolutionary songs and dances were performed, and marriage contracts were printed on paper decorated with the Syrian free flag. They were not only marriages between two revolutionaries, but they were also celebrated under the aegis of the Syrian revolution and Free Syria.

Maya's engagement party (*kateb al ketab*) took place in her mother's flat. Whereas her sisters had large parties for their engagements and marriages before the revolution, she had to accept that there would be only 10 female and 10 male guests, who would have separate 'parties' in two different rooms of the flat. Maya's mother wrote a list of five dishes that would be served and prepared at home. Maya, to her great displeasure, was wearing Raya's wedding dress and a few accessories she had found. Moreover, the guests were mainly Umm Yazan's and Ali's friends, as no family members were present. On the day, Ali came with two men, one of whom belonged to the Free Syrian Lawyers while the other was a sheikh. They brought a paper headed with the revolutionary flag and symbols on which to write the contract. This was a purely symbolic move as their engagement (*kateb al ketab*), albeit de facto a religious marriage, could not be a legal marriage unless it was registered with official authority. Apart from the fiancé and the brother's signature, they added the symbolic sum of US$100 they had agreed on. They had first proposed to write the amount in Syrian pounds, but Umm Yazan refused as she deemed it no longer a safe currency.

There was actually no marriage ceremony after the engagement 'party'. Although it was meant to take place several months after her engagement and before Ali's departure to Europe, in order to ensure that Maya could ask for family reunification, they finally decided to embark on the perilous journey together. Their date of departure was suddenly fixed only a couple of days before it took place (see Conclusion). Ali had managed to find a smuggler who was giving them a good price to travel on a supposedly safer route that crossed a river rather than the sea. There was thus no time to organise a ceremony. When I asked Umm Yazan about Maya and Ali's marital status (were they engaged or married?), she explained that they would be married as soon as they left her house and consummated the marriage. She added that they were already religiously married[28] and that their union was religiously *halal*, although socially they would have been expected to have a public ceremony sanctioning the first. This was quite far removed from the way Maya had imagined her marriage, and was a source of great distress for her. She could not reconcile with the idea of starting her married life on the horrendous journey to Greece, where she would have to sleep in tents at best and where she would not be able to wash properly nor have any intimacy for the weeks to come.

## Social changes as revolutionary transformations

'The revolution has mainly happened in people's houses,' Nour told me as we sat with her sister Raya on their mother's balcony. As the conversation shifted to Raya's pregnancy, Nour said: 'I'd really like to have a girl, but with the husband I have, I am happy I don't have one! I don't want him to oppress (*yazlem*) her the way he oppresses me!' With this, Nour links the social changes women are fighting for in the aftermath of the revolution to the initial cause of the revolution itself (*zulm*). The struggle against *zulm*, inside and outside Syria, in the political and intimate domains, was thus still ongoing.

For my displaced interlocutors, the 2011 revolution changed from a political to a social project, or rather from a public to an intimate project, albeit still a political one (personal and political became synonymous), as it was equally a struggle against *zulm*. Processes of social transformations were understood by my interlocutors, as in Theda Skocpol's definition of social revolution (1979), as bringing both social and political change, although in my interlocutors' case, social change was to precede and lead to a future political rupture rather than being the result of it, as in Skocpol's model. For my interlocutors, social revolution was thus not an attempt to eradicate social inequalities by state institutions (see Wilson 2016: 148). Rather, my interlocutors understood the political revolution to have switched in nature and objectives and to have turned to the social field. In other terms, their revolution, although defeated on the 'superficial' level of politics (Elliot 2017) produced a series of deep ruptures in the social field: within the *beit*, in gendered relations, roles, norms, and practices.

This shift of the defeated revolution from the 'political' to the social and intimate domains can be interpreted through the idea of depth of rupture.[29] Despite having failed to produce a rupture on the political level at the scale of the Syrian state, the Syrian revolution was experienced as an irreversible rupture by my interlocutors on the level of the social fabric and in the domain of gendered relations, roles, and norms. In other words, the social transformations, experienced as a radical rupture, have outlived the Syrian revolution's defeat. Furthermore, this rupture is qualified by my interlocutors as 'irreversible' and 'long term', deeper than the defeat on the political level, and appears as the condition of possibility for a future and irreversible revolution to occur in the political realm as well. This in-depth rupture was thus understood as the real revolutionary transformation – the radical rupture – that will eventually lead to a political revolution in the future. The depth of the rupture was thus judged by its permanence, radicalness, and future revolutionary potential, while social rupture was perceived, and became, a revolutionary entity and a transformative force in its own right.

Hence, despite the defeat of the revolution in the political realm as the revolutionaries' presence inside, and their power of leverage in politics, drastically diminished, this political defeat did not stop the ruptures that had already affected the social field. Yet, in order to grasp these ruptures and the transformations to which it led, it is necessary not to look at this series of changes from the counter-revolutionary moment, which would entail a teleological reading, but rather to follow and look into the multiple temporalities of revolutionary action, mobilisation, and failure (Haugbolle and Bandak 2017: 194). Such a vantage point allows light to be shed on the unforeseen consequences of revolution and, I argue, the shifting of focus to the social transformations of defeated revolutionary events. By shifting its focus to the smaller scale of the social domain, discussing the deep social transformations that took place in the revolutionary process and its aftermath, and highlighting their legacy in Syrians' everyday lives and social fields, I show that revolutionary transformations can outlive revolution's defeat.

Moreover, this scalar shift is completed by a temporal shift that re-centres the temporal focus by exploring the near and distant horizons of revolution and examining its short and *longue durée*. This analytical distinction is supported by an ethnographic one: revolution was a constant and shifting object of debate for the people I lived among, and so were its effects. My interlocutors differentiated between long- and short-term changes, and in-depth and superficial transformations, to distinguish social from political consequences of the revolution. If, in the early years of the revolution, my interlocutors expected large-scale political changes and the downfall of the regime (*isqat al-nizam*), these claims were challenged by the revolution's defeat and their experience in the liberated areas and in displacement. Being increasingly convinced that they could not overthrow the regime in the near future, the strategy voiced by those among my interlocutors who identified as *nasheteen* and worked in civil society organisations and local councils was to change society at its very core in order to produce long-term and irreversible transformations. There was thus a shift in my interlocutors' understanding of what revolutionary action and aims could and should be, which was the result of their experience and their witnessing the practices associated with social transformations inside and outside Syria.

## Notes

1   See Chapter 4. See also Schielke (2015, Chapter 9) on anger as a revolutionary feeling fuelling struggle against counter-revolutionary movements.
2   The concept of resistance has been the object of various critiques in anthropology for being too broad (e.g. Brown 1996), exoticising, and pathologising (Theodossopoulos 2014), in response to which the study of resistance has been divided into several fields that, however, all seem related to the political domain (Theodossopoulos 2014: 418).
3   I use the term 'resistance' to index these processes against forms of authority that were understood as *zulm* in social and familial spheres and in Syrians' everyday life, following the nuanced and de-romanticised use of 'resistance' by Lila Abu-Lughod (1990). In her study of Bedouin women's

poetry and subversive practices towards marriage and clothing habits, Abu-Lughod has shown how, by tracking acts of everyday resistance within local communities, families, gender relations, and generational hierarchies, one discovers that 'where there is resistance, there is power' (1990: 42). She further argues that such small and local forms of resistance are not specifically linked to 'the overthrow of the system or even to ideologies of emancipation' (1990: 41), something which, I demonstrate, strongly resonates with my interlocutors' experience. By taking resistance as an ethnographic concept, I do not counterpose political and social or hidden and public forms of resistance (see Scott 1990 for discussion of the concepts of 'off stage' and 'on stage' resistance); rather, I present the continuity my interlocutors perceived in their political struggles and in the transformations of their social and intimate lives.

4  On this debate see also Chancellor (2020), Ghazzawi (2014) and Taha (2020).

5  See Aubin-Boltanksi and Khalbous 2020 on this very topic. https://syria-lexicon.pubpub.org/pub/2yfycrt0/release/2.

6  Interestingly, the parallel that women established between state and patriarchal oppressive authority resonates with John Borneman's work on son–father relations in Syria (2007). In his ethnographic episodes set in the Aleppo souk, Borneman argues that the authority of leaders and fathers have a similar shape in Syria: both are presented and justified as a patrilineal construct. Yet this form of authority had already been compromised before the revolution, for fathers became increasingly unable to guarantee jobs for their children or participate in Syria's public life. In a similar vein, Bashar did not manage to match his father's economic and political achievements and thus ran the risk of his authority also being contested. Borneman interprets the wobbling of patriarchal authority as leading to a challenge, both within the home and of the regime, that could lead to regime change. His link between political and patriarchal authorities echoes my interlocutors' analysis.

7  This resonates with Sherine Hafez's (2012) analysis of the Egyptian uprising: women's participation in street protests and other revolutionary activities and the downfall of Mubarak destabilised the 'patriarchal bargain' (Kandiyoti 1988) at the scale of the state and led to a reshaping of the patriarchal organisation of the home. Hafez shows that these power dynamics characterise men–women relations as well as the relation between the Egyptian people and Mubarak, thereby referencing the widespread metaphor of the leader as a father (Hafez 2012).

8  Jessica Winegar argues that in places and at times when women's mobility and access to public space are reduced, one must carefully observe changes within the household (2012). Winegar claims that the Egyptian revolution was only possible because of the hidden labour of women within their homes – as caretakers and caregivers for children outside of schools and as cooks for those who were camping on Tahrir and other squares.

9  I develop my discussion of Syrian women's changing clothing practices and their discourse on revolution, displacement and resistance elsewhere (Al-Khalili 2019).

10  Similar recounting of life in pre-revolutionary Syria can be found in Al-Attar (2014) and Fedda (2013).

11  Suad Joseph defines the patrilineal logic in the following terms: 'Children belong to their fathers and, in some respects, are properties of their fathers', they are incorporated into their father's genealogical line and take his 'religion, his citizenship, his ethnic and national identity, his political loyalties, and his local and familial allegiances' (Joseph 1999d: 175).

12  In Joseph's terms, the father is not the only depository of patriarchal authority since 'men have been encouraged to control and be responsible for their female kin [and] women have been called upon to serve and to regard male kin as their protectors' (1999b: 11).

13  In her work on nationalist women in Belfast in the 1970s, Begoña Aretxaga shows that women's involvement in the struggle against the British similarly was 'a time of self-discovery and political education, which provided a necessary space for reflecting on gender social positions' (1998: 54). Further, women's participation in popular resistance created tensions within their homes and redefined their role as mothers. Aretxaga argues that women's involvement in politics (due to men's absence in prison or in hiding, their restricted movement by the British-imposed curfew, and their being primary targets of army violence) led to the emergence of a new political consciousness and 'gender trouble' (1998). Aretxaga thus demonstrates that the political and domestic fields cannot be conceived of separately: 'the practices of resistance undertaken by women constitute a privileged scenario wherein to examine the mechanisms of social change' (1998: 55). Inspired by Butler's work on shifting gender significations, Aretxaga argues that female resistance led to political and personal transformations (1998).

14 See also Malkki (1995) on Hutu refugees in Tanzania and Peteet (1991) on Palestinian refugees in Lebanon.

15 See also Allen 2006; Khalili 2006; Peteet 1991.

16 The absence of (male) kin was, however, not always positively perceived by women themselves. Indeed, if on the one hand neolocal residence allowed women to move and make decisions more freely, on the other it left them to carry out housework and childcare alone (Peteet 1991: 34).

17 It is not uncommon for women to go to malls, cafés or restaurants in Gaziantep, where they share space with men. Moreover, unlike the coffee shop, which remains a space for (older) men playing cards and smoking – and which should not be confused with the café – most spaces in the city are non-sex-segregated, and women can be found circulating alone in all public spaces.

18 This specific example does not contradict the fact that many women who had been imprisoned by the regime were often repudiated by their husband, ostracised by their family, or had their marriage prospects blighted due to rape and sexual violence – used as methods of torture in regime jails – which caused women to be deemed impure as a result.

19 In Syria children belong to the father and his family (see Chatty 2018), both traditionally and by law, and in the case of divorce or repudiation the father has the right to keep his children (see Rabo 2011).

20 This resonates with Julie Peteet's (1991) ethnography of Palestinian women displaced to Lebanon, in which she describes the changes in women's lives and gender relations as a consequence of their presence and involvement in the national resistance movement in the early 1980s.

21 Describing similar changes in marriage patterns to those I encountered, Peteet writes: 'The family as an arena for marital arrangements was being bypassed, as was corresponding family control over marriages. New spatial arenas open to women and alternative sources of authority empowered women enough to pursue marital strategies initially independent of the family' (1991: 181).

22 My interlocutors' most cherished belongings were their diplomas and their (marriage, birth, etc.) certificates, as the diplomas allowed those who had qualifications to hope for better employment or to resume their studies, while the certificates were needed for visa and family reunification processes (see Chapter 3).

23 Maria Kastrinou (2016) describes engagement processes in detail in her ethnography of the pre-war Druze community in Syria. See pages 100–3 in particular on the engagement process and celebrations.

24 In her work on Egyptian Bedouin women, Lila Abu-Lughod describes the rejection of marriages arranged by a woman's male relatives as a form of everyday and local resistance to their power (1990: 43). Moreover, she argues that, by looking at the transformation of marriage practices, one can grasp the profound shifts in women's social and economic lives (1990: 48). Similarly, in her work on marriage practices among the Druze community in Syria, Maria Kastrinou argues that marriages are 'intimate and violent sites of gendered, class and sectarian struggles. As sites of struggle, marriages tell us a lot about local power relations and politics' (2016: 1). Marriage practices thus become a vantage point from which to understand social and political struggles and change, for they bring together 'religious communities, authoritarian state policies and agents of neoliberal globalisation' 2016: 2.

25 Pre-revolutionary forms of marriage were endogamous, which did not necessarily mean that they took place between father's brother's son (FBS) and father's brother's daughter (FBD), but nevertheless within the close community.

26 See Joseph (1999d) on Lebanon.

27 Compare with Kastrinou 2016: 103–15 on marriage ceremonies before the revolution.

28 The engagement party is actually a religious marriage that used to be later sanctioned when it was registered with the state. This registration was the occasion of making the marriage public to the state, through the establishment of an official contract, and the community, through a wedding party (see Kastrinou 2016: 100–55).

29 In her work on the aftermath of the Tunisian uprising, Elliot argues that the revolutionary events were recalled and experienced by her interlocutors as giving rise to both deep/permanent and superficial/impermanent ruptures (2017). In her case, although the revolution was deemed successful, leading to the downfall of Ben Ali, it did not lead to changes on the political level; nonetheless, it was experienced as a deep rupture within her interlocutors' selves. Elliot suggests that, to make sense of this apparent contradiction, one needs to understand that rupture operates at different depths (2017: 2). Thus the absence of rupture on the superficial level, which Elliot defines as the political and economic realm, does not necessary imply the absence of a deeper rupture that she locates within her interlocutors' selves.

**Figure 6.1:** Cemetery. © Zouhir al-Shimale

# 6

# Making sense of the revolution's unexpected consequences: martyrdom, predestination, tragedy

In the protests in our neighbourhood [in Aleppo] before the revolution became armed, a lot of youths (*shabab*) were martyred. They were the best of the *shabab*. The day that my youngest son was martyred, a lot of young men were injured, but he was the only one who was martyred. In Islam we believe in destiny (*qada wa qadar*): before someone is born, everything is written (*maktub*).

This reflection was voiced by Umm Ahmad in one of our weekly encounters, which almost invariably came back to her five sons, three of whom had been martyred while two had disappeared at the hands of the regime. In her narrative, Umm Ahmad clearly links the uprising, martyrdom, and destiny, meanwhile observing that her youngest son's death in an anti-Assad protest made him a *shaheed* (martyr).

The martyr's iconography and language were omnipresent in the Syrian revolution. Visually the high probability and sometimes willingness to sacrifice oneself for the revolution – and its equivalent, dying a martyr – was alluded to by protesters wearing white funerary clothes. Moreover, martyrs' funerals were often the places to stage revolutionary protests. Yassar remembered the funerals of the first protesters killed in Deraa: 'The crowd was bigger at the funerals than at the protests themselves! … Actually, the funerals became new sites of protests'. Martyrdom was also a theme of many revolutionary songs and slogans. The protesters were singing together '*Janna janna janna, janna ya watana*' (paradise, paradise, paradise, paradise you are our homeland), a song that became an anthem of the revolution after Abdel Basset Sarout – a former football player and soon revolutionary icon – sang it in Homs's central square. Among other slogans in which the figure of martyrs appeared, the protesters shouted and wrote on banners: *'al-janna rahiin shuhada' b-l malayin'* (the martyrs will enter paradise in their millions).

Taking as its starting point the idea that self-sacrifice is defining of revolutionary subjects and revolution (see Chapter 2; Holbraad 2014; Cherstich et al. 2020), I analyse *shaheed* (martyr) as the politico-religious instantiation of revolutionary self-sacrifice among my interlocutors. The term of martyr has many iterations in the anthropological and historical literature on revolution. Reading through it, one is struck by the omnipresence of the term 'martyr' to describe the dead revolutionaries in a wide range of contexts (for instance Alexievich 2016; Holbraad 2014; Khalili 2006; Wahnich 2003). In the Syrian context, the term *shaheed* stands against a number of practices that are linked to *karama* (dignity) and are reflected in protesters' chants, summed up in the dichotomy 'dignity or death'.

Dwelling on the polysemic character and the indexical nature of 'shaheed', this chapter shows the ambivalences and ambiguities inherent to its understanding by my interlocutors. *Shuhada'* (the plural of *shaheed*) are linked to widespread ideas of futurity that can be framed within a historico-secular or cosmologico-religious spatio-temporality (Al-Khalili 2022b). Among a vast majority of interlocutors, *shaheed* was understood within an Islamic framework, and was reflected in narratives and practices that were tightly linked to destiny locally referred to as *qadar* or *maktub* (written).[1] Here I solely focus on the Islamic Sunni framework for ethnographic and analytical reasons. Islam was the most salient and developed framework among the mainly Sunni Syrians with whom I lived. If other frameworks offer partial explanations for the revolution's consequences, Islam is a cosmology that proposes a theory that grasps the revolution's consequences, ruptures, and disruptions and brings them into a coherent whole. Moreover, Sunni understandings and uses of martyrdom and destiny in the Syrian revolution appeared across political and sectarian lines as it 'afforded a political milieu to spread and perpetuate a movement that massive numbers of peoples could identify with' (Ghamari-Tabrizi 2016: 19). Indeed, this religious narrative is simultaneously a political discourse and moral admonition: ideas of death and understandings of the afterlife define what a good and dignified life should be. The use of the idioms of destiny and martyrdom by the vast majority of my interlocutors seems to encompass the differences in terms of piety, religious conservatism and commitment. But it did run deeper than linguistic occurrences, for burial practices, rituals and relations to time were also shaped by predestination and martyrdom.[2] Dying a martyr is thus a good death: it is dying for a just and higher cause. Whether these are understood in secular or religious terms, or both, they are not necessarily in contradiction.

In a context of ferocious repression against the revolution and its actors – a context characterised by mass killing, enforced disappearance, invisibilisation of the revolution by the regime's counter-narrative and actions, erasure of traces of the regime's atrocities,[3] and annihilation of revolutionary localities[4] – the focus on Syrian martyrs and understandings of destiny among Syrian survivors and witnesses is an exercise in anthropological tracing. It is a tracing of the invisible (the dead) and the invisibilised (the defeated) in the aftermaths of mass political violence as the revolution's ends and endings remain unclear (see Al-Khalili 2022b; Haugbolle and Bandak 2017; Mittermaier 2019; Napolitano 2015; Navaro 2020; Trouillot 1995). It can thus be described as an anthropological exercise in reading the Syrian revolution 'through the lens of al-ghayb, the unknown and invisible' (Mittermaier 2019: 18). As such, the narratives, memories and dreams of martyrs' relatives have to be understood as narrative and mnemonic traces of the early years of the revolution. They, the survivors, are the only ones left to give a voice to those who fell in the revolution's violent repression.

Two figures of witnesses emerge through such tracing: the martyr (shaheed, etymologically 'the witness'), a dead witness who testifies of his violent death in front of God on Judgement Day, and the survivor, the living witness who can testify in front of a human court.[5] Two temporalities and registers are signalled by this figure: a cosmological and historical time, and a divine and human regime of justice. This presents a different temporality and history – a non-linear and non-secular one – that could be thought of in terms of a heterotemporality or heterohistory (Chakrabarty 2000). In other words, taking revolution beyond the Enlightenment frame (Ghamari-Tabrizi 2016) and grasping it through an Islamic temporality – one marked by the Afterlife and Judgement Day – and the Sunni concept of predestination, broadly understood as life being predetermined (or as death being already written) opens up to a redefinition of revolutionary action and temporality.

Focusing on predestination and martyrdom, this chapter thus interrogates the relation between divine and human will in individual and collective practices and actions. How do my interlocutors' understandings of martyrdom and destiny radically reconfigure revolutionary temporality and political action: how is the urgency to act oriented towards imminent individual and collective endings? Moreover, examining martyrdom and destiny by giving significant space to witnesses' narratives that speak of God's presence in their lives and their complex power relations with Him is also a way to inflect my ethnographic writing and make space for my interlocutors' God in it (Mittermaier 2021: 22, 30; Schielke 2019: 4).

## Performing martyrdom: making sense of individual loss

> Ahmad was killed under torture. We got his body twenty days after his death. His blood was still pouring from his body. I put him on a mattress but the mattress became soaked with blood. When I hugged him his smell was so good that I could not get enough of it. His smell was like a perfume. The house was scented with musk for a week after we buried him. [Umm Ahmad pauses as she cannot restrain her sobs any longer.] You know the faces of the dead become yellow, but my son's face remained pink! He was dead, martyred, and he was still pink as if the blood was still circulating in his body. You would think he was alive, that he was sleeping. Even when my husband took him to the cemetery he opened his hands and they were not stiff!

In Umm Ahmad's narration of her son's death one perceives the religious and political dimensions of the establishment and cultivation of martyrdom. Although the tears were rolling down Umm Ahmad's cheeks, her face sometimes showed a small smile as she remembered keeping funerary vigil over Ahmad. In this description, Umm Ahmad gives abundant details of bodily signs that point towards his martyrdom. The smell of musk released by a martyr's body and the smile on his face were often reported by mothers and wives of martyrs as implicit proof of their martyrdom. The martyr's smell, skin tone, and blood did not look like those of other dead people because 'the martyr is not dead, he is alive' said Umm Ahmad. On another occasion, speaking of the smile on her youngest son's face despite his body showing signs of severe torture, she developed the theme:

> When the angel of death [malak al mawt] comes, if you are a good person, when you see him coming you are happy [tnbassat], you are not afraid of death. But if you are a bad person, an unbeliever [kafr], someone who did bad things, then you don't want to die, you are scared of death. You can see this feeling on people's faces when they die.

However, not only bodily signs, but the circumstances of death were central to one's being a martyr, something I was reminded of by Umm Khaled, whose husband and a son were martyred fighting against the regime army around their small town. Dying while defending one's homeland, house, or family are all situations cited in the Quran that lead to one's martyrdom, she explained (see Asad 2007; Ghannam 2014).[6] Yet she added a moral condition to the religious signs and circumstances of death necessary to make one a martyr. Umm Khaled claimed that it was not enough to fight (peacefully or not) against the regime; she remembered one specific man who had poor morals and died while fighting on the side of the rebels among her relatives. To her, this man could not be a martyr, as joining the rebellion did not absolve him from his sins. She even suspected that he had joined the rebels for the wrong reasons: probably to die as a *shaheed* (martyr) and try to compensate for his sinful life, she suggested. Yet 'ultimately it is up to God; we cannot say whether one is a *shaheed*', Umm Khaled conceded.

The uncertainty surrounding martyrdom was thus tied to religious argumentation and debates among my interlocutors. Attempts to estimate whether someone is a martyr – like efforts to determine what actions will be regarded as good deeds and facilitate entry to Paradise (Mittermaier 2013) – can never be definitive. In fact, believers state that no one knows how God will calculate on Judgement Day: the Day of Calculation (*yawm al hisab*). Although there are some indications about the 'points' gained or lost through specific actions (such as praying in a group, giving alms during Ramadan and so on), several stories in the Quran and Hadith remind believers of the complexity of this calculation. In some cases, a single good deed can absolve all one's sins, rendering it unclear whether good deeds always need to exceed sinful ones (see Mittermaier 2013: 286). Having good morals, fighting for justice, and exhibiting the signs of martyrdom are thus not enough to be certain someone is a martyr since, ultimately, martyrdom is predestined before one's birth, as Umm Khaled pointed out.

Despite religious texts stating who may be considered a martyr – someone who drowns or burns, or who dies while fleeing war or tyranny (see Asad 2007; Ghannam 2014) – doubts and arguments about martyrdom persist. Accepting that humans can never be certain who are the martyrs requires the acceptance of God's power and of humans' inability to read His ways. Moreover, the hierarchies of sacrifice explored in Chapter 2 here translate into hierarchies of martyrdom. Those who drowned at sea, as they were not involved in revolutionary actions when dying, were not understood as martyrs in the same way as those who died while protesting or fighting against the regime. A differentiation already exists in the Quran as those who die while fighting against oppression are martyrs of this life and the next (*shaheed al dunia wa al akhira*), while the others are martyrs of the afterlife (*shaheed al akhira*), a difference marked by how they are buried. Among my interlocutors, the hierarchy differentiated those who drowned while fleeing to Europe, those who fought against the regime, and those who died under the rubble of their homes. Although all are considered martyrs, they are not the same kind of martyr: the drowned are washed before being buried, while those who died fighting, under shelling,[7] in demonstrations, and under torture are not washed before being buried. They keep their blood and their clothes when they are buried to bear witness to their martyrdom on Judgement Day.

Some of these distinctions were objects of debate, with some of my interlocutors refusing to consider those who died at sea martyrs as they did not perceive crossing the sea as a sacrifice but rather as taking an unnecessary dangerous risk (see Pandolfo 2007). Justifying why she did not identify those who died making the sea crossing as martyrs, Umm Kamel, the widow of a martyred policeman from the Aleppo countryside whom I met on one of my visits to a *dar al aytam* (orphanage), told me:

> The sea is very dangerous. It is wrong for people to flee by sea with their children. Why not stay in Turkey? Life is hard here, it's true, but it's harder to go by sea than to live in a *dar al aytam* or in a camp here.

This exclusion of those who drown from the status of martyr questions the fine line between being (and potentially dying) in a dangerous situation and putting oneself in unnecessary danger. This line separates self-sacrifice as martyrdom from suicide (see below).[8] Yet the doubts about martyr status were also framed by political debates and positions by my interlocutors.

## Martyr: a political status?

> Why did they arrest them [her sons]? Why did they kill them? They were peaceful protesters. They were asking for *'adaleh* [justice], the end of the *zulm* [oppression] and the *fasad* [corruption]. My sons were saying that either they would live in dignity in their country or they'd rather die. They refused to leave the country!

Umm Ahmad linked her sons' involvement in the revolution to their death at the hands of the regime. What made her sons martyrs was that they were fighting for a just cause and were ready to sacrifice themselves for it. Through the stories of their sons' and husbands' lives and deaths, the women with whom I lived constructed them as freedom fighters: they fought (with weapons and/or by peaceful means) against the regime's corruption and oppression, for freedom and justice. Umm Ahmad often repeated, 'I was scared for my sons but I knew they were right to participate in the revolution'. She drew a portrait of ethical and respectful youth when describing them. 'My children were very respectful [*muhtarabin*],' she often said.

Moreover, Umm Ahmad, who regretted never completing middle-school as she was married at 14, had pushed her children to study hard. As a result, despite being from an impoverished background, she had sent most of her children to university. She presented her sons as bright and knowledgeable:

> Ahmad used to study history. He knew a lot. He spoke ancient languages. He was an encyclopaedia *mashallah*! All my sons went to university. They always passed all their exams.

She often showed me the diplomas and notebooks of her martyred and detained sons as she recounted their achievements (see Chapter 4). These artefacts bore witness to their intelligence and success and were signs that they were good and respectful young men. Umm Ahmad also listed characteristics and habits of her sons that reinforced this persona: they helped people, volunteered in the local mosques, had good grades at school, went to university. She described their characters in laudatory ways: they were good with her, did not tell her what to do, never spoke to her unkindly, always listened to her; they did not complain about anything and nor did they fight among themselves. She once said about her eldest son with emotion and admiration:

> Before Ahmad was martyred he had an operation. I went to visit him in the hospital and he asked me to help him pray. I told him there is no need, God allows the sick not to pray. He told me, 'No I'm fine, just help me pray'. He had a very tender heart!

All these qualities were what made Umm Ahmad's sons martyrs, and with these discourses on the practices of her sons' good lives, Umm Ahmad participated in creating this status. Through Umm Ahmad's portraits of pious and respectful youth, the concept of a 'good ending' – 'the death befalling a Muslim while or immediately after doing a pious deed' (Ghannam 2014: 6) – is expanded to their lives more broadly. This was also underlined by Umm Khaled, who echoed Umm Ahmad's words, saying: 'We've lost the best of the *shabab*', referring to the martyrs. In a monologue directed to her friend Umm Zayd on one of our visits to her, Umm Khaled expressed her frustration with her sons as well as her ambivalent motherly feelings:

> Are the others' sons [those fighting and martyred] better than ours [hers and Umm Zayd's]? I don't understand why they left not finishing what they started. It's true that after they arrived in Turkey I tried to force them not to go back. When I learned that my husband and my son were *shuhada'*, I didn't want them to go back. But later? Why didn't they go back later? Why did they give up?

In a context where martyr status is dependent on one's good life and good ending, and is therefore also created through survivors' narratives, martyrs' life stories and portraits were not only testimonies to or mnemonic traces of their lives, but ultimately have a performative effect: the depiction of the deceased as good and ethical subjects was what made them martyrs.[9] Umm Ahmad's description of her sons as good people, and Umm Khaled's admission of her disappointment in her sons because they had not returned to Syria to continue to fight, and their description of the martyrs as the best of youth, illustrate how young men are made martyrs by these performative narratives (see Ghannam 2014). Yet these narratives also functioned as a political tool since, by claiming martyrs, the revolutionaries performatively put themselves in the right, establishing their cause as the just one. In the Quran, martyrs are those fighting for justice. This resonates with a religious reading of the concept of *zulm*, and its opposite *'adaleh* (justice), both of which are central to Islamic political thought (Dabashi 2011; Qutb 1953).

In a highly polarised context, wherein revolutionaries and regime supporters both claim martyrs, signs of martyrdom are thus collected and exhibited as proof of one's fighting for a just cause as well as in order to seek justice in this world. Moreover, by defining their dead as martyrs, each side denies this status to their adversaries: for instance, regime supporters tend to demonise rebel fighters and call martyrs those dead while fighting on the side of the regime (see Bandak 2015); Islamist groups claim martyrs by borrowing the vocabulary of Islamic jihad, understood as armed struggle against infidels, thereby referencing and activating an essentialised 'culture of death' (Asad 2007). Such inclusion and exclusion of martyrs by opposing sides in the conflict demonstrate that martyrdom is a politico-religious indexical assignation. Hence, to my interlocutors and friends, there could only be martyrs on one side, since martyrdom is an indicator of the rightfulness of a struggle, and of God's siding with it. A martyr was thus necessarily someone sacrificing himself for the just cause, the revolution.

## Premonitory dreams and visual representations of martyrs

In addition to narratives, pictures of the dead were a crucial part of performatively establishing their martyrdom, and were highly political tools that participated in the indexicality of martyrdom. In early 2015 I was sitting in a café with Rami, a young man from the Homs countryside introduced in Chapter 1. It was the day after his cousin's death while fighting against the regime in northern Syria, and Rami narrated the circumstances. Taking out his phone, he showed me a picture of his cousin's face. 'See, he is smiling although he is dead! This means that he is *shaheed*'. As if to convince me of the truth of his words he showed me a series of pictures of martyrs, mostly FSA fighters. They were all smiling despite the violent circumstances of their death and the sometimes long periods of time before their bodies were found. By that stage of my fieldwork I had grown accustomed to seeing the pictures of dead people that were widely circulating on social media but I tried to avoid looking directly at the pictures Rami was presenting as I still felt uneasy about it.

Rami then began comparing the images of martyrs with gruesome pictures of regular army soldiers' corpses, 'half-rotted', he specified, even when they were found within days of death, he added. For Rami these signs provided clear evidence of the rebels' and revolutionaries' martyrdom and prove that the regime fighters did not qualify for that designation. During my fieldwork, many pictures of dead martyrs appeared on Facebook, where they circulated among pro-revolution groups and the martyrs' relatives' pages.[10] Here, the pictures of dead martyrs seemed to be used to perform martyrdom through the exhibition of its signs, as well as to display the regime's crimes, rather than solely to remember them as individuals.

Umm Ahmad and Umm Khaled often replaced their Whatsapp profile pictures with one of their living relatives. Umm Khaled finally got a montage of the pictures of all her sons with their martyred brother. Half of the picture was taken up by the martyr's face, the remainder by her two remaining sons. She explained that martyrs' pictures have several functions, including that of commemoration, but also of providing proof (*tawsiq*) – here that young men had been violently killed. But these proofs were not only to establish their status in the thereafter but also in the here and now, when published on social media. These scarred bodies can be read as traces since they make 'elsewhere(s) and other-times' resonate in the present (Napolitano 2015: 57), and are witnesses or lived memories of defeated and invisibilised events, as they embody the revolution's repression.

Umm Khaled, speaking with me about her new profile photo featuring her martyred son, commented on the practice of taking pictures of martyrs and publishing them, explaining that it was a novel trend, although it had been technically possible earlier.

> It allows the families to show that their sons are really martyrs. It is a proof of their martyrdom and also of the crimes of the regime. It works as a testimony against the regime. It is like a proof [*tawsiq*] of Bashar's crimes. We are in a situation of war and *zulm* so everything has to be recorded. These pictures show that the martyrs are innocent people, not terrorists!

In another mode, premonitory dreams also contributed to framing people as martyrs. They were believed to come from God and, as such, comprised the most certain proof of a loved one's martyrdom, despite being an intimate experience that could not be shared.

> I saw my husband: he was travelling and dressed in a wedding suit. I asked him, 'Why are you travelling? Where are you travelling?' I saw from the dream that he was going to travel and leave me. He would go somewhere and I wouldn't be with him. I had this dream a month before he was martyred. I also dreamed that there was a martyr in front of our door. People were carrying a martyr back to our place and when I saw him I was very sad and I got scared. In the dream I told my husband, 'Open the door and see who it is'. When he opened the door I saw that the martyr's body was in front of it. I cried a lot. The *shaheed* in this dream was my son.

Umm Khaled remembered these two dreams with emotion as she was narrating the days preceding her son and husband's martyrdom and the events that led up to it. Commenting on her dreams, she said that she knew it was not a 'normal' dream (*hulm 'adi*). 'A voice came; I don't know what the voice was. It said, "Don't worry you're not going to die. You're not going to die before you are eighty".' Umm Khaled later expanded on this voice: 'it came from elsewhere', she said, without specifying whose it was as she did not know that herself. What was clear, however, was that it sent a divine message. In this context, the dreams of the widows and mothers of martyrs are considered signs sent by God to announce a martyrdom. But martyrdom is not only a predestined death. Martyrs are chosen by God, and losing one's life as a martyr is an honour that grants a special status in the afterlife.

## Martyrdom: a predestined death better than life itself?

> Ahmad used to tell me: 'Mother don't be scared! Don't be scared because no one dies before his day has come. And one's death will come anywhere one is.' And he was right! Death comes when it has to and that's all [*bidu yiji al mawt, bidu yiji u khalas*].

Umm Ahmad reported her eldest son's words as we sat on the floor of her home's main room with her daughter around a *subya* (wood-burning hearth), the only source of heat in the house. The idea that death is predestined and happens at the hour fixed by God before birth was the most widespread understanding of destiny among my interlocutors. Umm Ahmad remembered how her son told her on another occasion that 'he who is destined to die will die even if he is inside his house'. This reflects the common Islamic belief – not peculiar to martyrs – that all deaths are pre-written, and that one will die anywhere and whatever one does at the hour thus fixed. Such a sentence was often repeated by my friends and interlocutors when they explained going inside or staying in Syria.

Umm Ahmad had taken it upon herself not only to tell me about her sons' deaths but also to teach me about Islam. Her daughter supported her in this endeavour with the explicit aim of converting me to Islam. Our weekly conversations included emotional moments when she spoke of her sons' tragic destiny, and more didactic ones when she taught me about Islam. Explaining to me her understanding of martyrdom, Umm Ahmad paraphrased the *ayat al shuhada'* (the verse of the martyrs) in colloquial Arabic: 'Those who are killed in the cause of God, do not call them dead. They are alive though you cannot perceive that life.' Her daughter then recited the Quranic verse in its original version.[11] Umm Ahmad later added that a martyr is said to be in paradise and to be able to choose seventy of his family members to join him there. Martyrdom can thus be understood as the best way to die[12] – a death that is sometimes seen as better than life itself – and an honour for the martyr's family, a sentiment rendered by the sentence, 'Allah yikramna' ('God honoured us').

Umm Ahmad expressed an ambivalent and painful sense of relief as she compared her martyred sons' fates with that of her detained sons. Comparing the incomparable, she stated that it was easier to have relatives martyred than detained. She could at least find some solace in the fact that the martyr's time had come: he met the death he was destined to meet. Those in jail, however, could be facing torture, rape, a lack or absence of food and medicine: 'they live in constant suffering', Umm Ahmad said. Umm Ahmad knew that her martyred sons 'are with God now', whereas she did not know anything about the whereabouts and fate of her detained sons. This absence of certitude gave rise to the tremendous pain that haunted the living. Expressing her ambivalent feelings and emotions, which shifted between maternal love, fear for her sons, support for the revolution, and attempts to receive her sons' martyrdom as an honour that should be met with happiness, Umm Ahmad said, strengthening her voice to hold back a sob:

> I am with the revolution. But I was really scared for them [her sons], sometimes I wanted them to leave the country. I'm a mother after all! When someone is *shaheed* people should be happy not sad because he is alive with God. But the grief is still there because you lose a person dear to you. There is a difference between a dead person and a *shaheed* [she said, trying to bring the conversation back to our more detached discussion of religious matters]. When you enter the house of a dead person you feel sad but when Mohammad was martyred we felt happy. It's true that there is sadness inside of us too but there is also happiness because when you have a martyr you don't consider that you have lost someone.

Despite the status of martyr having to be carefully carved through oral performance of their death and life and the collection of signs (visual and virtual), I argue that the shaping of the status is not only post facto. Future martyrs prepare themselves to meet their destiny, or rather they act towards becoming martyrs to try to actualise what they believed and wished to be their predetermined fate. In other words, the martyrs are those ready to sacrifice themselves for the revolution and a better future while simultaneously hoping, through their self-sacrifice for a just cause, to meet the best death possible. Acting towards becoming a *shaheed* can seem paradoxical, since martyrdom is something that must be self-cultivated but cannot be self-actualised. As Umm Khaled reminded me, 'ultimately it is up to God; we cannot say whether one is a *shaheed*'. A person's preparedness and actions can never guarantee certain outcomes when dealing with divine power.[13] One never knows whether one's actions will lead to martyrdom since it remains a divine decree fixed before one's birth.

Hence, 'technologies of immortality' (Ghannam 2014) are not only mobilised by martyrs' relatives to cultivate their martyr status; the *shabab* themselves played an active part in shaping and actualising their destiny as martyrs. In order to 'precipitate their destiny' (Elliot 2016a: 494) one had to live a good life, and to desire and invite such destiny by accepting one's own self-sacrifice and acting accordingly. Yet some ambiguities persist in this willingness to precipitate one's destiny as a martyr. Indeed, can one really desire to die, even if this death is imagined as better than life itself (see Blanchot 1982; Mittermaier 2015; Ramzy 2015)?

## Accepting self-sacrifice: acting to become a martyr?

> When Salah was martyred five months after his [youngest] brother, Ahmad [the eldest brother] was very affected. He had thought that it was his turn to be martyred. He didn't think it would happen to Salah first. My sons were not scared of being arrested or martyred. They told me, 'We know this is the road ahead. This will happen, don't get sad. You need to get used to it.'

Umm Ahmad, telling me about her sons' spirit in the revolution's early years, cast light on the mindset of those preparing to meet martyrdom. Remembering Ahmad's feelings at the time of Salah's death, a month before Ahmad was himself martyred, Umm Ahmad told me that he was crying. Ahmad was longing for martyrdom and to be reunited with his brother, as they had gone to school together and participated in the revolution alongside each other. Umm Khaled similarly remembered how her late husband used to come home lamenting that he was not yet a martyr as he told her about companions who had been martyred that day, thus reflecting the understanding that the best are martyred, that martyrdom is an honour and a death better than life itself.

Longing for a specific destiny has been described, in the recent literature on predestination, as an active process since a sense of destiny guides humans' actions in an uncertain world, while always leaving its outcomes unpredictable (for example see Elliot 2016a; Gaibazzi 2012;

2015a; Menin 2015; Schielke 2015). In their narratives my interlocutors' relatives appear to try their best to reach martyrdom despite not knowing whether this is what God has planned for them. In this sense, destiny is conceived as an interaction between human and divine wills, between human action and divine determinism, rather than an elimination of human agency.[14] Predestination, despite coming from elsewhere and being pre-written, needs human action and self-cultivation to be actualised. The future martyrs' actions are thus meant to precipitate their destiny and to realise it rather than to change or to create one of their own, introducing a tension between divine power and human action, between being acted upon by an elsewhere and cultivating themselves.[15]

Hence, the cultivation of the self to become a martyr through pious actions and a readiness to make the ultimate sacrifice cannot change people's fate, but can prepare them to meet their fate. A person's actions can never lead to certain outcomes when dealing with divine power: since, one never knows whether one's actions will lead to martyrdom because it is predetermined before birth, and the ultimate decision, the final calculation, is a divine one. Acting towards becoming a martyr can thus seem like a paradox, since martyrdom is something that only comes from God, yet must be cultivated.[16] Here, although one cannot choose to be a martyr, since it is something written before birth, one should, however, act like a martyr in order to become one: acting like a martyr or working towards martyrdom is understood as actualising destiny rather than creating it.

But how can one be sure that one is not modifying one's date of death by acting as a martyr? There appears to be a fine line between legitimate self-sacrifice leading to martyrdom, and suicide – a grave sin in Islam (see Hamdy 2009; Pandolfo 2007). This debate over destiny and the possibility of changing it is important in order to understand my interlocutors' desire and preparations for being and becoming a martyr (that is, for self-sacrifice) without altering their destiny – in other words, sacrificing oneself without killing oneself.[17] The most widespread understanding of martyrdom among my friends and interlocutors was linked to the knowledge that one should not put oneself in situations where death is unavoidable, as this would alter one's destiny by changing one's time of death. The difference between the two was hotly debated among my interlocutors. What was acceptable danger and what was not? In the context of violent repression and war in which death lurks everywhere, what was the difference between a dangerous situation – in which, if it were so ordained, one would die at the appointed hour without modifying destiny – and a suicidal situation in which death was inevitable, thereby interfering with destiny?

The debate over martyrdom and suicide was linked to several questions among the Syrians I lived with. Can God's plan be altered? Are there actions that might change one's foreordained time of death? Moreover, by embarking on a perilous journey, does one accomplish or oppose God's plan?[18] As I show below, my interlocutors argued the pros and cons of staying in or leaving their homes and countries, and over their understanding of self-sacrifice as martyrdom or suicide when they discussed fellow Syrians fleeing, staying under the bombs, or joining the armed struggle.

Attempting to explain this difference, Umm Ahmad used her own story to illustrate this fine line. She described how she fled Syria with her family after her male relatives became wanted by Daesh for having participated in the revolution.[19] She added that although they had lived for many years under indiscriminate shelling, which meant that death had been a strong possibility, there had however been a chance of survival. It was thus not destiny-altering to live under shellfire in one's own home, as death would not come before its appointed hour, echoing the often repeated sentence, 'One will die wherever one is when one's time comes'. However, after Daesh had established a checkpoint just outside Umm Ahmad's home, she said that they had to flee. Staying in this house would have been suicide as it meant certain arrest and the death sentence for the males of the family. The fine line between destined death and suicide is thus drawn between certain and uncertain death, necessary and unnecessary risks. This is why the family fled to Turkey for they were sure that the men would be arrested and killed by Daesh if they stayed.

If, for some, accepting one's possible self-sacrifice for the revolution turned to a longing for martyrdom, not all my interlocutors deeply involved in the revolution believed they were destined to be martyrs, longed for it, nor acted to become martyrs. This state of mind was expressed through choosing different fields of activity, different places of residence and different modes of operation. Yassar once laughingly said in a gathering, 'we knew we were not good enough to be martyrs!', meaning that he and his group of friends were not 'pious enough' to become martyrs.

Yassar, who regularly entered Syria's liberated areas, explained his relation to death, sacrifice, and revolutionary action in the following terms.

> We went to protest and we knew we could die. Then we went to the
> liberated areas to protest and later to live there and we knew we

could die too. And now I go inside Syria and yes it is very dangerous. But I don't do it the same way: I am very much prepared, I plan everything in its smallest details … I believe that the revolution is worth dying for. I knew all the risks from the beginning, which is why when I woke up after my injury I was smiling. I knew this could happen and I didn't regret any of the things I did although this injury meant I would never be able to live the way I did before the revolution … But if I were to do it all over again, I would do it the same way.

The places where Yassar was going were often under intense shelling but this did not stop him from going there frequently despite knowing that the chance of dying was high (see Chapter 2). He had already escaped death several times: during his violent detention at the hands of the regime, and while he was gravely injured by a shell that killed the people standing around him.

Yassar, who as the son of a local sheikh and Islamic scholar had a pious upbringing, but defined himself as secular, explained his survival of the shell that killed those nearby and left him injured as something incomprehensible and, because he could not make sense of it, he said that only divine intervention could explain it. 'When, despite all your efforts to succeed or to reach something, you are stuck, this is where you can see destiny,' he once told me. Something that could not be explained, such as his miracle survival, was a sign of God's presence and of a predetermined destiny. After he survived the shelling, he became intimately convinced that if he had survived the shell, he was not destined to die in the revolution. Yet this did not mean that he put himself into inescapable dangers. On the contrary, he was now preparing his trips to Syria very carefully. Here, the feeling that one's destiny is not to be a martyr also leads to another kind of work on oneself, and another orientation of one's activities. As with precipitating the meeting with one's destiny as a martyr, work is required to actualise this other desired destiny.[20]

The belief that destiny is pre-written incites rather than cancels human actions. Fulfilling or meeting one's destiny is actually inseparable from journeying, since one has to navigate an unpredictable world full of potentialities (see Gaibazzi 2015). In the case of displaced Syrian revolutionaries, fulfilling their destiny meant continuing their struggle – continuing to fight for their 'cause' – hence their continuing to enter Syria despite the high risk of arrest and death. If dying as a martyr was a strong possibility for which they prepared themselves through their actions, then surviving the revolution was also a possible destiny, and putting oneself in unnecessary danger could mean thwarting one's predestined path.

Martyrdom was a possibility that one should be ready for, yet even when they acted towards becoming a martyr, the revolutionaries knew it was not in their hands, and, therefore, that they should carefully stay on the side of martyred self-sacrifice rather than of suicide (see Abu Zein's story in Chapter 2).

## Predestination as a theory of political action

> When someone is created, his destiny is written: it is written how long he will live, if his life will be happy, what his work will be, how many children he will have. God has written how everyone will live his life. Everything that happened with me was written even before I was born. Before anyone is born, God has written what will happen in his life.

Umm Ahmad once said this to me in an attempt to explain what she meant by *maktub* (written/destiny) as I sat next to her with her daughter, Sara, while sipping coffee. Her words reflected a rather widespread definition among my interlocutors, although there were many arguments about the extent of what is pre-written. This debate was shaped around several questions: Does destiny only fix one's day of birth and life or is everything one does pre-written? Are decisions and actions determined by a divine power or chosen by a free human agent? Moreover, what about collective actions: are only individual lives pre-written or is history's course also pre-written? These questions push one to explore the ways in which my interlocutors make sense of the series of unexpected and unpredictable transformations that resulted from revolutionary actions and events, describing how they explain the revolution, its violent repression (on a collective and individual scale), its defeat, and the tragic consequences in their lives.

> Everything that is happening in Syria was written by God! You could ask where the good is in what's happening in Syria now. For a long time, there have been millions of reasons for the revolution to happen. Why did it happen now? This was written! Everything is written. The people who are going to Europe, the ones who die at sea, everything!

Sara, who usually listened in silence to her mother's stories, intervened as our conversation turned to the understanding of the revolution as a foreordained event. The question of the extension of destiny from the individual to collective, and the intimate to historical scales was a point of debate for many of my more pious interlocutors, as it came to theological questions about freedom, agency and history. They asked whether they entered freely into the revolution or if it was predetermined. They raised questions about the revolution itself: Was it an act of human or divine will? Was the revolution pre-written, the same as one's life? Furthermore, how could one make sense of the revolution's failure as part of a divine plan? These questions deepen the understanding of the links between human agency and freedom, divine predestination, and the consequences of political actions and events. During this conversation, I asked how human freedom should be positioned in relation to predestination. Umm Ahmad answered by rhetorically asking: 'If humans made no choices and decisions, why would there be the need for a final judgement?' 'The only reason for Judgement Day is that even if destiny is pre-written people still choose between good and evil actions along the path designed by God', Sara suggested, reflecting the Ashari school's understanding of destiny.

Sara later reformulated the relation between divine destiny and human agency in metaphoric terms:

> There is choice because you don't know that this will happen so you still choose. It's like a film. You are a spectator and God is the one who wrote it. You have the choice to watch it or stop watching it.

In this interpretation, destiny appears as a way to understand what it means for humans to act as a moral category that directs how one acts, or a moral orientation of time (see Schielke 2015: 220–3). Rather than providing them with a fixed route or a fatalistic approach to life, destiny helped my interlocutors make sense of their actions in an uncertain world. This is what led them to get involved with and pursue their involvement in the revolution: in order to meet their destiny, they had to fight against oppression within the frame drawn by their desired destiny. They thus had the choice to protest or stay home, to be involved in peaceful or armed actions, and so on. Participating in the revolution was therefore a matter of free will.

However, if we go back to Umm Ahmad's first words – 'Everything that is happening in Syria was written by God' – destiny seems to become not only a theory of revolutionary actions but also a theory of revolutionary events. If one follows Umm Ahmad's description of continuity between the individual and collective scales when it comes to destiny, it seems that, as with Mittermaier's Sufi interlocutors, 'even a hypervisible, activist-driven event such as the uprising is enfolded in *al-ghayb* as God moved the people … the uprising was driven by a divine force; history is only seemingly made by humans' (2019: 19). Drawing on Umm Ahmad's words, I argue that destiny becomes a theory of revolutionary action in the Syrian context. I thus expand Samuli Schielke's definition of destiny as a theory of action – a theory of the unintended consequences of people's actions in a world that people do not control (2015) – translating it to a different scale: that of politico-historical events. Destiny, as a theory of action, is closely tied to interrogations of the consequences of political actions, since for most of my interlocutors there was a tendency to understand both revolutionaries' deaths and the revolution's defeat as predestined.

## Revolution's destiny

But extending the understanding of individual predestination to a collective and historical scale – to political events and the course of history – did not go unproblematised for my interlocutors; on the contrary, it was a topic of complex debate for many. Towards the end of my fieldwork, in spring 2016, facing an increasingly obvious defeat, my interlocutors had doubts about the revolution's success. Bringing individual and collective losses together and regarding the consequences of the revolution on her own life, Umm Khaled concluded: 'In the end I say that this is what God wrote for us and that nothing is up to us'. She later added: 'Everybody is against us! No one wants the revolution to succeed. I hope my son and husband didn't die in vain'. 'Let his death not be for nothing!' was a sentence often repeated by the martyrs' relatives who profoundly hoped that their sacrifice would eventually lead to the success of the revolution.

If the fact that they had martyrs seemed to indicate the righteousness of their cause, how could my interlocutors make sense of the revolution's defeat? The revolution's violent repression, its setbacks and its final defeat were broadly understood by my interlocutors as a divine test at a collective scale, in the same way as the martyrdom of loved ones were at an individual scale. Rather than weakening faith, this unexpected outcome of their political struggle had the effect of deepening and strengthening the faith of martyrs' widows and mothers, since it was understood as a test from God. Women, in particular, had to cultivate resilience (*sumud*) and patience (*saber*) (see Chapters 2 and 5). But the revolution's defeat also sent the revolution's end(ing) and the hope for justice for those killed to another time and another form of justice: the afterlife and the divine.

When something like what happened to me happens to you, you need to be patient [*tsburi*], because this is what God has written, and it is not up to you. This is my destiny [*qadari*], this is *qada wa qadar* [destiny]. You need to get used to it.

Umm Ahmad, nicknamed Umm Saber (mother of patience) by fellow Syrians, often repeated that patience is required in order to accept a destiny such as hers. She saw the loss of three of her sons as a series of hardships that God had put in her way, which she understood as a test of her faith (*iman*) that actually led to its strengthening, whereas others would see this as a sign of absence of divine justice and a deep shaking of their beliefs. She was certain that there was a reason behind what happened to her, but a divine one: one that she could not understand yet and now, but which would be revealed to her on Judgement Day.

My second visit to the field in the summer of 2014 coincided with the Israeli attack on Gaza, which prompted some of my interlocutors to say that this could, and for some must, be a sign of the 'end times'. They understood the concurrence of the Gaza and Syrian wars as the fulfilment of a Hadith announcing that in the end times there would be a war in the Levant between Muslims and Jews, and later a war of all nations against Muslims.[21] Commenting on the links between the end of time, predestination and the Syrian revolution, Umm Ahmad said:

In one of the Hadiths it is written that there will be a war in Palestine at the end of times. It is also mentioned that there will be a war in Ghouta during the same period.

These kinds of comments were mainly made by my pious interlocutors and resonate with the understanding of destiny as a theory of action and its consequences (Schielke 2015) that would make sense on a collective rather than individual scale. Here destiny appears as a reminder that after one has done one's share, the outcomes of one's actions are no longer in one's own hands and must simply be accepted (Gaibazzi 2015; Schielke 2015). My ethnography shows that this principle is particularly acute in the case of revolutionary action, for the imminence of positive or negative endings renders action urgent and intimately linked to human freedom.

I thus argue that destiny can be understood as a theory of individual and collective political actions and their tragic outcomes. In other words, destiny appears as a theory that helps make sense of the unintended results of political actions and events. In this sense, looking at revolution through the lens of predestination means making sense of revolution's unexpected consequences for, as in the case of individual actions and destiny, the future always remains an unreached horizon and always unfolds differently than it was expected to. Revolution can thus be understood through destiny (as a theory of collective political action), for political action is particularly susceptible to failure: it rarely goes as it was expected to. This line of thinking resonates with David Scott's work (2014) on the failed Grenada revolution, in which he shows that the ineradicable contingency of revolutionary action makes it especially prone to tragic (unexpected) consequences. Drawing on Bradley's paradox of human action in time – 'that men start a course of events but can neither calculate nor control it' (1991: 31) – Scott shows that political action often has tragic outcomes as they almost never meet actors' expectations. In the Syrian context, these tragic outcomes of political actions are being read through destiny understood as a theory of human action and political events. Both their aims continuously appear as horizons that remain unattainable, and those who try to reach them are inevitably left facing unexpected results.

But looking at revolution through destiny also means understanding revolution as being oriented towards a pre-written yet unknown future which leads to a reimagining of revolution from the perspective of the end of times. This invites us to rethink what the temporality of political action means. Here again, my interlocutors' understanding of the temporality of political action through predetermined futures and endings does echo Scott's conclusion on the Grenada revolution's failure in relation to time and temporality: this failure provoked 'an accentuated experience of temporality, of time as *conspicuous*' (2014: 2; emphasis original). As I show in Chapters 1 and 4, the experience and meaning of modern historical time is challenged in the aftermaths of the Syrian revolution and particularly in the aftermaths of its defeat, for history is experienced as cyclical rather than linear and the time is experienced as out-of-joint and punctuated rather than cumulative, progressive and oriented in a unique direction (see Scott 2014: 5–7; Ghamari-Tabrizi 2016).

Understood through Islamic cosmology, the experience of historical time is thus interpreted by some of my interlocutors as predetermined: the revolution's defeat is perceived as having a divine meaning that will be uncovered on Judgement Day. But by casting revolution within a cosmological time, its defeat is not necessarily seen as tragic, nor are the deaths of revolutionaries. Although I have shown that my friends' and interlocutors' feelings towards the revolution's and revolutionaries' endings are ambivalent, they were broadly understood as part of a divine plan. Here, revolutionary time and action are oriented towards personal and collective destinies that appear as individual and cosmological endings.

## Living in the midst of defeat: cultivating patience and faith, and hoping for a better future

Reflecting on the numerous martyrs and the revolution's defeat, Umm Khaled said: 'There is nothing else but to say "*ya rab*" [oh Lord], God is one. We need patience, patience.' This reflects two temporalities of destiny: it was an urge to act to precipitate one's destiny in the revolution's first years, and it became a tool to reflect on revolutionary actions and events after the revolution's defeat. Moreover, although there is no agreement among my interlocutors over the extent of predestination at the individual and collective scales, there was a common understanding that when things are unintelligible to human minds, there is always a divine plan. 'You may not understand today or tomorrow but eventually God will reveal why you went through everything you did', as a friend worded it in a Facebook post at the time of violent attacks on her hometown in Ghouta. While my interlocutors did not concur and sometimes did not know which parts of individual and collective paths were predestined, there was a consensus that there must be a reason behind the unexpected outcomes of individual and collective actions, and behind the unexpected course of history and the unfolding of revolutionary events. Most believed that God was actually testing them through these sacrifices and defeats, and that they should place and renew their faith in God. Only God knew what was happening, but there was meaning in all of this that would eventually be revealed.

Ideas and practices central to revolutionary process are thus reconfigured in light of Islamic predestination and martyrdom: revolutionary actions are urgent in a context where collective and individual endings are imminent. In this context, revolutionary actions appear as an anticipation of destiny; revolutionary actors hope to actualise a predetermined future in the revolutionary present and to meet desired endings. Furthermore, destiny becomes a moral frame to revolutionary actions and a theory to understand *ex post facto*[22] the unexpected consequences of collective and personal actions and events. Ultimately, the linear chronology of history is replaced by a cosmological non-linear time in which the failed revolution's tragic outcome is understood in light of Judgement Day and God's unknown calculation.

To come back to the figure of the witness, the *shaheed*, it is both a historical and cosmological figure in the Syrian context: it brings together historical and apocalyptic endings, utopian and prophetic temporalities. The aftermaths of the defeated revolution thus resonate with the afterlife and with the apocalyptic ending of the world. In this sense, this chapter is an attempt not only to map out the ways in which 'the invisible can make history', but also to retrace historical and cosmological events through the invisible. This contributes to showing 'how attending to invisible actors can open up new ways for thinking about memory, history, and violence' (Mittermaier 2019: 28). Moreover, it demonstrates how history and violence appear through the absence/presence of disappeared actors and witnesses. This ultimately means asking how unknown and invisible revolutionary events, actions and actors can inflect and create an anthropology of defeat. Indeed, with the revolution's defeat, historical and cosmological times seem to be colluding. This is very much visible in the figure of the *shaheed* – both the historical witness in front of other humans and the cosmological witness in front of God. In both cases, the *shaheed* needs to present proof of the crimes committed against them. In fact, both survivors and martyrs 'carry history on themselves, since they are a physical embodiment, a historical relation carried on the self' (Trouillot 1995: 149). The coexistence or co-absence of these two kinds of witnesses can be understood as a 'heterotemporality' (Chakrabarty, in Mittermaier 2012: 395). In the Syrian case, that means writing the history of the revolution in a way that brings together cosmological (pre-written/predestined) history and secular history.

In tracing the Syrian revolution through witnesses' (*shuhada'*) testimonies, I aimed to not reify *al-ghayb* but rather to let it inflect my writing and theorising, thus taking my cue from Mittermaier (2019). It led me to attempt to account for mass political violence and its history beyond the framework and language imposed by the Enlightenment frame and leave space in stories of the Syrian uprising and revolution for the invisible and the absent (whether it be God, predestination, martyrs or dream-visions). This, in other terms, allows different temporal frames to coexist, forming a 'temporal multiplicity' (Ssorin-Chaikov 2017) in which different histories and times replace one another and change over time, and according to my interlocutors. In this chapter, destiny thus appears not only as a cosmological but also as a moral frame of revolutionary actions, as well as providing an *ex post facto* theory of the revolution's defeat and the course of history. I thus argue that the Islamic concept of predestination can be understood as a theory of individual and collective political actions and their tragic outcomes. In other words, it helps to clarify Syrians' understanding – through the lens of Islam – of the ruptures and disruptions that marked their lives during and in the aftermath of the revolution.

# Notes

1  Most of my interlocutors understood the violent repression of the revolution, forced displacement, personal losses, and war through Islamic narratives and concepts, although some also mobilise non-religious explanatory frameworks to make sense of violent and premature death, the halting of revolution, and individual and collective hardships (see Proudfoot 2022 on non-religious understandings of martyrdom). Some chose secular or 'scientific' narratives while others prefer conspiracy theories to explain the events they have witnessed.

2  This has been similarly studied in the Palestinian and Iranian contexts (e.g. Ghamari-Tabrizi 2016; Khalili 2007; Peteet 1994), in which revolutionaries come from diverse political and religious paths; the figure of the *shaheed* is central to political actions in the context of mass violence.

3  Secret mass graves, absence of bodies and destruction of bodies are common in Assad's Syria. See Weizmal (2019) on Sednaya's crematorium and Munif (2020) on necropolitics in Syria.

4  For instance some of *rif dimashq* towns were bombed to the ground after their forced evacuation. See Vignal (2021) on destruction and Munif (2020) on urbicide.

5  This has been the case in trials against Syrian officials condemned for crimes against humanity in Germany.

6  Martyrdom has been most famously studied in the context of political violence (e.g. Asad 2007; Cook 2007; Mitchell 2012; Shalinksy 1993) and, more specifically, in order to understand suicide bombing as a form of self-sacrifice (see for instance Asad 2007; Naaman 2007). The texts belonging to the 'discursive tradition' of the anthropology of Islam derive their understanding of martyrdom from their interpretation of the Quran and the Hadith. Talal Asad's study on suicide bombing is a classic example of this tradition, in which he develops the religious definitions of martyrdom through his reading of the Quran (2007). A number of studies researching the Palestinian situation offer more secular ways to make sense of self-sacrifice (e.g. Allen 2006; 2009; Hage 2003; Khalili 2006), and in other contexts have adopted an approach closer to the anthropology of Islam's 'lived tradition' (e.g. Ghannam 2014; Mittermaier 2015; Pandolfo 2007). There are also more recent studies of martyrdom in the context of the Arab Revolutions that argue that 'engagement with death, martyrdom, and afterlife is indispensable if we want to understand the making of pasts and futures in a revolutionary present' (Mittermaier 2015: 583; see also Ghannam 2014; Bandak 2015; Ramzy 2015; Rozen 2015; Gilman 2015).

7  A fatwa was issued in the liberated areas making those dying under the rubble of their houses *shuhada' al dunia* for, although they did not directly fight against the regime, they were seen as similarly resisting and sacrificing their lives in the fight. This was, at the same time, a pragmatic response to the high number of people dying in shelling (something for which there is obviously no direct reference in the Quran or Hadith), according to Ahmad, a doctor working in the liberated areas before being displaced to Gaziantep.

8  See Pandolfo 2007; Mittermaier 2015; Rozen 2015; Willerslev 2009 on this topic.

9  See Farha Ghannam's work on the performative effects of death narratives in the Egyptian context (2014).

10  This was quite unlike the use of pictures of martyrs in the Palestinian context, which were those taken in life and displayed in Palestinian homes and towns (cf. Allen 2006; Buch 2010; Khalili 2007).

11  See Surah N.2 Al Baqr. Ayat N. 154.

12  See also Ramzy (2015) on the meaning of martyrdom for Egyptian Copts and its understanding as being more valuable than life itself.

13  See also Mittermaier (2011; 2013) on the necessity to cultivate oneself to receive dreams but the impossibility to make them happen through such cultivation.

14  The various understandings of their articulations have led authors to comprehend destiny in radically different ways. In his project of defining Protestant destiny, Max Weber (1996) contrasts it with the Islamic version. In his writing, Islamic destiny is understood as fatalism: a 'well-rounded, metaphysically satisfying conception of the world' (Weber 1996: 132). In other words, it is the belief that human destiny, actions, and outcomes are controlled by metaphysical forces. In this understanding of fatalism, while humans cannot control the outcomes of their actions, they can nonetheless inflect their identity 'by being virtuous, carrying God's will, or accumulating merit' (Elder 1966: 228). Yet conceiving of destiny as fatalism implies a radical lack of human agency and portrays Muslim subjects as inactive and submissive. The clash of

civilisations scholarship builds on Weber's (1991, originally published 1922) opposition between Christian predestination as leaving space for the exercise of free will, and Islamic predestination defined as an irrational form of fatalism (summarised in Acevedo 2008). Huntington (1996), Fukuyama (1992), and Lewis (1993) portray Islam in a caricatured way as a fatalistic religion and world view, describing Islamic destiny as going against self-empowerment and individualism and as 'plac[ing] the burden of life's outcomes at the hands of omnipotent, metaphysical forces' (Acevedo 2008: 1712). The basic theory of these authors is that Muslim individuals believe that they do not have control over their lives and actions, as they believe this control belongs to a sacred authority. They define Islam as requiring obedience to cosmological forces, and as an absence of personal freedom and agency. In fact, they conflate the idea of Islamic predestination with fatalism and submission. To Acevedo, however, the primary error in interpreting Islam as a fatalistic religion is 'in not properly addressing the cosmologically oriented dimensions of personal efficacy and the reliance that individuals may place on metaphysical powers to determine worldly outcomes' (Acevedo 2008: 1740). The Islamic conception of destiny is thus an interaction between humans' and God's will, between human action and divine determinism, rather than an elimination of human agency.

15  A similar tension between a life predestined by a divine power and the necessity to work to meet what has been pre-written is explored in Alice Elliot's Moroccan women seeking to meet their destined spouses (2016a).

16  In her article on dream-visions in a Cairene Sufi circle, Amira Mittermaier (2012) explains a similar idea – that divine dreams do not happen without any action on the part of the dreamer; even though the dreamer does not produce the dream, she should, however, prepare herself to receive it. Self-cultivation is part of receiving a divine dream, although the dreamer cannot trigger it solely by her action as it depends only on God's will.

17  This recalls the debate over migration among Moroccan youth, in which they ask themselves whether risking one's life to cross the Mediterranean and reach Europe is suicide or jihad (personal struggle understood as a form of self-cultivation) (Pandolfo 2007).

18  These are questions that the literature on illness, migration, and death explores in detail. For instance, Hamdy (2009) highlights the fear her interlocutors had of interfering with their destiny and modifying their time of death by seeking or not seeking treatment: seeking or refusing treatment could both thwart God's plan and lead one to modify one's destiny by potentially lengthening or shortening one's life, as God's will and one's own destiny are unknowable.

19  See Chapter 1 for an explanation of relations between Daesh and the Syrian regime.

20  This resonates with Paolo Gaibazzi's study of Gambian Soninke men (2012; 2015) where he describes the young men's aspiration to migrate as being closely related to ideas of destiny that nonetheless do not lead to a fatalistic waiting for their destiny to realise itself by itself, but rather to a series of actions to realise their desired destiny.

21  See Mittermaier (2012) on religious interpretations of historical events.

22  I borrow the use of this phrase in this context from Gaibazzi 2015.

**Figure 7.1:** The revolution a decade on. © Ali Haj Suleiman

# Conclusion: rescaling the revolution

'*Suriyya khalas*' (Syria is over) Umm Yazan told me with tears in her eyes as we took a break from packing and sat on her balcony enjoying the fresh breeze after a long, hot summer day. It was August 2015 and I had received a message from her that morning telling me that all her family were leaving the next day for İzmir. She added that we would probably not meet again. When I asked why, she mysteriously texted back, 'I don't know'. I asked if she was going to cross to Europe (İzmir is the place where most Syrians embarked in the rubber boats that took them to the Greek islands). 'Come, we will speak,' she answered. On my way to her place I tried to make sense of her message. Umm Yazan's daughter Maya and her fiancé were supposed to be crossing the Mediterranean soon, but Umm Yazan had never mentioned that she was thinking of leaving as well. After her plans to go back to Syria's liberated areas with her daughter Nour and her family failed, she seemed to have settled on staying in Turkey while waiting for her husband to join her.

When I arrived at her place Umm Yazan was sitting on her bed facing a chest of drawers. She was preparing to leave the house. She tied a *qumteh* (the piece of fabric women put under their hijab) around her neck and pulled it back over her head to keep her hair in place. She took one of her light scarves and folded it over her head before fixing it under her chin with a pin that she had kept between her lips during this process. Taking the small wooden stick from a pot of black *henneh*, she rapidly drew a line along her eyelid. She then reached for two boxes, each containing a set of jewellery: a necklace, a ring, earrings, and a bracelet. She put them deep into her handbag. Answering my question she explained, 'This is Sara's wedding jewellery from her first marriage. I'm going to sell it in the *carci* ['market' in Turkish]. I'm expecting 400 dollars from this one and 200 dollars from that one; this is all gold. Sara's first husband was a very rich man!'

As Umm Yazan left the flat, her daughters Maya and Nour, who had already begun packing, explained that their mother had suddenly decided to leave and go with Nour and her husband to İzmir. Maya and her fiancé were preparing to cross the Mediterranean and Umm Yazan did not want to stay alone in Gaziantep. I started to help Maya and Nour. As we made our way between the piles of clothes, suitcases, and garbage bags full of shoes and other accessories, Maya lamented: 'We had to leave everything behind in Syria, and now we have to do it all over again.' Not only the flat and their belongings but their lives seemed to have been turned upside down as they were forced to give up, to surrender and definitively leave what they had first thought would be a temporary location while waiting to return to their hometown. As we were emptying the closets in Maya's room, Nour cursed Bashar, 'Ya ibn al-kalb!' (son of a dog). She cursed him for putting them in this situation, and then for not allowing them the choice of staying or going back. Nour understood her family's forced departure as a continuation of Assad's strategy of making Sunni families flee their city and their land, and had no regret concerning the revolution or its militarisation. 'Bashar only understands force', she said.

Packing up their clothes brought back many memories. As Raya joined us, she also went through the piles to see if she had left any behind when she got married. She suddenly caught sight of some black trousers her sisters had put to one side. They had holes here and there from sitting in them for several months, but this did not affect her enthusiasm. 'Do you remember those trousers?!' she exclaimed. 'Those are the trousers I was wearing while I was in jail! Aren't they? [Addressing Nour:] Look at those trousers! Aren't those the trousers you and mum brought me in jail?' She moved them to the pile of clothes she wanted to take with her. Later on, after her mother came back from the 'gold market', Raya ran to her mother's bedroom to show her the trousers. She wanted to be sure they were the pair her mother had brought her in jail. Raya became very emotional as the piece of clothing awoke memories: of the beginning of the revolution, of detention, of a time when they still hoped the revolution could succeed. Just as Umm Yazan was turning her back on Syria and the revolution, when they were trying to forget the past to start new lives elsewhere, the past was coming back to them, carried by the various items they came across. Later, when we were taking a couple of bags out of a cupboard, Nour found keys in one of the bags she wanted to take with her. Nour and Maya laughed. 'Those are the keys to our house in Syria,' Maya said, turning to me. They put them to one side. 'Keep them with you,' Maya said to Nour, who was staying in Turkey. 'Insha'allah we will open this door again!'

We interrupted the packing to prepare dinner and I sat in the kitchen peeling vegetables with Nour. Her husband, who was sitting on the balcony, asked me if I wanted to join him to see videos of his 'work' (*sheghel*). I agreed. I did not realise he meant 'revolutionary work' (*sheghel b-thawra*). In Syria he had been a fighter and used to document the fighting, destruction, and massacres. We sat next to one another on the balcony and he started to show me short videoclips. As we watched them he pointed at the people he had fought alongside who were appearing on the screen. He slowly gave their war names and told me their fate: 'Martyred, martyred, also martyred, martyred …' The list of martyrs was very long; only two of his comrades were still alive, either fighting or injured. He explained that he was still planning to go back, expressing his disapproval of his mother-in-law's intention to flee further, which he perceived as fulfilling the wishes of the Assad regime. Umm Yazan, who had joined us on the balcony, commented with a bitter laugh: 'I cannot go back unless Assad leaves. It's either me or him! We cannot live in the same country. Not anymore!' Umm Yazan had lost hope in the revolution and in a future in Syria. Starting a monologue she said:

> I don't know what's going on in Syria right now. The revolution was not like this. This is not our revolution. This is a war not a revolution! Now everybody is fighting everybody … A revolution is between the people and the regime, but now there are too many states fighting in Syria. This is not our revolution; look how many countries are fighting in Syria? … What's the reason for these countries fighting in Syria? Why are the Iranians and Russians fighting in Syria? Why?! We didn't want a war. I'm not saying that a revolution should be peaceful, but we didn't want a war! We started with peaceful demonstration.

The next morning, Umm Yazan's decision was made. She had been informed during the night that a group of Raya's friends were planning to cross the Mediterranean and she had decided that she would join them with her youngest daughter and try to reach Sara, who had settled in Germany. It was not only the loss of the revolutionary horizon, and of hope in a future in Syria, that encouraged her to flee further. It was also the fact that in Germany she saw the chance to reconstitute a *beit* with her daughter's family and her son (see Chapter 5), whereas the degrading conditions in Turkey were an obstacle to her desire to settle in the country more permanently. Furthermore, she had recently lost her job and would soon not be able to pay the increasing rent on her flat (see Chapter 3).

She sat on her bed in her prayer clothes, only taking off the upper part; she was too busy to take off the bottom layer. She was trying to organise her personal belongings, emptying her chest of drawers and the little bedside table. She held a pocket-size Quran in her hands, not knowing what to do with it. It was the Quran she read from every morning, and she could not imagine leaving it behind, but it was also too precious to risk losing it or getting it ruined with seawater. She decided not to take it, but, thinking of the need to have a copy of the holy text with her, she said she could download a PDF file of the Quran onto her phone to protect her during the perilous journey. Umm Yazan held a small rucksack between her legs in which she was trying to organise everything; it all had to fit into this single bag as she would not be allowed to embark with anything more. She turned to her prayer carpet, which would probably not fit, so she opted for a scarf she had never worn and could therefore use to pray on.

As I was about to leave their flat, Umm Yazan insisted that I take a black handbag she wanted me to have to remember her by. As she gave it to me I opened it to make sure it was empty, remembering the keys that were found in one of the bags the day before. Inside the bag I found a little green packet containing a very small piece of paper with printed writing. Umm Yazan screamed with joy: 'Give it to me! This is the verse for travellers.' She seemed happy and relieved that she had found a copy of the holy text she could easily carry with her. 'This is to protect travellers!' she said in a joyful voice. It must have been a bag that one of her daughters had carried when travelling to Turkey, the verse placed inside it to protect her.

## Of ruptures, disruptions and continuities

This book has explored the effects of a series of ruptures and disruptions that the Syrian revolution and its repression has imposed on Syrians' lifeworlds. Tracing the intended, unexpected, and tragic consequences of the events that began in 2011, it has demonstrated that, despite its defeat in the political field at the scale of the nation-state, the Syrian revolution has been a powerful transformative entity that has affected Syrians' lives and world in multi-scalar and multi-dimensional ways. In other words, *al-thawra* appears as a cosmogonic or world-making force.

The ruptures and disruptions enacted and witnessed by Syrians have been primarily of a spatio-temporal nature. If the initial events can be said to have generated a temporal rupture within Syrians' collective history and personal genealogies – although inscribed within the continuity of Syria's contentious politics on the *longue durée* (Chapter 1) – its effects, in the first phase of the uprising and in the initial phase of my fieldwork (when the Syrian–Turkish border was still open), have been mainly spatial. The brutal repression of the uprising quickly led to a series of spatial ruptures and disruptions that created a novel geography and new relations with space, establishing various insides through the liberation of some parts of Syria and a division between inside (*juwwa*) and outside (*barra*) through enforced displacement. Such spatial phenomena had repercussions on the intimate scale: new kinds of subjects appeared as a sense of revolutionary self emerged and was cultivated through movement between inside (*juwwa*) and outside (*barra*) (Chapter 2). This spatial reconfiguration also had an impact on Syrians' everyday lives, as they were cut off from inside after the EU–Turkey deal (after which the Syrian–Turkish border closed), and as they found themselves living an increasingly uncertain and precarious life as *diyuf* (guests) in Gaziantep (Chapter 3). The reshaping of Syrians' geography did not only have intimate and daily effects, it also had temporal effects: displacement in the aftermath of a thwarted revolution was experienced as a suspended present stuck between a utopian and heroic past (the revolutionary time inside – *juwwa*) and a tragic future in which the only hope lies in a different (that is, successful) repetition of the past (Chapter 4). The series of intended and unexpected consequences that marked Syrians' lifeworlds as a result of spatio-temporal ruptures and disruptions also inflected Syrians' social relations, roles, and norms. *Barra* (outside), the defeated revolution was experienced as a revolutionary process that, despite failing politically, had concrete impacts on the social domain. The revolution was thus reframed in its aftermath and in the *longue durée* as a social upheaval (Chapter 5). Yet how has this phenomenon, which led to a multiplicity of spatio-temporal reconfigurations, been grasped by my interlocutors? The cosmological concepts of destiny and martyrdom have had a central role in rescaling the revolution's defeat within a larger, divine, spatio-temporal frame, helping to make sense of it (Chapter 6).

## An ethnographic archive?

But perhaps this book ends up doing something slightly different from what it had first aimed to. Despite an increasing number of academic publications and artistic productions[1], there has been an 'invisibilisation' or 'erasure' (Trouillot 1995: 95) of the Syrian non-violent revolutionary moment through wide media coverage framing the events as a civil war and an endless conflict. If there has been a hypervisibility of certain forms of violence, usually highly orchestrated murders by jihadi groups, there is simultaneously a corresponding invisibilisation of the peaceful revolutionary movement, legacy, and its ferocious repression by the Assad regime. This is a paradox since the horror of the revolution's repression is reported by millions of images and videos (Boëx and Devictor 2021) of the destruction, the sieges, the victims of chemical weapons, and Syrians tortured and killed in Assad's jails, which seem to constitute 'formulas of erasure' or 'silence' (Trouillot 1995: 95).

This book can thus also be read as an archive of the invisibilised Syrian revolution – its non-violent and defeated actors: those who mainly opposed the militarisation of the revolution, and the Islamist and jihadi factions that appeared on the ground. It is also an invitation to look at the realities of revolutionary actors and subjects that often appear on the margins: pious and conservative middle-aged housewives. Moreover, and maybe most importantly, through the act of showing what is being invisibilised and forgotten, one can enhance and broaden the collective political imagination in learning from Syrian revolutionary political experience.

The book's main question can thus be reformulated as: What traces does a revolution, its repression, and defeat leave on people's bodies, self, and social and gendered norms, as well as lifeworlds? Such an ethnographic endeavour turns out to be an attempt to locate the silenced revolution's traces in different domains and on various scales of Syrian lifeworlds – in other words, to draw a fragmented picture of the revolution's afterlives through the (re)collection of linguistic, mnemonic, material and bodily marks. It does so through the ethnographic exploration of revolutionary Syrians' stories of involvement in the 2011 revolution and through the recounting of the transformations of their lifeworlds in displacement. Such an ethnography of the Syrian revolution and its defeat can only be fragmentary. This simultaneously suggests the rethinking of anthropologists' methodological tools of enquiry as well as anthropological concepts, and proposes to walk away from an ontology and epistemology inherited from the Enlightenment (Ghamari-Tabrizi 2016; Trouillot 1995) and open up to its subjects' conceptions and perceptions of the invisible *al-ghayb* (Bubandt et al. 2019; Mittermaier 2019).

In this sense this ethnography not only brings ethnographic 'examples' but shows the 'exemplar' experiences of my interlocutors (see Højer and Bandak 2015). In that way it resonates with a wider field of archiving of the revolution – mainly literary, artistic and oral archives (for instance Al-Attar 2013; 2014; 2017; Al-Dik 2016; Al-Haj Saleh 2016b; Al-Kateab 2019;

Coquio et al. 2022; Farah 2021; Fayyad 2019; Mermier 2018; Pearlman 2017; Sulaiman 2018; Yazigi 2018) – that I interpret as being set against the backdrop of this meticulously planned invisibilisation by the Assad regime (see Al-Haj Saleh 2016b; Al-Khalili 2022a; Chehayed and De Vaulx d'Arcy 2021; Munif 2020). I have tried to bring some of this very rich written content, as well as online written content – from Facebook posts to tweets, articles, (self-)published essays, novels and theatre works – into dialogue with my own writing. I am, however, not able to do justice to all the brilliant works published since 2011 given the enormous proportion this corpus has reached since the start of the revolution – a revolution that has also been an explosion of words and a liberation of creativity that has brought about a great development of written and artistic works.

## Revolution's migratory horizons

I finish with a last scene that shows how revolutionary practices are themselves transformed through further exile. In summer 2016 I went to visit a friend, Ahmad, in a camp near Thessaloniki where he was detained for several months after crossing the Mediterranean in the hope of reaching Sweden. Deep in the Greek countryside, I found that Ahmad and his friends – with whom he had lived and worked through the revolution in their besieged neighbourhood and with whom he embarked in a dinghy to reach Greece – had reproduced a similar way of organising life as when they were under siege. Those aged 17 to 27 took it upon themselves to alleviate the hardships of residents' lives by filling the gap left by the camp's administration and the lack of resources deployed in it. The food was of poor quality and insufficient, especially during Ramadan; children were left without school or activities, pregnant women without healthcare, infants and toddlers did not have appropriate clothes, food, or beds, and the camp infrastructure was dilapidated or non-existent. The young people decided to construct a common space with a kitchen where people could bring food or recook the food they had. They also renovated a small house in the middle of the camp where they organised activities and classes for the children, and opened a small infirmary. Most of them had had experience in one of those fields while living under siege: some had been in charge of children's activities, others were trained by nurses and doctors as first aiders, and all of them still had the revolutionary spirit and energy to 'help the people' despite finding themselves in a similarly precarious situation. They also managed to collect donations from Greek volunteers and activists they had met while stuck in Idomeni a couple of months earlier.

The continuation of revolutionary work in and through exile was thus also echoed in refugee camps in Greece. Such an example shows the resilience of the revolutionary spirit within Syrian selves. But such action can only be understood as revolutionary, and as a mark of revolutionary transformation within Syrians' lifeworlds, if one understands revolution as creating a deep rupture within people's selves and a radical shift of their lifeworlds. Ultimately it is yet another illustration of the reconfiguration of revolution as a transformational entity through time and space, one that suggests analysing Syrian refugees' lifeworlds in Europe in relation to the evolving revolutionary process inside Syria. It is also another example of the importance of ethnographically analysing the rich nexus between revolution and migration. In Greece, new spatio-temporal horizons emerged. My interlocutors dreamed of reaching Western Europe, where they imagined they would be treated with dignity, according to impartial laws, and where they would have the chance to live a good life – a life that they imagined to be not unlike the one they dreamed of, and rose up to create, in 2011.

## Notes

1 See Al-Dik 2016; Al-Kateab 2019; Boëx and Pinto 2018; Boissière 2015; Burgat and Paoli 2013a; Farah 2021; Hassabo and Rey 2015; Halasa et al. 2014; Munif 2020; Pearlman 2017; Sulaiman 2018; Suerbaum 2022; Proudfoot 2022.

# References

Abdulhadi, R. 2003. 'Where is home? Fragmented lives, border crossings, and the politics of exile', *Radical History Review* 86: 89–101.

Abu-Lughod, L. 1990. 'The romance of resistance: tracing transformations of power through Bedouin women', *American Ethnologist* 17 (1): 41–55.

Abu-Lughod, L. 1991. 'Writing against culture'. In *Recapturing Anthropology: Working in the present*, edited by R. Fox, 137–62. Santa Fe: School of American Research Press.

Abu-Lughod, L. 2012. 'Living the "revolution" in an Egyptian village: moral action in a national space', *American Ethnologist* 39 (1): 21–5.

Abu-Nahleh, L. 2006. 'Six families: survival and mobility in times of crisis'. In *Living Palestine: Family survival, resistance, and mobility under occupation*, edited by L. Taraki, 103–84. New York: Syracuse University Press.

Acevedo, G. 2008. 'Islamic fatalism and the clash of civilizations: an appraisal of a contentious and dubious theory', *Social Forces* 86 (4): 1711–52.

Achcar, G. 2013. *The People Want: A radical exploration of the Arab uprising*. London: Saqi.

Agamben, G. 1998. *Homo Sacer: Sovereign power and bare life*. Trans. Daniel Heller-Roazen. Stanford: Stanford University Press.

Agamben, G. 2015. *Stasis: Civil war as a political paradigm*. Stanford: Stanford University Press.

Agier, M. 2002. 'Between war and city: towards an urban anthropology of refugee camps', *Sage* 3 (3): 317–41.

Aita, S. 2007. 'L'Economie de la Syrie peut-elle devenir sociale? Vous avez dit "économie sociale de marché?"'. In *La Syrie au présent*, edited by B. Dupret, Z. Ghazzal, Y. Courbage and M. al-Dbiyat, 541–81. Paris: Actes Sud.

Al-Aswad, H. 2020. *I'da'at a'la ba'd a'sbāb fashal al-ṯawra al-sūriyya*. Doha: Harmoon Center for Contemporary Studies.

Al-Attar, M. 2013. *Trojan Women* [film]. https://vimeo.com/266944123.

Al-Attar, M. 2014. *Antigone of Shatila* [film]. https://vimeo.com/130179483.

Al-Attar, M. 2017. *Aleppo: A portrait of an absence*. https://archiv.hkw.de/en/app/mediathek/gallery/why_are_we_here_now_aleppo.

Al-Dik, M. 2016. *A l'Est de Damas, au bout du monde: Témoignage d'un révolutionnaire syrien*. Trans. N. Bontemps. Paris: Don Quichotte.

Al-Haj Saleh, Y. 2015. *Récits d'une Syrie oubliée: Sortir la mémoire des prisons*. Trans. M. Babut and N. Bontemps. Paris: Les Prairies Ordinaires.

Al-Haj Saleh, Y. 2016a. 'La Syrie ne s'est pas démocratisée, c'est le monde qui s'est syrianisé', *Libération*, 9 May. http://www.liberation.fr/debats/2016/05/09/yassin-al-haj-saleh-la-syrie-ne-s-est-pas-democratisee-c-est-le-monde-qui-s-est-syrianise_1451478.

Al-Haj Saleh, Y. 2016b. *La Question syrienne*. Trans. Z. Majed, F. Mardam-Bey and N. L. Aïssaoui. Paris: Actes Sud.

Al-Haj Saleh, Y. 2017a. 'The Palestinization of Syrians', *Aljumhuriya*, 27 June. http://www.yassinhs.com/2017/06/27/the-palestinization-of-syrians/.

Al-Haj Saleh, Y. 2017b. *The Impossible Revolution: Making sense of the Syrian tragedy*. Trans. I. Mahmood. London: Hurst.

Al-Haj Saleh, Y. 2020. 'About dignity and humiliation, and the dignity of the humiliated', Aljumhuriya.net. https://cutt.ly/Nnx2hUO (in Arabic).

Al-Haj Saleh, Y. 2021. *Al-faẓī'a wa tmaṯṯluhu: Mudwalāt fī shakl sūriyyā al-muḥarrab wa tashakkulihā al-'asīr*. Beirut: Dār al-Jadīd.

Al-Kallas, W. and Aubin-Boltanski, E. 2022. 'Refuser d'être complice: nuances de gris en temps de guerre', *Terrain: Anthropologie & sciences humaines* 77: 130–7.

Al-Kateab, W. 2019. *For Sama* [film], ITN Productions, Frontline – WGBH, Chanel 4.

Al-Khalil, S. 2016. *Yawmiyyāt al-ḥiṣār fī Dūmā 2013*. Beirut: Arab Institute for Research and Publishing.

Al-Khalili, C. (as Loris-Rodionoff, C.) 2017a. 'Démocratie rebelle, l'invention des conseils locaux pendant la révolution syrienne', *Vacarme* 79: 48–55.

Al-Khalili, C. (as Florino, M. [pseudonym]) 2017b. 'Récits de Raqqa la nuit', *Vacarme* 79: 58–63.

Al-Khalili, C. (as Loris-Rodionoff, C.) 2018. 'Résistance féminine à Ildeb: itinéraire d'une activiste', *Vacarme* 82: 40–5.

Al-Khalili, C. (as Loris-Rodionoff, C.) 2019. 'Of Revolutionary Transformations: Life in displacement at the Syrian–Turkish border'. PhD thesis. London: UCL. https://discovery.ucl.ac.uk/id/eprint/10071605/.

Al-Khalili, C. 2021. 'Halaqas, relational subjects, and revolutionary committees in Syria', *Focaal: Journal of Global and Historical Anthropology* 91: 50–66.

Al-Khalili, C. 2022a. 'Towards an anthropology of defeat: rethinking the Syrian revolution's aftermaths', *Condition Humaine/Conditions Politiques: Revue internationale d'anthropologie du politique* 4. http://revues.mshparisnord.fr/chcp/index.php?id=888.

Al-Khalili, C. 2022b. 'Destiny in time of revolution: urgent actions and imminent endings', *Social Anthropology/Anthropologie Sociale* 30 (4): 70–89.

Al-Khalili, C. 2023. 'Rescaling hospitality: everyday displacement at the Syrian–Turkish Border', *American Ethnologist* 50 (2): 309–20. https://doi.org/10.1111/amet.13144.

Al-Khalili, C., Ansari, N., Lamrani, M. and Uzel, K. (eds.) 2023. *Revolution beyond the Event: The afterlives of radical politics*. London: UCL Press. https://www.uclpress.co.uk/products/180039.

Al-Mehdi, D. 2019. 'The tribulations, and deportations, of Syrian guests in Turkey', *Refugee Hosts*, 31 July. https://refugeehosts.org/2019/07/31/the-tribulations-and-deportations-of-syrian-guests-in-turkey/.

Al-Om, T. 2018. 'Emergence of the political voice of Syria's civil society: the non-violent movements of the Syrian uprising'. In *The Syrian Uprising: Domestic origins and early trajectory*, edited by R. Hinnebusch and O. Imady, 159–72. New York: Routledge.

Al-Sarraj, M. 2011. *'Aṣr al-dam*. Beirut: Dār al-Adāb.

Al-Zahre, N. 2021. 'De la dignité et de la reconnaissance qui ne vient pas'. In *Mots de chair et de sang: Écrire le corps en Syrie (2011–2021)*, edited by E. Aubin-Boltanski and N. Chehayed, 29–47. Beirut: Presses de L'IFPO.

Alexievich, S. 2016. *Secondhand Time: The last of the Soviets*. New York: Random House.

Alhayek, K. 2015. 'Untold stories of Syrian women surviving war', *Syria Studies* 7 (1): 1–30.

Alkan, H. 2021. 'The gift of hospitality and the (un)welcoming of Syrian migrants in Turkey', *American Ethnologist* 48 (2): 1–12.

Allan, D. 2014. *Refugees of the Revolution: Experiences of Palestinian exile*. Stanford: Stanford University Press.

Allen, L. 2006. 'The polyvalent politics of martyr commemorations in the Palestinian Intifada', *History and Memory* 18 (2): 107–38.

Allen, L. 2008. 'Getting by the occupation: how violence became normal during the second Palestinian Intifada', *Cultural Anthropology* 23 (3): 453–87.

Allen, L. 2009. 'Martyr bodies in the media: human rights, aesthetics, and the politics of immediation in the Palestinian Intifada', *American Ethnologist* 36 (1): 161–80.

Allison, A. 2012. 'Ordinary refugees: social precarity and soul in 21st century Japan', *Anthropological Quarterly* 85 (2): 345–70.

Amar, A. 2021. 'Ṭawratān wa laysat ṭawra wāḥida : kayfa nafhamu al-ṭawra al-sūriyya fī ḏikrāhā al-'ashira?', *Al-jazeera,* 21 March. Accessed 8 May 2023. https://www.aljazeera.net/midan/reality/politics/2021/3/21/قصد-ثورت-ن-اذامل-نيترو-ش-فلت-ا-لثور.

Amnesty International. 2015. 'Syria: "We had nowhere else to go": forced displacement and demolitions in northern Syria'. Accessed 7 May 2023. https://www.amnesty.org/en/documents/mde24/2503/2015/en/.

Anderson, P. 2023. *Exchange Ideologies: Commerce, language, and patriarchy in preconflict Aleppo*. Ithaca, NY: Cornell University Press.

Antoun, R. 1991. 'Ethnicity, clientship, and class: their changing meaning'. In *Syria: Society, culture and polity*, edited by R. Antoun and D. Quataert, 1–13. Albany: State University of New York Press.

Appadurai, A. 2002. 'Deep democracy: urban governmentality and the horizon of politics', *Public Culture* 14 (1): 23–43.

Appadurai, A. 2013. *The Future as a Cultural Fact: Essays on the global condition*. London: Verso.

Arendt, H. 1965. *On Revolution*. New York: Penguin Books.

Aretxaga, B. 1998. *Shattering Silence: Women, nationalism, and political subjectivity in Northern Ireland*. Princeton: Princeton University Press.

Armbrust, W. 2017. 'Trickster defeats the revolution: Egypt as the vanguard of the new authoritarianism', *Middle East Critique* 26 (3): 221–39.

Armbrust, W. 2019. *Martyrs and Tricksters: An ethnography of the Egyptian revolution*. Princeton: Princeton University Press.

Asad, T. 2003. *Formations of the Secular: Christianity, Islam, modernity*. Stanford: Stanford University Press.

Asad, T. 2007. *On Suicide Bombing*. New York: Columbia University Press.

Asad, T. 2018. *Secular Translations: Nation-state, modern self and calculative reason*. New York: Columbia University Press.

Attia, K. 2016. *Réfléchir la mémoire* [film], 48 minutes.

Aubin-Boltanksi, E. and Khalbous, O. 2020. 'Qualifier l'engagement des Syriennes dans la revolution: les retournements du mot حرائر (femmes libres)', *Lexique Vivant de La Révolution et de La Guerre En Syrie*, June. https://doi.org/10.21428/3633fae9.e30065a4.

Auyero, J. 2011. 'Patients of the state: an ethnographic account of poor people's waiting', *Latin American Research Review* 46 (1): 5–29.

Ayalon, A. 1987. 'From Fitna to Thawra', *Studia Islamica* 66: 145–74.

Aziz, O. 2013. 'al auraq as siassieh lfiker al majles al mahalieh'. https://www.facebook.com/note.php?note_id=143690742461532.

Baban, F., Ilcan, S. and Rygiel, K. 2017. 'Syrian refugees in Turkey: pathways to precarity, differential inclusion, and negotiated citizenship rights', *Journal of Ethnic and Migration Studies* 43 (1): 41–57. https://doi.org/10.1080/1369183X.2016.1192996.

Baczko, A., Dorronsoro, G. and Quesnay, A. 2017. *Civil War in Syria: Mobilization and competing social order*. Cambridge: Cambridge University Press.

Badiou, A. 2003. *Saint Paul: The foundation of universalism*. Stanford: Stanford University Press.

Badiou, A. 2011. *Le Réveil de l'Histoire*. Paris: Lignes.

Bandak, A. 2015. 'Reckoning with the inevitable: death and dying among Syrian Christians during the uprising', *Ethnos* 80 (5): 671–91.

Barnes, R. 1974. *Kédang*. Oxford: Clarendon.

Bartolomei, E. 2018. 'Sectarianism and the battle of narratives in the context of the Syrian uprising'. In *The Syrian Uprising: Domestic origins and early trajectory*, edited by R. Hinnebusch and O. Imady, 223–41. New York: Routledge.

Batatu, H. 1999. *Syria's Peasantry: The descendants of its lesser rural notables, and their politics*. Princeton: Princeton University Press.

Belhadj, S. and Kienle, E. 2007. 'Y a-t-il de varies transformations politiques internes en Syrie?'. In *La Syrie au présent*, edited by B. Dupret, Z. Ghazzal, Y. Courbage and M. al-Dbiyat, 687–729. Paris: Actes Sud.

Benveniste, E. 1969. *Le vocabulaire des institutions indo-européenes*. Paris: Les Éditions de Minuit.

Ben-Yehoyada, N. 2011. 'The moral perils of Mediterraneanism: second-generation immigrants practicing personhood between Sicily and Tunisia', *Journal of Modern Italian Studies* 16 (3): 386–403.

Ben-Yehoyada, N. 2014. 'Transnational political cosmology: a central Mediterranean example', *Comparative Studies in Society and History* 56 (4): 870–901.

Ben-Yehoyada, N. 2015. '"Follow me, and I will make you fishers of men": the moral and political scales of migration in the central Mediterranean', *Journal of the Royal Anthropological Institute* 22 (1): 183–202.

Bergson, H. 1908. *Matière et mémoire: Essai sur la relation du corps à l'esprit*. Paris: Félix Alcan.

Betts, A., Ali, A. and Memisoglu, F. 2017. *Local Politics and the Syrian Refugee Crisis: Exploring responses in Turkey, Lebanon, and Jordan*. Oxford: Refugee Studies Centre.

Bhabha, H. 1994. *The Location of Culture*. London: Routledge.

Bille, M., Hatrup, F. and Sørensen, T. 2010a. *An Anthropology of Absence: Materializations of transcendence and loss*. New York. Springer.

Bille, M., Hatrup, F. and Sørensen, T. 2010b. 'Introduction: an anthropology of absence'. In *An Anthropology of Absence: Materializations of transcendence and loss*, edited by M. Bille, F. Hatrup and T. Sørensen, 3–23. New York: Springer.

Blanchot, M. 1982. *The Space of Literature*. Lincoln: University of Nebraska Press.

Boëx, C. and Devictor, A. 2021. *Syrie, une nouvelle ère des images: De la révolte au conflit transnational*. Paris: CNRS Éditions.

Boëx, C. and Pinto, P. 2018. 'Restituer la densité et la diversité des liens entre le religieux et le politique', *Archives de sciences sociales des religions* 181: 11–23.

Boissière, T. 2015. 'L'anthropologie face au conflit syrien: replacer la société au cœur de l'analyse', *Revue des mondes musulmans et de la Méditerranée* 138: 117–30.

Borneman, J. 2007. *Syrian Episodes: Sons, fathers, and an anthropologist in Aleppo*. Princeton: Princeton University Press.

Bourdieu, P. 1972. *Esquisse d'une théorie de la pratique: precede de trois etudes d'ethnologie kabyle*. Paris: Librairie Droz.

Bradley, A. C. 1991. *Shakespearean Tragedy: Lectures on Hamlet, Othello, King Lear and Macbeth*. New York: Penguin.

Brink, J. 1991. 'The effect of emigration of husbands on the status of their wives: an Egyptian case', *International Journal of Middle East Studies* 23: 201–11.

Brønd, T. 2017. 'The most beautiful friendship: revolution, war and ends of social gravity in Syria', *Middle East Critique* 26 (3): 283–96.

Brown, M. F. 1996. 'On resisting resistance', *American Anthropologist* 98 (4): 729–35.

Bryant, R. 2014. 'History's remainders: on time and objects after conflict in Cyprus', *American Ethnologist* 41 (4): 681–97.

Bryant, R. 2016. 'On critical times: return, repetition, and the uncanny present', *History and Anthropology* 27 (1): 19–31.

Bubandt, N., Rytter, M. and Suhr, C. 2019. 'A second look at invisibility: Al-Ghayb, Islam, ethnography', *Contemporary Islam* 13: 1–16.

Buch, L. 2010. 'Derivative presence: loss and lives in limbo in the West Bank'. In *An Anthropology of Absence: Materializations of transcendence and loss*, edited by M. Bille, F. Hastrup and T. Sørensen, 83–98. New York: Springer.

Buch Segal, L. 2013. 'Enduring presents: living a prison sentence as the wife of a detainee in Israel'. In *Times of Security: Ethnographies of fear, protest and the future*, edited by M. Holbraad and M. Pedersen, 122–41. London: Routledge.

Buch Segal, L. 2016. *No Place for Grief: Martyrs, prisoners, and mourning in contemporary Palestine*. Philadelphia: University of Pennsylvania Press.

Burgat, F., Chehayed, J., Paoli, B. and Sartori, M. 2013. 'La puissance politique des slogans de la révolution'. In *Pas de Printemps pour la Syrie: Les clés pour comprendre les acteurs et les défis de la crise (2011–2013)*, edited by F. Burgat and B. Paoli, 185–95. Paris: La Découverte.

Burgat, F. and Paoli, B. (eds.) 2013a. *Pas de Printemps pour la Syrie: Les clés pour comprendre les acteurs et les défis de la crise (2011–2013)*. Paris: La Découverte.

Burgat, F. and Paoli, B. 2013b. 'Introduction: quelles clés pour comprendre le drame syrien?' . In *Pas de Printemps pour la Syrie: Les clés pour comprendre les acteurs et les défis de la crise (2011–2013)*, edited by F. Burgat and B. Paoli, 7–16. Paris: La Découverte.

Butler, J. 2000. *Antigone's Claim: Kinship between life and death*. New York: Columbia University Press.

Candea, M. 2012. 'Derrida en Corse? Hospitality as scale-free abstraction', *Journal of the Royal Anthropological Institute* 18: 34–48.

Candea, M. and Da Col, G. 2012. 'The return to hospitality', *Journal of the Royal Anthropological Institute* 18: 1–19.

Carpi, E. and Şenoğuz, P. 2019. 'Refugee hospitality in Lebanon and Turkey: on making "the other"', *International Migration* 47 (2): 126–42.

Carroll, T., Jeevendrampillai, D., Parkhurst, A. and Shackelford, J. (eds.) 2017. *The Material Culture of Failure: When things go wrong*. London: Bloomsbury Academic.

Caton, S. C. 1987. 'Power, persuasion, and language: a critique of the segmentary model in the Middle East', *International Journal of Middle East Studies* 19: 77–101.

Cavidan, S. 2012. 'The New Draft Law on Foreigners and International Protection in Turkey', *Oxford Monitor of Forced Migration* 2 (2): 38–47.

Chakrabarty, D. 2000. *Provincializing Europe: Postcolonial thought and historical difference*. Princeton: Princeton University Press.

Chancellor, A. 2020. 'The women want the fall of the (gendered) regime: in what ways are Syrian women challenging state feminism through an online feminist counter-public?', *Cornell International Affairs Review* 13: 137–83.

Chatty, D. 2017. 'The duty to be generous (karam): alternatives to rights-based asylum in the Middle East', *Journal of the British Academy* 5: 177–99. https://doi.org/10.5871/jba/005.177.

Chatty, D. 2018. *Syria: The making and unmaking of a refugee state*. London: Hurst.

Chehayed, N. and De Vaulx d'Arcy, G. 2021. *La destructivité en oeuvres: Essai sur l'art syrien contemporain*. Beirut: Presses de l'IFPO.

Cheng, Y. 2009. *Creating the 'New Man': From Enlightenment ideals to socialist realities*. Honolulu: University of Hawai'i Press.

Cherstich, I., Holbraad, M. and Tassi, N. 2020. *Anthropologies of Revolution: Forging time, people, and worlds*. Berkeley: University of California Press.

Çifçi, D. 2018. 'Political incongruity between the Kurds and the "opposition" in the Syrian uprising'. In *The Syrian Uprising: Domestic origins and early trajectory*, edited by R. Hinnebusch and O. Imady, 309–28. New York: Routledge.

Cook, D. 2007. *Martyrdom in Islam*. Cambridge: Cambridge University Press.

Coquio, C., Hubrecht, N., Mansour, L. and Mardam-Bey, F. 2022. *Syrie le pays brûlé: Le livre noir des Assad (1970–2021)*. Paris: Seuil.

Crapanzano, V. 2003. 'Reflections on hope as a category of social and psychological analysis', *Cultural Anthropology* 18 (1): 3–32.

Dabashi, H. 2011. *Shi'ism: A religion of protest*. Cambridge, MA: Harvard University Press.

Dağtaş, S. 2017. 'Whose *misafirs*? Negotiating difference along the Turkish–Syrian border', *International Journal of Middle East Studies* 49: 661–79.

Dahi, O. 2011. 'A Syrian drama: a taxonomy of a revolution'. https://www.joshualandis.com/blog/a-syrian-drama-a-taxonomy-of-a-revolution-by-omar-dahi/.

Daoudy, M. 2020. *The Origins of the Syrian Conflict: Climate change and human security*. Cambridge: Cambridge University Press.

Das, V. 2018. 'On singularity and the event'. In *Recovering the Human Subject: Everyday creativity and decision*, edited by J. Laidlaw, B. Bodenhorn and M. Holbraad, 53–73. Cambridge: Cambridge University Press.

Davies, R. P. 1949. 'Syrian Arabic kinship terms', *Southwestern Journal of Anthropology* 5 (3): 244–52.

Davis, J. 1986. *Libyan Politics: Tribe and revolution: An account of the Zuwaya and their government*. London: I. B. Tauris.

Day, S., Papataxiarchis, E. and Stewart, C. (eds.) 1999. *Lilies of the Field: Marginal people who live for the moment*. Oxford: Westview Press.

De Haas, H. and Van Rooij, A. (2010) 'Migration as emancipation? The impact of internal and international migration on the position of women in rural Morocco', *Oxford Development Studies* 38 (1): 43–62.

Deleuze, G. 1993 [Originally published 1968]. *Différence et Répétition*. Paris: PUF.

Deleuze, G. and Guattari, F. 1975. *Kafka: Pour une littérature mineure*. Paris: Les Editions de Minuit.

Derrida, J. 1995. 'The time is out of joint'. In *Deconstruction Is/In America*, edited by A. Haverkamp, 14–38. New York: NYU Press.

Derrida, J. 1997. *De L'hospitalité*. Paris: Calmann-Levy.

Diken, B. 2004. 'From refugee camps to gated communities: biopolitics and the end of the city', *Citizenship Studies* 8 (1): 83–106.

Dubois, S. 2013. 'Les chants se révoltent'. In *Pas de Printemps pour la Syrie: Les clés pour comprendre les acteurs et les défis de la crise (2011–2013)*, edited by F. Burgat and B. Paoli, 196–200. Paris: La Découverte.

Elder, J. 1966. 'Fatalism in India: a comparison between Hindus and Muslims', *Anthropological Quarterly* 39 (3): 227–43.

Elliot, A. 2016a. 'The makeup of destiny: predestination and the labor of hope in a Moroccan emigrant town', *American Ethnologist* 43 (3): 488–99.

Elliot, A. 2016b. 'Gender'. In *Keywords of Mobility: Critical engagements*, edited by N. B. Salazar and K. Jarayam, 73–92. New York: Berghahn.

Elliot, A. 2017. 'Permanent rupture: Tunis style', Paper given at the UCL Rupture Conference, 13/02/2017.

Elliot, A. 2021. *The Outside: Migration as life in Morocco*. Bloomington: Indiana University Press.

Elshtain, J. B. 1987. *Women and War*. New York: Basic Books.

Elyachar, J. 2012a. 'Writing the revolution: dilemmas of ethnographic writing after the January 25th revolution in Egypt', Hot Spots, *Cultural Anthropology* website. https://culanth.org/fieldsights/209-writing-the-revolution-dilemmas-of-ethnographic-writing-after-the-january-25th-revolution-in-egypt.

Elyachar, J. and Winegar, J. 2012. Revolution and counterrevolution in Egypt a year after January 25th. *Cultural Anthropology* website. https://culanth.org/fieldsights/208-revolution-and-counter-revolution-in-egypt-a-year-after-january-25th.

Fanon, F. 1967. *The Wretched of the Earth*. Harmondsworth: Penguin.

Farah, R. 2021. *Our memory belongs to us* [film].

Fassin, D. 2007. 'Humanitarianism as politics of life', *Public Culture* 19 (3): 499–520.

Fassin, D. 2010. 'Noli me tangere: the moral untouchability of humanitarianism'. In *Forces of Compassion: Humanitarianism between ethics and politics*, edited by E. Bornstein and P. Redfield, 35–52. Santa Fe: SAR Press.

Fassin, D. 2011. 'Policing borders, producing boundaries: the governmentality of immigration in dark times', *Annual Review of Anthropology* 40: 213–26.

Fassin, D. 2012. *Humanitarian Reason: A moral history of the present*. Berkeley: University of California Press.

Fassin, D. 2013. 'The precarious truth of asylum', *Public Culture* 69 (1): 39–63.

Fausto, C. 2012. 'The friend, the enemy, and the anthropologist: hostility and hospitality among the Parakanã (Amazonia, Brazil)', *Journal of the Royal Anthropological Institute* 18: 196–209.

Favier, A. 2016. 'Local governance dynamics in opposition-controlled areas in Syria'. In *Inside Wars: Local dynamics of conflicts in Libya and Syria*, edited by L. Narbone, A. Favier and V. Collombier, 6–16. Fiesole: European University Institute.

Fayyad, F. 2019. *The cave* [film].

Fedda, Y. 2014. *Queens of Syria* [film].

Foucault, M. 1986. 'Of other spaces', *Diacritics* 16 (1): 22–7.

Foucault, M. 1994. *Dits et Ecrits*, vol. 3. Paris: Gallimard.

Foucault, M. 1997. *Ethics, Subjectivity, and Truth: Essential works of Foucault, 1954–1984*. New York: New Press.

Foucault, M. 1999. 'About the beginning of the hermeneutics of the self'. In *Religion and Culture*, edited by J. Carrette, 158–81. New York: Routledge [Originally published 1980].

Fukuyama, F. 1992. *The End of History and the Last Man*. New York: Free Press.

Gaibazzi, P. 2012. '"God's time is the best": religious imagination and the wait for emigration in The Gambia'. In *The Global Horizon: Expectations of migration in Africa and the Middle East*, edited by K. Graw and S. Schielke, 121–36. Leuven: Leuven University Press.

Gaibazzi, P. 2015. 'The quest for luck: fate, fortune, work and the unexpected among Gambian Soninke hustlers', *Critical African Studies* 7 (3): 227–42.

Gell, A. 1992. *The Anthropology of Time*. Oxford: Berg.

Ghamari-Tabrizi, B. 2016. *Foucault in Iran: Islamic revolution after the Enlightenment*. Minneapolis: University of Minnesota Press.

Ghannam, F. 2002. *Remaking the Modern: Space, relocation and the politics of identity in a global Cairo*. Berkeley: University of California Press.

Ghannam, F. 2011. 'Mobility, liminality, and embodiment in urban Egypt', *American Ethnologist* 38 (4): 790–800.

Ghannam, F. 2012. 'Meanings and feelings: local interpretations of the use of violence in the Egyptian revolution', *American Ethnologist* 39 (1): 32–6.

Ghannam, F. 2013. *Live and Die Like a Man: Gender dynamics in urban Egypt*. Stanford: Stanford University Press.

Ghannam, F. 2014. 'Technologies of immortality, "good endings", and martyrdom in urban Egypt', *Ethnos* 80 (5): 1–19.

Ghazzawi, R. 2014. 'Seeing the women in revolutionary Syria'. Accessed 8 May 2023. https://www.opendemocracy.net/en/north-africa-west-asia/seeing-women-in-revolutionary-syria/.

Gilman, D. 2015. 'The martyr pop moment: depoliticizing martyrdom', *Ethnos* 80 (5): 692–709.

Gilsenan, M. 1996. *Lords of the Lebanese Marches*. New York: Tauris.

Göle, N. 2002. 'Islam in public: new visibilities and new imaginaries', *Public Culture* 14 (1): 173–90.

Goody, J. 1990. 'Marriage and property in the Arab world'. In *The Oriental, the Ancient and the Primitive: Systems of marriage and the family in the pre-industrial societies of Eurasia*, 361–82. Cambridge: Cambridge University Press.

Graw, K. and Schielke, S. (eds.) 2012a. *The Global Horizon: Expectations of migration in Africa and the Middle East*. Leuven: Leuven University Press.

Graw, K. and Schielke, S. 2012b. 'Introduction: reflections on migratory expectations in Africa and beyond'. In *The Global Horizon: Expectations of migration in Africa and the Middle East*, edited by K. Graw and S. Shielke, 7–22. Leuven: Leuven University Press.

Grosz, E. 1999. *Becomings: Explorations in time, memory, and futures*. Ithaca, NY: Cornell University Press.

Guevara, E. and Castro, F. 2009. *Socialism and Man in Cuba*. New York: Pathfinder Press.

Gupta, A. 1995. 'Blurred boundaries: the discourse of corruption, the culture of politics, and the imagined state', *American Ethnologist* 22 (2): 375–402. https://doi.org/10.1525/ae.1995.22.2.02a00090.

Guyer, J. 2007. 'Prophecy and the near future: thoughts in macroeconomic, evangalical and punctuated time', *American Ethnologist* 34 (3): 409–21.

HadžiMuhamedović, S. 2018. *Waiting for Elijah: Time and encounter in a Bosnian landscape*. New York: Berghhan.

Hafez, S. 2012. 'No longer a bargain: women, masculinity, and the Egyptian uprising', *American Ethnologist* 39 (1): 37–42.

Hage, G. 2003. '"Comes a time we are all enthusiasm": understanding Palestinian suicide bombers in times of exighophobia', *Public Culture* 15 (1): 65–89.

Hage, G. 2005. 'A not so multi-sited ethnography of a not so imagined community', *Anthropological Theory* 5 (4): 463–75.

Hage, G. 2009a. *Waiting*. Melbourne: Melbourne University Publishing.

Hage, G. 2009b. 'Waiting out the crisis: on stuckedness and governmentality'. In *Waiting*, edited by G. Hage, 97–107. Melbourne: Melbourne University Publishing.

Hage, G. 2018. 'Afterword'. In *Ethnographies of Waiting: Doubt, hope and uncertainty*, edited by M. Janeja and A. Bandak, 203–9. London: Bloomsbury Academic.

Halasa, M., Omareen, Z. and Mahfoud, N. 2014. *Syria Speaks: Art and culture from the frontline*. London: Saqi.

Hamdy, S. 2009. 'Islam, fatalism, and medical intervention: lessons from Egypt on the cultivation of forbearance (sabr) and reliance on God (tawakkul)', *Anthropological Quarterly* 82 (1): 173–96.

Harkin, J. 2018. 'Demands for dignity and the Syrian uprising'. In *The Syrian Uprising: Domestic origins and early trajectory*, edited by R. Hinnebusch and O. Imady, 173–87. New York: Routledge.

Hassabo, C. and Rey, M. 2015. 'L'événement en révolution: réflexions autour des cas syrien et égyptien', *Revue des mondes musulmans et de la Méditerranée* 138: 29–46.

Haugbolle, S. 2016. 'In defense of ideology: notes on experience and revolution'. https://pomeps.org/2016/05/31/in-defense-of-ideology-notes-on-experience-and-revolution/.

Haugbolle, S. and Bandak, A. 2017. 'The ends of revolution: rethinking ideology and time in the Arab uprisings', *Middle East Critique* 26 (3): 191–204.

Hegland, M. 2014. *Days of Revolution: Political unrest in an Iranian village*. Stanford: Stanford University Press.

Herzfeld, M. 1987. '"As in your own house": hospitality, ethnography, and the stereotype of Mediterranean society'. In *Honor and Shame and the Unity of the Mediterranean*, edited by D. Gilmore, 75–89. Washington, DC: American Anthropological Association.

Herzfeld, M. 1989. *The Poetics of Manhood: Contest and identity in a Cretan mountain village*. Princeton: Princeton University Press.

Hinnebusch, R. 1991. 'Class and state in Ba'thist Syria'. In *Syria: Society, culture and polity*, edited by R. Antoun and D. Quataert, 29–49. Albany: State University of New York Press.

Hinnebusch, R. and Imady, O. (eds.) 2018a. *The Syrian Uprising: Domestic origins and early trajectory*. New York: Routledge.

Hinnebusch, R. and Imady, O. (eds.) 2018b. 'Introduction: origins of the Syrian uprising: from structure to agency'. In *The Syrian Uprising: Domestic origins and early trajectory*, edited by R. Hinnebusch and O. Imady, 1–11. New York: Routledge.

Hodges, M. 2008. 'Rethinking time's arrow: Bergson, Deleuze and the anthropology of time', *Anthropological Theory* 8: 399–429.

Højer, L. and Bandak, A. 2015. 'Introduction: the power of example', *Journal of the Royal Anthropological Institute* 21 (S1): 1–17. https://doi.org/10.1111/1467-9655.12173.

Holbraad, M. 2004. 'Religious "speculation": the rise of Ifá cults and consumption in post-Soviet Cuba', *Journal of Latin American Studies* 36 (4): 643–63.

Holbraad, M. 2014. 'Revolución o muerte: self-sacrifice and the ontology of Cuban revolution', *Ethnos* 79 (3): 1–23.

Holbraad, M. and Pedersen, M. 2012. 'Revolutionary securitization: an anthropological extension of securitization theory', *International Theory* 4 (2): 165–97.

hooks, b. 1984. *Feminist Theory: From margin to center*. New York: Routledge.

Human Rights Watch. 2015. 'If the dead could speak: mass death and torture in Syria's detention facilities'. Accessed 7 May 2023. https://www.hrw.org/report/2015/12/16/if-dead-could-speak/mass-deaths-and-torture-syrias-detention-facilities.

Humphrey, C. 1983. *Karl Marx Collective: Economy, society, and religion in a Siberian collective farm*. Cambridge: Cambridge University Press.

Humphrey, C. 2008. 'Reassembling individual subjects: events and decisions in troubled times', *Anthropological Theory* 8 (4): 357–80.

Humphrey, C. 2012. 'Hospitality and tone: holding patterns for strangeness in rural Mongolia', *Journal of the Royal Anthropological Institute* 18 (S1): 63–75.

Huntington, S. 1996. *The Clash of Civilizations and the Remaking of World Order*. New York: Simon and Schuster.

Ismail, S. 2011. 'The Syrian uprising: imagining and performing the nation studies', *Ethnicity and Nationalism* 11 (3): 538–49.

Ismail, S. 2018. *The Rule of Violence: Subjectivity, memory and government in Syria*. Cambridge: Cambridge University Press.

Janeja, M. and Bandak, A. (eds.) 2018. *Ethnographies of Waiting: Doubt, hope and uncertainty*. London: Bloomsbury Academic.

Jean-Klein, I. 2000. 'Mothercraft, statecraft, and subjectivity in the Palestinian Intifada', *American Ethnologist* 27 (1): 100–27.

Jean-Klein, I. 2003. 'Into committees, out of the house? Familiar forms in the organization of Palestinian committee activism during the first Intifada', *American Ethnologist* 30 (4): 556–77.

Joseph, S. 1993. 'Connectivity and patriarchy among urban working-class Arab families in Lebanon', *Ethos* 21 (4): 452–84.

Joseph, S. 1999a. *Intimate Selving in Arab Families: Gender, self, patriarchy*. Syracuse, NY: Syracuse University Press.

Joseph, S. 1999b. 'Theories and dynamics of gender, self, and identity in Arab families'. In *Intimate Selving in Arab Families: Gender, self, patriarchy*, edited by S. Joseph, 1–21. Syracuse, NY: Syracuse University Press.

Joseph, S. 1999c. 'Brother–Sister relationships: connectivity, love, and power in the reproduction of patriarchy in Lebanon'. In *Intimate Selving in Arab Families: Gender, self, patriarchy*, edited by S. Joseph, 113–41. Syracuse, NY: Syracuse University Press.

Joseph, S. 1999d. 'My son/myself, my mother/myself: paradoxical relationalities of patriarchal connectivities'. In *Intimate Selving in Arab Families: Gender, self, patriarchy*, edited by S. Joseph, 174–91. Syracuse, NY: Syracuse University Press.

Kandiyoti, D. 1988. 'Bargaining with patriarchy', *Gender and Society* 2 (3): 274–90.

Karabet, A. 2010. *Al-rahīl ila al-majhūl, yawmiyyātī fī-l-sujūn al-sūriyya* . Alexandria: Dār Jidār.

Kastrinou, M. 2016. *Power, Sect and the State in Syria: The politics of marriage and identity amongst the Druze*. London: I. B. Tauris.

Kastrinou, M. and Knoerk, H. n.d. 'To the future guest of Lesvos: hospitality among Syrian refugees in Greece'. Unpublished manuscript.

Kelly, T. 2006. 'Documented lives: fear and the uncertainties of law during the second Palestinian Intifada', *Journal of the Royal Anthropological Institute* 12 (1): 89–107.

Khalifa, K. 2006. *Madīḥ al-karāhiya*. Beirut: Dār al-Adāb.

Khalifa, K. 2013. *Lā sakākīn fī matābikh hādhihi al-madina*. Cairo: Dār al-ʿAīn.

Khalifa, K. 2016. *Al-mawt ʿamal shāqq*. Beirut: Dār Naufal, Hachette-Antoine.

Khalifa, M. 2007. *Al-qawqʿa: yawmiyyāt mutalaṣṣiṣ*. Beirut: Dār al-Adāb.

Khalili, L. 2004. 'Grassroots commemorations: remembering the land in the camps of Lebanon', *Journal of Palestine Studies* 34 (1): 6–22.

Khalili, L. 2006. *Heroes and Martyrs of Palestine: The politics of national commemorations*. Cambridge: Cambridge University Press.

Kharkhordin, O. 1999. *The Collective and the Individual in Russia: A study of practices*. Berkeley: University of California Press.

Khosravi, S. 2017. *Precarious Lives: Waiting and hope in Iran*. Philadelphia: University of Pennsylvania Press.

Khuri, F. I. 1981. 'Classification, meaning and usage of Arabic status and kinship terms', *International Journal of Sociology of the Family* 11 (2): 347–66.

Khuri, F. I. 1991. 'The Alawis of Syria: religious ideology and organization'. In *Syria: Society, culture and polity*, edited by R. Antoun and D. Quataert, 49–63. Albany: State University of New York Press.

Khuri, F. I. 2004. *Being a Druze*. London: Druze Heritage Foundation.

Kienle, E. 1991. 'Entre jama'a et classe: le pouvoir politique en Syrie contemporaine', *Revue du monde musulman et de la Méditerranée* 59/60: 211–39.

Koselleck, R. 1985. *Futures Past: On the semantics of historical time*. Cambridge, MA: MIT Press.

Kublitz, A. 2013. 'Seizing catastrophes: the temporality of Nakba among Palestinians in Denmark'. In *Times of Security: Ethnographies of fear, protest and the future*, edited by M. Holbraad and M. Pedersen, 103–22. London: Routledge.

Kwon, H. 2008. *Ghosts of War in Vietnam*. Cambridge: Cambridge University Press.

Lakha, S. 2009. 'Waiting to return home: modes of immigrant waiting'. In *Waiting*, edited by G. Hage, 121–35. Melbourne: Melbourne University Publishing.

Lan, D. 1985. *Guns and Rain: Guerrillas and spirit mediums in Zimbabwe*. London: James Currey.

Leach, E. 1950. 'Primitive calendars', *Oceania* 20: 245–62.

Le Caisne, G. 2015. *Opération César: Au cœur de la machine de mort syrienne*. Paris: Stock.

Lewis, B. 1993. *Islam in History*. Chicago: Open Court.

Llera-Blanes, R. and Oustinova-Stjepanovic, G. (eds.) 2015. *Being Godless: Ethnographies of atheism and non-religion*. New York: Berghahn.

Loiseau, M. 2017. *Syrie le cri étouffé* [film].

Longuenesse, E. 1979. 'The class nature of the state in Syria: contribution to an analysis', *MERIP Reports* 77: 3–11.

Longuenesse, E. 1994. 'Ingénieurs et médecins dans le changement social en Syrie', *Maghreb-Machrek* 4: 59–71.

Longuenesse, E. 1995. 'Ingénieurs et médecins en Syrie: formation, emploi, statut social', *Tiers Monde* 36 (143): 499–513.

Longuenesse, E. and Ruiz de Elvira Carrascal, L. 2016. 'La société syrienne, entre résilience et fragmentation', *Confluences Méditerranée* 4 (99): 9–18.

Mahmood, S. 2001a. 'Feminist theory, embodiment, and the docile agent: some reflections on the Egyptian Islamic revival', *Cultural Anthropology* 16 (2): 202–36.

Mahmood, S. 2001b. 'Rehearsed spontaneity and the conventionality of ritual: disciplines of "salat"', *American Ethnologist* 28 (4): 827–53.

Mahmood, S. 2005. *Politics of Piety: The Islamic revival and the feminist subject*. Princeton: Princeton University Press.

Mahmud, R. 2016. 'Les Syriens à Gaziantep: entre dynamisme et défis', *Confluences Méditerranée* 4 (99): 75–85.

Malik, N. 2009. 'Waiting for Imam Mahdi and development: the case of Pakistan'. In *Waiting*, edited by G. Hage, 54–66. Melbourne: Melbourne University Publishing.

Malkki, L. 1995. *Purity and Exile: Violence, memory and national cosmology among Hutu refugees in Tanzania*. Chicago: University of Chicago Press.

Manning, P. 2007. 'Rose-colored glasses? Color revolutions and cartoon chaos in postsocialist Georgia', *Cultural Anthropology* 22 (2): 171–213.

Mao, Z. 1976. *Quotations from Chairman Mao Tse Tung*. Austin: University of Texas Press.

Mardam-Bey, F. 2022. 'Introduction'. In *Syrie le pays brûlé: Le livre noir des Assad (1970–2021)*, edited by C. Coquio, N. Hubrecht, L. Mansour and F. Mardam-Bey, 29–31. Paris: Seuil.

Marsden, M. 2009a. 'A tour not so grand: mobile Muslims in northern Pakistan', *Journal of the Royal Anthropological Institute* 15: 57–75.

Marsden, M. 2009b. 'Talking the talk', *Anthropology Today* 25 (2): 20–4.

Marsden, M. 2011a. 'A tour not so grand: mobile Muslims in northern Pakistan'. In *Fragments of the Afghan Frontier*, by M. Marsden and B. D. Hopkins, 111–37. London: Hurst.

Marsden, M. 2011b. 'Muslim cosmopolitans? Transnational village life on the frontiers of South and Central Asia'. In *Fragments of the Afghan Frontier*, by M. Marsden and B. D. Hopkins, 137–77. London: Hurst.

Marsden, M. 2012. 'Fatal embrace: trading in hospitality on the frontiers of South and Central Asia', *Journal of the Royal Anthropological Institute* 18: 117–30.

Mazeau, G. 2013. 'La ronde des révolutions', *La Vie des Idées*. Accessed 8 May 2023. https://laviedesidees.fr/La-ronde-des-revolutions.

Mbembe, A. 2019. *Necropolitics*. Durham, NC: Duke University Press.

Menin, L. 2015. 'The impasse of modernity: personal agency, divine destiny, and the unpredictability of intimate relationships in Morocco', *Journal of the Royal Anthropological Institute* 21: 892–910.

Mermier, F. 2018. *Écrits libres de Syrie: De la révolution à la guerre*. Paris: Classiques Garnier.

Michaud, Y. 2000. 'Des modes de subjectivation aux techniques de soi: Foucault et les identites de notre temps', *Cités* 2: 11–39.

Minnegal, M. 2009. 'The time is right: waiting, reciprocity and sociality'. In *Waiting*, edited by G. Hage, 89–97. Melbourne: Melbourne University Publishing.

Mitchell, J. W. 2012. *Martyrdom: A very short introduction*. Oxford: Oxford University Press.

Mitchell, T. 1990. 'Everyday metaphors of power', *Theory and Society* 19 (5): 545–77.

Mittermaier, A. 2011. *Dreams that Matter: Egyptian landscapes of the imagination*. Berkeley: University of California Press.

Mittermaier, A. 2012. 'Dreams from elsewhere: Muslim subjectivities beyond the trope of self-cultivation', *Journal of the Royal Anthropological Institute* 18: 247–65.

Mittermaier, A. 2013. 'Trading with God: Islam, calculation and excess'. In *A Companion to the Anthropology of Religion*, edited by J. Boddy and M. Lambek, 274–93. Hoboken, NJ: John Wiley.

Mittermaier, A. 2014. 'Bread, freedom, social justice: the Egyptian uprising and a Sufi Khidma', *Cultural Anthropology* 29 (1): 54–79.

Mittermaier, A. 2015. 'Death and martyrdom in the Arab uprisings: an introduction', *Ethnos* 80 (5): 583–604.

Mittermaier, A. 2019. 'The unknown in the Egyptian uprising: towards an anthropology of al-Ghayb', *Contemporary Islam* 13: 17–31.

Mittermaier, A. 2021. 'Beyond the human horizon', *Religion and Society: Advances in Research* 12: 21–38.

Miyazaki, H. 2004. *The Method of Hope: Anthropology, philosophy, and Fijian knowledge*. Stanford: Stanford University Press.

Miyazaki, H. 2006. 'Economy of dreams: hope in global capitalism and its critique', *Cultural Anthropology* 21 (2): 147–72.

Mundy, M. 1995. *Domestic Government: Kinship, community and polity in north Yemen*. London: I. B. Tauris.

Munif, Y. 2020. *The Syrian Revolution: Between the politics of life and the geopolitics of death*. London: Pluto Press.

Naaman, D. 2007. 'Brides of Palestine/angels of death: media, gender, and performance in the case of the Palestinian female suicide bombers', *Signs* 32 (4): 933–55.

Napolitano, V. 2015. 'Anthropology and traces', *Anthropological Theory* 15: 47–67.

Navaro, Y. 2020. 'The aftermath of mass violence: a negative methodology', *Annual Review of Anthropology* 49: 161–73.

Navaro-Yashin, Y. 2012. *The Make-Believe Space: Affective geography in a postwar polity*. Durham, NC: Duke University Press.

Nechayev, S. 1869. *The Revolutionary Catechism*. https://www.marxists.org/subject/anarchism/nechayev/catechism.htm.

Nielsen, M. 2011. 'Futures within: reversible time and house-building in Maputo, Mozambique', *Anthropological Theory* 11 (4): 397–423.

Oustinova-Stjepanovic, G. 2011. 'Performative Failure among Islamic Mystics in Urban Macedonia'. PhD dissertation, London: UCL.

Oustinova-Stjepanovic, G. 2017. 'A catalogue of vice: a sense of failure and incapacity to act among Roma Muslims in Macedonia', *Journal of the Royal Anthropological Institute* 23 (2): 338–55.

Özden, S. 2013. 'Syrian refugees in Turkey', Migration Policy Centre (MPC), *MPC Research Report* 2013/05. http://www.migrationpolicycentre.eu/docs/MPC-RR-2013-05.pdf.

Pandolfo, S. 2007. '"The burning": finitude and the politico-theological imagination of illegal migration', *Anthropological Theory* 7 (3): 329–63.

Parrott, R. F. 2010. 'Bringing home the dead: photographs, family imaginaries and moral remains'. In *An Anthropology of Absence: Materializations of transcendence and loss*, edited by M. Bille, F. Hatrup and T. Sørensen, 131–46. New York: Springer.

Pearlman, W. 2017. *We Crossed a Bridge and it Trembled: Voices from Syria*. New York: HarperCollins.

Pedersen, M. 2012. 'A day in the Cadillac: the work of hope in urban Mongolia', *Social Analysis* 56 (2): 136–51.

Pedersen, M. 2016. 'Moving to remain the same: An anthropological theory of nomadism'. In *Comparative Metaphysics: Ontology after anthropology*, edited by P. Charbonnier, G. Salmon and P. Skafish, 221–46. London: Rowman and Littlefield.

Peteet, J. 1991. *Gender in Crisis: Women and the Palestinian resistance movement*. New York: Columbia University Press.

Peteet, J. 1994. 'Male gender and rituals of resistance in the Palestinian "Intifada": a cultural politics of violence', *American Ethnologist* 21 (1): 31–49.

Picard, E. 1980. 'La Syrie de 1946 à 1979'. In *La Syrie d'aujourd'hui*, edited by A. Raymond, 143–84. Paris: Editions du CNRS.

Pierret, T. 2013. *Religion and State in Syria: The Sunni ulama from coup to revolution*. Cambridge: Cambridge University Press.

Pinto, P. 2007a. 'Religions and religiosité en Syrie'. In *La Syrie au présent*, edited by B. Dupret, Z. Ghazzal, Y. Courbage and M. al-Dbiyat, 323–59. Paris: Actes Sud.

Pinto, P. 2007b. 'Le soufisme en Syrie'. In *La Syrie au présent*, edited by B. Dupret, Z. Ghazzal, Y. Courbage and M. al-Dbiyat, 389–99. Paris: Actes Sud.

Piot, C. 2010. *Nostalgia for the Future: West Africa after the Cold War*. Chicago: University of Chicago Press.

Pitt-Rivers, J. 2012. 'The law of hospitality', *HAU: Journal of Ethnographic Theory* 2 (1): 501–17.

Potter, S. H. and Potter, J. M. 1990. *China's Peasants: The anthropology of a revolution*. Cambridge: Cambridge University Press.

Proudfoot, P. 2022. *Rebel Workers: Revolution and loss among Syrian labourers in Lebanon*. Manchester: Manchester University Press.

Qutb, S. 1953. *Social Justice in Islam*. Trans. J. B. Hardie. New York: Islamic Publications International.

Rabo, A. 2011. 'Legal pluralism and family law in Syria'. In *The Governance of Legal Pluralism*, edited by W. Zips and M. Weilenmann, 213–34. London: Global Book Marketing.

Ramzy, C. M. 2015. 'To die is gain: singing a heavenly citizenship among Egypt's Coptic Christians', *Ethnos* 80 (5): 649–70.

Reed, A. 2011. 'Hope on remand', *Journal of the Royal Anthropological Institute* 17 (3): 527–44.

Ridd, R. and Callaway, H. (eds.) 1986. *Caught up in Conflict: Women's responses to political strife*. London: Macmillan Education.

Robbins, J. 2007. 'Continuity thinking and the problem of Christian culture: belief, time, and the anthropology of Christianity', *Current Anthropology* 48 (1): 5–38.

Rosello, M. 2001. *Postcolonial Hospitality: The immigrant as guest*. Stanford: Stanford University Press.

Rotter, R. 2016. 'Waiting in the asylum determination process: just an empty interlude?', *Time and Society* 25 (1): 80–101.

Rozakou, Katerina. 2012. 'The biopolitics of hospitality in Greece: humanitarianism and the management of refugees', *American Ethnologist* 39 (3): 562–77. https://doi.org/10.1111/j.1548-1425.2012.01381.x.

Rozen, J. 2015. 'Civics lesson: ambivalence, contestation, and curricular change in Tunisia', *Ethnos* 80 (5): 605–29.

Ruiz de Elvira Carrascal, L. 2014. 'Retour sur la révolution syrienne: conditions de depart et premières mobilisations', *Annuaire français de relations internationales* 15: 673–89.

Rundell, J. 2009. 'Temporal horizons of modernity and modalities of waiting'. In *Waiting*, edited by G. Hage, 39–54. Melbourne: Melbourne University Publishing.

Sabea, H. 2012. 'A "Time out of Time": Tahrir, the political and the imaginary in the context of the January 25th revolution in Egypt'. *Cultural Anthropology* website. https://culanth.org/fieldsights/211-a-time-out-of-time-tahrir-the-political-and-the-imaginary-in-the-context-of-the-january-25th-revolution-in-egypt.

Said, E. 1979. *Orientalism*. New York: Vintage Books.

Said, S. 2018. 'The uprising and the economic interests of the Syrian military-mercantile complex'. In *The Syrian Uprising: Domestic origins and early trajectory*, edited by R. Hinnebusch and O. Imady, 56–76. New York: Routledge.

Sakhi, M. 2022. 'Protivogosudarstvennye politiki v sirijskoj revoljucii: primer osvobozhdennyh zon', *Jetnograficheskoe Obozrenie* 2: 45–60.

Salamandra, C. 2013. 'Sectarianism in Syria: anthropological reflections', *Middle East Critique* 22 (3): 303–6.

Salih, R. 2016. 'Reading Hannah Arendt in the Middle East: refugees, sovereignty, humanity', Paper presented at the Centre on Conflict, Right and Justice, London, 16 November.

Sanbar, E. 2001. 'Out of place, out of time', *Mediterranean Historical Review* 16 (1): 87–94.

Sanyal, R. 2011. 'Squatting in camps: building and insurgency in spaces of refuge', *Urban Studies* 48 (5): 877–90.

Saouli, A. 2018. 'The tragedy of Ba'thist state-building'. In *The Syrian Uprising: Domestic origins and early trajectory*, edited by R. Hinnebusch and O. Imady, 12–29. New York: Routledge.

Sayigh, R. 1995. 'Palestinians in Lebanon: harsh present, uncertain future', *Journal of Palestine Studies* 25 (1): 37–53.

Sayigh, R. 2005. 'A house is not a home: permanent impermanence of habitat for Palestinian expellees in Lebanon', *Holy Land Studies: A Multidisciplinary Journal* 4 (1): 17–39.

Schielke, S. 2010. 'Second thoughts about the anthropology of Islam, or how to make sense of grand schemes in everyday life', *ZMO Working Papers* 2: 1–16.

Schielke, S. 2012a. 'Engaging the world on the Alexandria waterfront'. In *The Global Horizon: Expectations of migration in Africa and the Middle East*, edited by K. Graw and S. Schielke, 175–92. Leuven: Leuven University Press.

Schielke, S. 2012b. 'Writing anthropology of and for the revolution'. *Cultural Anthropology* website. https://culanth.org/fieldsights/239-writing-anthropology-of-and-for-the-revolution.

Schielke, S. 2015. *Egypt in the Future Tense: Hope, frustration, and ambivalence before and after 2011.* Bloomington: Indiana University Press.

Schielke, S. 2019. 'The power of God: four proposals for an anthropological engagement' (ZMO Programmatic Texts, 13). Berlin: Leibniz-Zentrum Moderner Orient (ZMO). https://nbn-resolving.org/urn:nbn:de:101:1-20190122095405433300142.

Schielke, S. 2020. *Dreaming of the Inevitable: Migration and the search for a good life between Egypt and the Gulf.* Cairo: American University of Cairo Press.

Schielke, S. and Debevec, L. 2012. *Ordinary Lives and Grand Schemes: An anthropology of everyday religion.* New York: Berghahn.

Schwartz, B. 1975. *Queuing and Waiting: Studies in the social organization of access and delay.* Chicago: University of Chicago Press.

Scott, D. 2014. *Omens of Adversity: Tragedy, time, memory, justice.* Durham, NC: Duke University Press.

Seifan, S. 2020. 'Burhān ġaliyūn fī "ʿaṭab al-ḏāt": fashalat al-ṯawra al-sūriyya aw tamma īfshāluhā' *Al-Araby.* Accessed 12 May 2023. https://tinyurl.com/kvkxwjnx.

Seurat, M. 1989. *L'Etat de Barbarie.* Paris: le Seuil.

Shah, A. 2009. 'In search of certainty in revolutionary India', *Dialectical Anthropology* 33 (3/4): 271–86.

Shalinsky, A. 1993. 'Women's roles in the Afghanistan *jihad*', *International Journal of Middle East Studies* 25 (4): 661–75. https://doi.org/10.1017/S0020743800059316.

Shryock, A. 2004. 'The new Jordanian hospitality: house, host, and guest in the culture of public display', *Comparative Studies in Society and History* 46 (1): 35–62.

Shryock, A. 2008. 'Thinking about hospitality, with Derrida, Kant, and the Balga Bedouin', *Anthropos* 103 (2): 405–21.

Shryock, A. 2009. 'Hospitality lessons: learning the shared language of Derrida and the Balga Bedouin', *Paragraph* 32 (1): 32–50.

Shryock, A. 2012. 'Breaking hospitality apart: bad hosts, bad guests, and the problem of sovereignty', *Journal of the Royal Anthropological Institute* 18: 20–33.

Skocpol, T. 1979. *States and Social Revolutions: A comparative analysis of France, Russia, and China.* New York: Cambridge University Press.

Smeets, S. and Beach, D. 2020. 'When success is an orphan: informal institutional governance and the EU–Turkey deal', *West European Politics* 43 (1): 129–58.

Ssorin-Chaikov, N. 2006. 'On heterochrony: birthday gifts to Stalin, 1949', *Journal of the Royal Anthropological Institute* 12 (2): 355–75.

Ssorin-Chaikov, N. 2017. *Two Lenins: A brief anthropology of time.* Chicago: Chicago University Press.

Starn, O. 1991. 'Missing the revolution: anthropologists and the war in Peru', *Cultural Anthropology* 6 (1): 63–91.

Suerbaum, M. 2022. *Masculinities and Displacement in the Middle East: Syrian refugees in Egypt.* London: I.B. Tauris.

Sulaiman, H. 2018. *Freedom Hospital: A Syrian story*. Northampton, MA: Interlink Books.

Sule, C. 2017. 'The Syrian civil war, sectarianism and political change at the Turkish–Syrian border', *Social Anthropology* 25 (2): 174–89.

Taha, D. M. 2020. '"Like a tree without leaves": Syrian refugee women and the shifting meaning of marriage', *Mashriq & Lahjar: Journal of Middle East and North African Migration Studies* 7 (1): 1–26.

Taneja, A. V. 2017. *Jinnealogy: Time, Islam, and ecological thought in the medieval ruins of Delhi*. Stanford: Stanford University Press.

Theodossopoulos, D. 2014. 'On de-pathologizing resistance', *History and Anthropology* 25 (4): 415–30.

Thomassen, B. 2017. 'Endnotes: wandering in the wilderness or entering the promised land?', *Middle East Critique* 26 (3): 297–307.

Ticktin, M. 2014. 'Transnational humanitarianism', *Annual Review of Anthropology* 43: 273–89.

Toğral Koca, B. 2016. 'Syrians in Turkey: from "guests" to "enemies"?', *New Perspectives on Turkey* 54: 55–75.

Trotsky, L. 1957. *Revolution and Literature*. New York: Russell and Russell.

Trouillot, M.-R. 1995. *Silencing the Past: Power and the production of history*. Boston: Beacon Press.

Turnbull, S. 2016. '"Stuck in the middle": waiting and uncertainty in immigration detention', *Time and Society* 25 (1): 61–79.

Turner, V. 1967. *The Forest of Symbols: Aspects of Ndembu ritual*. Ithaca, NY: Cornell University Press.

Turner, V. 1969. *The Ritual Process: Structure and anti-structure*. London: Routledge.

Ümit, D. 2014. 'Refugee crisis next door: Turkey and the Syrian refugees', *Nevşehir Hacı Bektaş Veli University Journal of Social Sciences* 3: 1–18.

Valverde, M. 2009. 'Jurisdiction and scale: legal "technicalities" as resources for theory', *Social and Legal Studies* 18 (2): 139–57. https://doi.org/10.1177/0964663909103622.

Van Gennep, A. 1961. *The Rites of Passage*. Trans. M. V. Vizedom and G. L. Caffee. London: Routledge.

Varzi, R. 2006. *Warring Souls: Youth, media and martyrdom in post-revolution Iran*. Durham, NC: Duke University Press.

Vigh, H. 2009. 'Wayward migration: on imagined futures and technological voids', *Ethnos* 74 (1): 91–109.

Vignal, L. 2021. *War-Torn: The unmaking of Syria 2011–2021*. London: Hurst.

Viveiros de Castro, E. 2003. 'And: after-dinner speech at "Anthropology and Science", the 5th Decennial Conference of the Association of Social Anthropologists of the UK and Commonwealth, 2003'. *Manchester Papers in Social Anthropology* 7: 1–6.

Viveiros de Castro, E. 2004. 'Perspectival anthropology and the method of controlled equivocation', *Tipiti* 2 (1): 2–22.

Viveiros de Castro, E. 2009. *Métaphysiques Cannibales*. Paris: Presses Universitaires de France.

Vom Bruck, G. 1997a. 'A house turned inside out: inhabiting space in a Yemeni city', *Journal of Material Culture* 2 (2): 139–72.

Vom Bruck, G. 1997b. 'Elusive bodies: the politics of aesthetics among Yemeni elite women', *Signs* 23: 175–214.

Wahnich, S. 2003. *La liberté ou la mort: Essai sur la terreur et le terrorisme*. Paris: La Fabrique.

Weber, M. 1991 [Originally published 1922]. *The Sociology of Religion*. Boston: Beacon Press.

Weber, M. 1996 [Originally published 1958]. *The Religion of India: The sociology of Hinduism and Buddhism*. Delhi: Munshiram Manoharlal.

Wedeen, L. 1998. 'Acting "as if": symbolic politics and social control in Syria', *Comparative Studies in Society and History* 40 (3): 503–23.

Wedeen, L. 1999. *Ambiguities of Domination: Politics, rhetoric and symbols in contemporary Syria*. Chicago: University of Chicago Press.

Wedeen, L. 2013. 'Ideology and humor in dark times: notes from Syria', *Critical Inquiry* 39: 841–73.

Weizmal, E. 2019. *Forensic Architecture: Violence at the threshold of detectability*. Princeton: Princeton University Press.

West, H. 2005. *Kupilikula: Governance and the invisible realm in Mozambique*. Chicago: University of Chicago Press.

Whyte, Z. 2011. 'Enter the myopticon: uncertain surveillance in the Danish asylum system', *Anthropology Today* 27 (3): 18–21.

Willerslev, R. 2009. 'The optimal sacrifice: a study of voluntary death among the Siberian Chukchi', *American Ethnologist* 36 (4): 693–704.

Wilson, A. 2016. *Sovereignty in Exile: A Saharan liberation movement governs*. Philadelphia: University of Pennsylvania Press.

Wilson, A. 2019a. 'Revolution'. In *The Cambridge Encyclopedia of Anthropology*, edited by F. Stein, S. Lazar, M. Candea, H. Diemberger, J. Robbins, A. Sanchez and R. Stasch. http://doi.org/10.29164/19rev.

Wilson, A. 2019b. 'Invisible veterans: defeated militants and enduring revolutionary social values in Dhufar, Oman', *Conflict and Society* 5 (1): 132–49.

Wilson, A. 2023. *Afterlives of Revolution: Everyday counterhistories in southern Oman*. Stanford: Stanford University Press.

Winegar, J. 2012. 'The privilege of revolution: gender, class, space, and affect in Egypt', *American Ethnologist* 39 (1): 67–70.

Worsley, P. 1961. 'The analysis of rebellion and revolution in modern British social anthropology', *Science & Society* 25 (1): 26–37.

Yassin Hassan, R. 2009. *Ḥurrās al-hawā'*. Beirut: al-Rayyas lil-Kutub wa-al-Nashr.

Yazbek, S. 2018. *Tis'a 'ashra imra'a: sūriyyāt yarawīn* . Beirut: Mnshūrāt al-matūsṭ.

Yazigi, S. 2018. *Qiṣṣa makān, qiṣṣa insān, bidāyāt al-ṭawra al-sūriyya 2011–2015*. Beirut: IFPO Press.

Yurchak, A. 2003. 'Soviet hegemony of form: everything was forever, until it was no more', *Comparative Studies in Society and History* 45 (3): 480–510.

Yurchak, A. 2015. 'Bodies of Lenin: the hidden science of communist sovereignty', *Representations* 129: 116–57. https://doi.org/10.1525/rep.2015.129.1.116.

Zaman, T. 2016. *Islamic Traditions of Refuge in the Crises of Iraq and Syria*. New York: Palgrave Macmillan.

Ziadeh, R. 2014. *The Years of Fear: The forcibly disappeared in Syria*. Washington, DC: Freedom House.

# Index

hospitality (*karam*) 86–9, 96–8, 99–100,
    108n15
  and jurisdictions 92–3, 94–5
  and Syrian 102–5
Humphrey, Caroline 80n14

Idlib 7, 71, 122
inside (*juwwa*) 21–2, 57, 59, 137, 191
  and continuity 71–5
  and manhood 75–7
  and revolutionary work 62, 63–5, 70
internally displaced people (IDP) 9, 63, 112
intimacy 23, 61–2, 138, 156
invisibility (*al-ghayb*) 15, 163, 183, 192
invisibilisation 15, 21, 163, 191–2, 193
Iran 51, 79n5
Iraq 40, 41, 103
irreversible changes (*ghir rdud*) 137–8
ISIS *see* Daesh
Islam *see* Quran; Shi'ite Islam; Sunni Islam
Islamists 4, 16, 46–7, 137, 168
islamiyyin (*Islamists*) 10, 24n13
Israel 39, 180
İzmir 144, 187–8

Jaysh al-Fatah 7
jihadists 16, 40–1, 168
Jordan 21, 90
Joseph, Suad 149, 158n11
Judgement Day 132, 163, 165, 178, 180, 181
justice (*'adaleh*) 30, 168
Justice and Development Party (AKP) 88, 106
*juwwa see* inside

*karama see* dignity
Kastrinou, Maria 159n24
Khalifa, Khaled 80n9
Khalifa, Mustafa: *The Shell* 54n24
Khosravi, Shahram 134n22
*kimliks* (identity documents) 2, 25n24, 85,
    86, 91, 94
Kublitz, Anja 128
Kurdish Democratic Union Party (PYD) 4,
    44–5

laws 93, 94–5
Lebanon 58, 90, 105, 113
Leila 96–7
liberated areas 3, 57, 62–7, 137, 184n7
Libyan revolution 39
life
  dignified life 95, 107–8, 162
  everyday life 86–7, 92–3, 118–19, 157n3
  ritual life 118
  social life 117–18
limbo 86, 111–12, 115–16
local councils (*al majales al mahaliyya*) 11, 17,
    18, 20, 64, 80n11
*longue durée see* duration
loss 31, 58, 179–80, 189
lower-middle classes 5, 9, 35–6

Manal 62, 65–6
manhood 75–7, 78
Mariam 140, 141–2
marriage 92, 150–5, 159n24
martyrs (*shaheed*) 9, 11, 122–3, 146–7, 182–3
  and actions 173–7
  and definition 164–6
  and political status 166–9
  and predestination 171–3
  and songs 161–2
  and suicide bombings 184n6
  and Sunni Islam 162–4
  and visual representation 169–71
massacres 6, 14, 30
Maya 150–1, 152–3, 154–5, 187–8
Mazeau, Guillaume 51
media 5, 192
Mediterranean 107, 117, 143–4, 187, 189,
    193
mentality (*'aqliyyeh*) 138
methodology (research) 4, 21–2, 192, 24n5,
    n6
middlemen 120–1, 124
migration 107, 116; *see also* refugees
Mittermaier, Amira 64, 178, 183
Mohammad 50–1
*muhajir* (follower of the Prophet) 88–9
Munif, Yasser 30
Muslim Brotherhood 6, 30, 39, 41
Muslims 88–9
Mustafa 113–14

*nasheteen* (activists) 8, 65, 140
Nasserist party 6, 41
nationalisation 5
necropolitics 30
new man 61–2, 79n7
NGOs (non-governmental organisations) 12
nostalgia 69, 101, 112, 131
Nour 75, 155–6, 187–9
Nura 112–13, 115, 123, 137

Omar 151
oppression (*zulm*) 16, 29–30, 32
  and counter-revolutionary forces 42–6
  and honour 33
  and Islamists 137
  and women 139, 140, 141–2
Ottoman Empire 88–9
outside (*barra*) 21–2, 59, 191
  and revolutionary work 62, 63–4, 70

Palestine 39, 79n3, 180
  and martyrdom 184n6
  and Nakba 111, 128
  and refugees 113
  and women 138, 146–7
participation 34–5
passports 92–3
past 125–30, 130–1

www.ingramcontent.com/pod-product-compliance
Ingram Content Group UK Ltd.
Pitfield, Milton Keynes, MK11 3LW, UK
UKHW051358151224
452469UK00002B/8